An Introduction to Medieval History

An Introduction to Medieval History

Paolo Delogu

Translated by Matthew Moran

Duckworth

First published in 2002 by
Gerald Duckworth & Co. Ltd.
61 Frith Street, London W1D 3JL
Tel: 020 7434 4242
Fax: 020 7434 4420
Email: enquiries@duckworth-publishers.co.uk
www.ducknet.co.uk

First published in Italian as *Introduzione allo studio della storia medievale* by Società Editrice Il Mulino, Bologna, Italy, in 1994.
© 1994 Società Editrice Il Mulino, Bologna.
Edizione in lingua inglese effettuata con
l'intermediazione dell'Agenzia Letteraria Eulama.

English translation © 2002 by Matthew Moran

A catalogue record for this book is available
from the British Library

ISBN 0 7156 3079 2

Typeset by Ray Davies
Printed in Great Britain by
Bookcraft (Bath) Ltd, Bath, Avon

Contents

Preface

This book originated in response to the experience of teaching history – and teaching medieval history – in a university context. In particular, its aim is to supplement the material provided by the standard text-books with a degree of information regarding the practice of historical research and its traditions, and the aims and the methods which it employs. Numerous texts, old and new, have been written with similar aims, though perhaps not so many that another such offering might seem superfluous. This, then, is the book's justification.

As for its success, this must be judged by teachers and students themselves in the course of teaching and research. I have endeavoured to achieve precisely what the book's title implies. This is an introduction, a structured profile of ideas and information intended to help students to take account of the purpose of their studies, and to encourage them to approach the Middle Ages at first-hand, rather than through the mediation of textbooks alone.

This objective explains the arrangement of the text and my treatment of the material. Some account of the history of historical research is inevitable in a book of this kind. My approach to the subject is intended to highlight certain key issues in order to persuade the reader that historical studies imply important questions that go beyond the simple recording of past events. In the same way, my account of the sources – another prerequisite of 'introductions' of this kind – is conceived as a history of their production, in order to highlight the formal and typological characteristics of the sources, and, moreover, to draw attention to their significance in the context of medieval culture.

Of course, the general ideas expressed by such a book as this may well be met with reservation by professional historians. However, it is my hope that these ideas will provide the basis for useful discussion in the seminar room. Likewise, there is scope for criticism of my choice of source material for discussion, and the implications of my treatment of that material in the pages that follow. Naturally, drastic choices are called for when writing a book of this kind, in order to keep it from taking on excessive length, or to prevent the text becoming a simple typological list. I privilege certain categories of evidence which have traditionally been at the heart of studies of medieval history, and these I set alongside rather less-familiar material in order to reveal at least something of the variety of sources available to students of the Middle Ages.

The text is nevertheless bulky. Yet it is my hope that certain themes will emerge from the detail, and that together these themes will provide readers with a framework of approaches to medieval history. However lengthy some of the chapters may seem, they are not intended as straightforward or self-contained repertories of essential information on specific subjects, but rather as lenses purposefully trained on unusual points of view.

I have not included any systematic account of historical method, however. My reason for this omission is that, removed from the practical experience of handling documents and their use for the writing of history, the prescription of principles and rules can easily become an airy and altogether fruitless business. The methods of historical research and reasoning are learned in practice, under the tutelage of teachers. No manual can pretend to substitute that experience. This is not to say that theory is entirely absent, however, as it would be impossible to write without theory, especially when dealing with such questions as periodization and the concept of historical sources.

Certain friends and colleagues kindly agreed to read parts of the book, therefore helping me to avoid at least the most obvious errors. Warm thanks go in particular to Giulia Barone, Paola Supino Martini, Alessia Rovelli and Paolo Cherubini. Notwithstanding the efforts of these individuals, all responsibility for the remaining omissions and infelicities rests with the author. I shall be very grateful to have such errors brought to my attention and to make them good as best I can.

Finally, I dedicate the book to students everywhere, with all best wishes.

Paolo Delogu

2002

Supplementary thanks must be added to this English edition, to all those who were involved with the enterprise and worked to carry it out. Richard Hodges recommended the translation, probably reminiscent of our passionate disputes on the Middle Ages at San Vincenzo al Volturno, Birka and other medieval sites across Europe. The translator faced a difficult task, the Italian phrasing being so different from the English (either as a consequence of the Latin heritage or the author's prolixity), that he had to work hard in order to create a clear and readable English text. Finally Deborah Blake of Duckworth patiently and efficiently coped with the author's claim to check and modify the text till the last minute. To all of them my sincere thanks together with the wishful omen that their cares prove to be worthwhile.

P.D.

Translator's Note

Paolo Delogu's *Introduzione allo studio della storia medievale* was first published in 1994, and immediately became a standard reference work for honours students in medieval history in Italy. Those familiar with the original text will see that certain changes have been made in preparing the present English edition. Above all, this book is rather shorter than the original in a number of respects. Professor Delogu concluded most chapters of the original work with plenteous bibliographies, material supported by a tremendous wealth of detailed information on medieval sources and bibliographies adjoined in appendices. For the present edition, references to secondary sources only are given, chapter by chapter, in a single list at the back of the book. While the present bibliography contains many of the references intended by the author, readers will note that it was compiled by the translator, with the interests and needs of an English-speaking audience in mind.

The appearance of this book is outrageously overdue. My thanks are due in the first place to the author, for his consistency and kind counsel. The idea of an English translation of the *Introduzione* was proposed by Richard Hodges; for his continued help and inspiration, my warm thanks to him. A special debt is due to Deborah Blake, at Duckworth, on account of her confidence and quiet encouragement – and for bearing with my spectacular tardiness in finishing the job. I am also grateful to Christopher Harper-Bill, Richard Deswarte, Oliver Gilkes, Edward Harris, John Mitchell, Lucy Nicholson, Alessandro Serio, and Chris Wickham, for assistance of various sorts. These apart, by far the best of my gratitude goes to Pippa, Seth and Stevie.

Norwich   Matthew Moran
February 2002

Introduction

The Middle Ages and contemporary culture

Why study medieval history? Any book that presents itself as an introduction to such a study cannot ignore this question, however crude and simplistic it may seem.

The most straightforward answer to the question is provided by the formal curricula followed in secondary schools and universities. As a subject, medieval history may be more or less obligatory for students in certain schools, as well as for some undergraduates. As such, medieval history is often only encountered in the classroom, and for many the encounter may be unwelcome, perhaps even unpleasant.

The curricula pursued by schools and universities are not merely ends in themselves; instead, in formal and structured ways, they reflect cultural values that have their roots in freedom of choice, and which are prompted by the value (and the pleasure) we associate with knowledge and learning. Approaching the question from this perspective, it would seem that there is every reason to count medieval history among the objects and preoccupations of intellectual and cultural life. Beyond this perspective, however, it may seem that the study of medieval history or, for that matter, the study of any period in history, has little or no relevance.

But if we consider the question as interested intellectuals, rather than as browbeaten students, we are immediately made aware of the paradoxical nature of the medieval as a concept.

The medieval past is commonly considered to be the very opposite of the values upon which modern consciousness and customs are based. Traditionalism and authoritarianism, deep social stratification, and a subsistence economy based predominantly on agriculture – these are fundamental aspects of medieval life which contrast markedly with the order and values developed by European society in the course of recent centuries. The spirit of critical inquiry, juridical and social egalitarianism, and economic prosperity based on industrial production – though they are now witnessing profound and unpredictable change, these conditions provide the matrix of modern consciousness and experience. Seen in this way, the history of the middle ages might assume some small significance, as a reflection of the first formation of values and forms of organization that reached their fullest development only in some later period. In other words, the medieval period might be interesting, if only for the way in which it seems to repress its own inherent qualities, thus giving way to the modern era.

Nevertheless, and notwithstanding the widespread tendency impulsively to reject the significance of medieval history, nowadays much lively curiosity is shown towards the most characteristic (and anti-modern) sides of medieval life – religious faith and beliefs, social and cultural primitivism and technological backwardness, to give just some instances. What results is the image of a simple, organic society, one driven by a powerful and singular ideological inspiration. Variations on this theme are present in the writings of famous historians, as well as in the theatre, cinema and in works of literature. They range from evocations of an exotic, distant world, to more or less open nostalgia for a world apparently unaffected by the ills of industrial and post-industrial society.

Such a contrast of perceptions is not without significance. It reveals that as a period in history, or even as a mode of civilization, the Middle Ages are a problem for the modern consciousness. The period provokes anxiety or disquiet, appearing sometimes as a danger to be exorcised, sometimes as an ideal to which to aspire. The problem stems from the fact that the medieval period is not so remote from the present as to allow us to approach it with disinterest. In effect, we are dealing with a relatively recent episode in the experience of European society. And the tangible remains of that experience are still apparent in the world in which we live, in the rural and urban landscape, in important religious and political concepts, and in certain aspects of the institutions that govern us.

To sum up, if we are looking for links between past and present, in order better to understand the nature of our cultural identity, then the Middle Ages are of far greater importance than classical antiquity, and scarcely less significant than the more familiar modern era. What better reason could there be recognize medieval history as the legitimate object of scholarly study?

The medieval has not become a disquieting concept only in recent times. In fact, one might say that the modern European consciousness has been constantly haunted by the significance of that millennium of history that preceded our own era. One might also say that, from its very beginnings, the modern world has defined itself in relation to the medieval world, by taking an aggressive stance, and much distance, in the face of its medieval legacy. In pursuing the problematic nature of the period in greater detail, the discussion now proceeds with a brief profile of ways in which the period has been perceived and valued in modern European culture. The following chapter is dedicated to the intellectual developments which have produced and transmitted the value judgements that continue to condition our attitudes and cultural orientation to this day.

1

The Middle Ages – the history
of an idea

The Italian humanists and the 'middle age'

It is commonly said that the concept of the Middle Ages was first developed by Italian humanists, as an antithesis to the ideals of the Renaissance. During the fourteenth and fifteenth centuries, Italian scholars and thinkers thought of themselves as living at a moment of profound change – a transformation characterized by the recovery of the literature and, still more, the spirit of classical antiquity. The humanists considered antiquity to be the source of ideal models of style and civilization. Closely linked as it was to a renewed conception of man, the re-conquest of learning and letters appeared to the humanists to signal the rebirth of antiquity after a long decline of cultural values and decadence in literary taste.

Similarly, the artists and art-theorists of the Renaissance claimed to have rediscovered the aesthetic and moral values as well as the advanced intellectual and technical skills inherent in ancient art, after centuries of neglect. Some humanist artists and writers developed a notion of the history of civilization based on three phases: classical antiquity (when the most highly developed human and cultural values had been formulated), an age of barbarity and decadence (following the fall of the Roman empire) and, finally, the Renaissance present, when the ideals of classical civilization were reborn.

Beginning with the barbarian invasions and ending with the rebirth of art and letters, the humanists' 'middle age' (or 'età di mezzo' in Italian) corresponds with what we now know as the medieval period of European history – or the Middle Ages. For Renaissance commentators, the 'middle age' was one of crudity and obscurity, characteristics that were long to be applied to the period. However, while it would seem that the idea of the Middle Ages was well defined already in the fifteenth century, we would be mistaken in thinking that Italian humanists considered all of history to be encompassed by philosophy or literature. In terms of politics, institutions and religion, Renaissance humanists knew that their present was not so much a return to antiquity as it was the outcome of a process set in course by the decline of the Roman empire – a continuous and uninterrupted process of development. Though they participated in the humanistic literary culture of their day, history writers such as Leonardo Bruni (*c.*1370-1444) and Flavio Biondo (1392-1463) considered the past to be divided between antiquity (before the fall of the Roman empire) and a later, more 'recent' epoch just prior to the present. It was in the latter period that the institutions familiar to fifteenth-century Italians had emerged, institutions such as the town, municipal government and the Church of Rome. As certainly as they appreciated what was new in the fields of culture, the arts and government, humanist historians did not deny or condemn the historical developments that had brought such novelties into being. This conception is fully developed in the historical works of Niccolò Machiavelli (1469-1527). In taking account of the conditions in Italy in his own day, Machiavelli referred to the formation of regional principalities and the political power of the papacy in preceding centuries. For Machiavelli, the history of Italy was conceived as a process of continuous development set in motion by the barbarian invasions.

This disparity of views is reflected in the terms used to refer to the 'middle age'. Probably the first specific designation of the period was made in 1469, by the bishop and humanist, Giovanni Andrea Bussi (1414/17-1475). In referring to the work of another famous humanist, Nicolaus Cusanus, Bussi praised Cusanus' considerable knowledge of Latin histories, both ancient writings and those of the *media tempestas*. In Bussi's use of the Latin term, *media* may be interpreted to mean 'intermediate', though it is more likely that Bussi intended it to refer to an age 'less ancient'. Therefore, in this earliest use of the concept, *media tempestas* refers to an epoch more recent than antiquity, though it does not imply that this is an intermediate period or an age clearly defined and now at an end.

It should not be said, therefore, that Italian Renaissance humanists extended their view of the poverty of the arts and learning in the post-Roman period to the history of that period as a whole. In the fifteenth century, commentators did not regard the 'middle age' as a period removed alike from the present and the ancient past. From the Renaissance to the present day, the idea of the Middle Ages has been developed – or constructed – by several centuries of historical discourse in Italy and Europe and beyond. As a concept, therefore, the Middle Ages has its own history. The progress of that history is the subject of this chapter.

The barbarian age in sixteenth-century European culture

During the sixteenth century, a number of French and German humanists returned to the problem of the three-way relationship between classical antiquity and a successive, intermediate era and the present. Like the Italians, these men were proudly aware that theirs was an age of great intellectual progress – a movement witnessed above all in the refined critical appreciation of ancient literature and Holy Scripture. The same men were fully engaged in the realities of political, institutional and religious life in their home countries, and, as such, they were concerned with identifying and promoting traditions of national history. In France, scholars such as Charles Dumoulin (1500-1566), Etienne Pasquier (1529-1615), and Claude Fauchet (1530-1602), gave voice to the interests of the élite groups engaged in the government of the kingdom, namely the classes of nobles and jurists. These writers set out to investigate and record the traditions of their own class as well as those of the monarchy. In sixteenth-century France, the recall to ancient culture did not have the same cultural references it presented to Italian humanists; on the contrary, French commentators considered the Italians' disdain for the barbarians to be an expression of Italian nationalism. It was to the barbarian age that French observers traced the origins of their national political institutions, especially the monarchy, and so it was to the barbarian age that the French addressed strongly patriotic sentiments. In this context, French historians developed the practice of philology, applying it to the study of the law, legislation and literature of France's feudal age.

Likewise in Germany – and already in the fifteenth century – historians, antiquarians and theologians, such as Hartmann Schedel (1440-1514) and Johan Verge (known as *Nauclerus*) (1425-1510), regarded the barbarian invasions and the medieval German empire with respect, as episodes affirming the role of the German people in the history of Europe. Subsequently the religious reform launched by Martin Luther further consolidated the national consciousness in this respect. The re-evaluation of German history that ensued was to be a key plank in the educational programme set up to propagate Reformation ideology. Johan Sleidan (*c.*1506-1556) and Philipp Melanchthon (1497-1560), Luther's close collaborator, together with his son-in-law, Kaspar Peucer (1525-1602), composed universal histories with which they vindicated the role of the German empire as defender of the Christian faith, while accusing the Roman Church of reducing the German people to a divided, marginal and impotent state.

Naturally the history of the Church occupied a prominent place in Protestant culture. Philipp Melanchthon and others among Luther's collaborators, such as the Englishman Robert Barnes (1495-1540), ended their historical writings with the conclusion that the Roman Church had progressively neglected the mission entrusted to the Apostles by Christ, becoming ever more worldly and concerned with promoting papal primacy. The result was corruption in the Church and the dereliction of Christ's work – a decline set in reverse by Luther's reform. These ideas were systematically developed in the *Historia Ecclesiastica* edited by Matthias Vlacic (1520-1575), the Istrian humanist better known by the latinized form of his name, Flacius Illyricus. Vlacic travelled to Germany in 1539, and became an eager campaigner for Luther. His great history was intended to illustrate the progressive degeneration of the Church, from its Apostolic origins to the thirteenth century, when, the reformers believed, the papacy had become the very embodiment of the antichrist. Numerous scholars collaborated in the preparation of Vlacic's grand project, many pursuing original archive research to the same end, though not all of this work was of the most rigorously critical or unbiased kind. The narrative of the *Historia Ecclesiastica* is divided into centuries, or *centuriae*; and thus it became known as the *Centuries of Magdeburg*, after the German city where it was prepared. Published in the years between 1559 and 1574, the *Centuries* are distinguished neither in their originality nor their objectivity. They did, however, achieve great popularity and wide circulation in the Protestant world, and they did much to articulate and enforce the Protestant worldview. In the process, the *Centuries* characterized an entire period of history, the medieval period, with the perceived standards of a single medieval institution – the Church. Chronologically, in its timing and duration, this is much the same period as the other 'middle age' recognized by Renaissance humanists, albeit with one important difference – for sixteenth-century Protestants, the middle age was precipitated not by the barbarian invasions, but by the progressive mundanity of the Church after the time of Constantine.

The polemic of Protestant historians attached a roundly negative connotation to the medieval centuries, one that emphasized the decadence of Christianity and the Church. However, Protestant texts also drew attention to other aspects of the period, which writers believed to be vital elements of German national culture – namely, the emergence of the German people and its empire.

The great cultural renewal witnessed in Europe in the fifteenth and sixteenth centuries established the idea that the present was separated from classical antiquity (or the early-Christian period) by a third age, a middle (or medieval) age. In the same context, the intermediate epoch was subject to mostly negative characterizations, though perceptions of that epoch's civilization remained so diverse that it was not yet recognized as a single, homogeneous period in history.

The Middle Ages in the culture of the seventeenth century

The notion of the Middle Ages as a distinct historical period was to mature, slowly, from the end of the 1500s and throughout the first decades of the seventeenth century. At this time, the monarchies of western Europe sought to discourage the writing of history as a vehicle for the interests of particular institutions or social groups, preferring to use it instead as a means of celebrating the antiquity of Church, monarchy, and nation.

A prominent aspect of scholarly activity in Europe from the end of the sixteenth century was the publication, in printed form, of the texts of medieval chronicles and numerous other documents found in the deposits of archives and libraries across the continent. This initiative was encouraged by the well-developed practice of philology, the historical study of language, which derived the logic of its methods from mathematics and physics. In France in the sixteenth century, Pierre Pithou (1539-1596), a jurist and magistrate to the royal court, published two collections of medieval chronicles relating to the history of France from the eighth to the thirteenth centuries. Later, in 1616, André Duchesne (1584-1640), court historian and geographer, published the chronicles of the duchy of Normandy, before beginning work on a huge collection of ancient documents for a history of France. Similarly, in Germany between 1601 and 1604, Heinrich Canisius (*c.*1550-1610), a professor of law at Ingolstadt, published the *Antiquae lections* (6 vols), containing the texts of religious, literary and narrative sources for the medieval period. In 1685 Johan Heinrich Boecker published the *Scriptores rerum Germanicarum*. And in England at this time, medieval sources for English history were published by William Camden (1551-1623), whose *Anglica, Normannica, Cambrica a veteribus scripta* appeared in 1603; and by Sir Henry Savile (1549-1622), author of *Rerum Anglicarum Scriptores post Bedam praecipui*, published after 1596.

By themselves, the discovery and publication of documents did not encourage writers and others to regard the medieval epoch as a distinct era in history or even a significant one, as the records in question were concerned above all with the deeds of medieval monarchs and their peoples. Yet growing awareness of the sources of medieval history did not fail to rouse the genuine curiosity of scholars for what they saw as the startling and unexpectedly original characteristics of medieval records, such as the large numbers of narrative or historical accounts produced in the period, and the peculiarities and technicalities of medieval Latin. In 1627, the Dutch scholar Johan Gerard Voss (1577-1649), or *Vossius* as he was to be known, published a dissertation on Latin historians. The texts he divided into three groups chronologically: his first group consists of ancient writers active before the end of the second century AD; the second is concerned with writers from the period between the third century and the time of Petrarch; and the third with historians of more recent times. In Vossius' account of the development of Latin historiography, the middle age is treated as an epoch distinct both from antiquity and the recent past, and one of comparably lesser achievement. In 1645, Vossius published a thesis on the peculiarities of what he called 'barbaric Latin', with which he acknowledged the originality of medieval Latin, while passing a mostly negative judgement on its quality.

The need for specialized dictionaries or vocabularies of medieval Latin was repeatedly expressed in these years. This demand was finally satisfied by a contribution that remains an essential tool in medieval studies to this day, if now in revised and expanded form. This is the *Glossarium ad scriptores mediae et infimae latinitatis* (3 vols), compiled by Charles Du Fresne Du Cange (1610-1688) and published in Paris in 1678. Du Cange was a man learned in the history, geography, archaeology, law and numismatics of France. In the *Glossarium* he invested the full extent of his extraordinary knowledge of the French sources. The result is rather more than a simple glossary. It is an encyclopaedic repertory of Latin terms in medieval usage, terms relating to concepts and institutions and the material culture of late antiquity and the Middle Ages. These terms were derived from all the wide range of juridical, narrative and other sources that the previous century of activity had made accessible to students of Du Cange's day. Significantly, the concept of 'middle' and 'lower' Latin referred to in the title implies no negative assessment of the subject – it simply refers to the distance between medieval and classical Latin in chronological terms. The *Glossarium* defines the antiquities, institutions, customs and concepts of the medieval period, with the aim of building up a more detailed knowledge of a period that must have seemed, to Du Cange and his contemporaries, to be becoming ever more remote and unfamiliar with the passing of time.

Much of the energy of seventeenth-century scholars was dedicated to ecclesiastical history. Already at the end of the sixteenth century, official Catholic culture had answered the Protestants' charges with an imposing historical work, the *Annales Ecclesiastici*, by Cardinal Cesare Baronio (1538-1607). Baronio set out the story of the Church year by year, from the birth of Christ to 1198. This history's great strength was provided by the very considerable scholarship of its author. In preparing his work, Baronio undertook intensive research amid the rich holdings of the Vatican Library, of which he was the prefect; his knowledge of the Vatican's vast resources furnished much unpublished material for his great project. The resulting history provided the Catholic Church with a formidable defence against the accusations of the Protestants, as well as a platform upon which to re-establish Rome's claim to papal primacy.

The Counter-Reformation movement produced its second great work of historical scholarship north of the Alps. This was the *Acta Sanctorum*. In 1643, at Anversa in Belgium, a small group of Jesuits led by Jean Bolland (1596-1665) set out to transcribe and publish printed texts of the lives of saints revered by the Catholic Church. To this end, they made use of the critical philological methods usually reserved for treatments of narrative and literary sources. Their motive was to provide a firm historical footing for the cult of saints and relics, which had been one of the favourite targets of Protestant critics. It was to be a daunting task, involving countless medieval records of the saints' miraculous lives and passions. Despite the scale of the task, in a remarkably short time Bolland and his associates saw to the publication of a series of volumes containing critical editions of the lives of the saints in the order of the liturgical calendar, with selected texts of proven authenticity and chronology, furnished with philological, historical and religious commentaries.

Another centre of Catholic learning at this time was the congregation of Benedictine monks of Saint-Germain-des-Prés, near Paris, who were known as the Maurists after St Maurus, one of the first followers of St Benedict, to whose cult they were dedicated. The rule of the community set great store by the study of ecclesiastical and especially monastic history, and its role in the monks' intellectual and spiritual formation. This encouraged the practice of exact scholarship in historical research. The same learned tradition produced such eminent figures as Jean Luc d'Achery (1609-1685) and Jean Mabillon (1632-1707), who prepared editions of unpublished texts of the writings of the Church fathers, the lives of Benedictine saints and other sources for monastic history. Through their activities, the Maurists perfected the methods of critical philological analysis. Moreover, the interests of the Maurists were not restricted to religious and literary sources. In a volume of the *Acta Sanctorum* dated 1675, the Jesuit scholar, Daniel Papebrock, published a dissertation outlining criteria for the identification of false documents, particularly medieval forgeries – the *Propylaeum antiquarium circa veri ac falsi discrimen in vetustis membranis*. Papebrock's findings led him to question the authenticity of some of the oldest documents in the archive of the abbey of Saint-Denis, near Paris, including the *diplomata* of Merovingian kings. Papebrock's remarkable claims failed to convince Saint-Germain's most celebrated scholar, Jean Mabillon. Troubled by Papebrock's statements and sceptical of his methods, Mabillon set about devising a means of systematically evaluating medieval documents based on their formal and material characteristics (script, style, external form, dating, signatures, seals and so forth). Mabillon set down the results in a treatise entitled *De re diplomatica* (1681). Mabillon's contribution remains the basis of the modern practice of medieval documentary analysis known as Diplomatics. Immediately upon its appearance, the book exerted a tremendous impact: Papebrock declared his acceptance of Mabillon's conclusions, while expressing his wish to come over to Mabillon's school. The scholarly activity of the Maurists continued into the following century, when it was extended to include the history of liturgy and Greek patristics.

Ecclesiastical scholars regarded the history of the Church as one of uninterrupted progress, from Christ's preaching to their own lifetime. Though they recognized no rupture in the course of the institution's history, Church historians identified many distinctive expressions of medieval religion and ecclesiastical life, and their observations contributed to the slowly altering image of the era. Hence, while the medieval period continued to be regarded in the seventeenth century as one of barbarism, progressively it must have seemed rather less threatening, and even more acceptable, on account of its manifestations of faith.

During the course of the seventeenth century, the medieval period was increasingly regarded as a distinct and autonomous era – an age at an end. Central to this understanding was a growing awareness that the modern era was decidedly original with respect to all periods in the past, classical as well as medieval.

Not only artists and writers, but also jurists, political philosophers, scientists and others now considered that theirs was a time of unmistakable change in a wide field of human endeavour. As well as the arts and humanities, this change affected economic and political systems, and the progress of science and morals – and even the very shape of the known world. In the second half of the seventeenth century, academic historians transferred this new consciousness into syntheses of universal history. The author of one such work was George Horn (1620-1670), professor of history at the university of Leiden, in the Netherlands. In his account of the career of humankind, the *Arca Noae, sive historia imperiorum et regnorum a condito orbe ad nostra tempora* (1666), Horn proposed a new periodization based on the separation of ancient (*vetus*) and recent (*recentior*) histories. Recent history Horn divided into two sub-phases: a *medium aevum*, or 'middle age'; and an *aevum recentius*, or recent era. In this account, the point of transition between medieval and recent history coincides with the European discovery of gunpowder and the printing press, and with the earliest voyages of discovery and with the new order of European states – as well as with the rebirth of the humanities. In another work, the *Historia ecclesiastica et politica*, Horn fixed the chronological terms of the 'middle age' between the fall of the Roman empire in 476 and the conquest of Constantinople by the Turks in 1453.

The division of universal history into three periods, ancient, medieval and modern, was taken up by a number of other seventeenth-century European scholars, including Gottfried Wilhelm Leibnitz (1646-1716), the philosopher and mathematician. At the same time, academic acceptance of the system was sanctioned by Christopher Keller (or *Cellarius*) (1638-1707), professor at the university of Halle. In 1675, Keller published a summary of ancient history prior to the birth of Christ, a text intended as an aid for the study of classical literature. Later, in the second edition of his history published in 1685, Keller extended the limits of ancient history up to the reign of the emperor Constantine, and the adoption of Christianity as the official religion of the Roman empire. For Keller, the institution of Christianity signalled a decisive turn in the course of ancient history. Three years later, Keller published his version of the *History of the Middle Ages from the Time of Constantine to the Conquest of Constantinople by the Turks*; this was followed by the *Historia Nova* (1696), a history of the sixteenth and seventeenth centuries. As textbooks, these works were enormously influential in establishing Keller's scheme of historical periodization, a scheme that made less of particular political and military events, and more of two crucial and overwhelming transformations – the establishment of the Church under the Roman empire on the one hand, and, on the other, the novelty of the modern age, its cultural achievement and geographical and technological discoveries. What is more, Keller passed a negative judgement over the intervening era, without the slightest concern for its proper characteristics.

Moral philosophy, the Middle Ages and the history of Europe

Once it had been closely defined in chronological terms, as a historical period, the medieval epoch became the object of a rather different sort of historical reflection during the eighteenth century. At this time, the characteristics of medieval civilization were evaluated by comparison with those of the modern epoch. This development was brought on by the marriage of scholarship and moral philosophy in the context of the Enlightenment debate on the progress of society and humankind.

Eighteenth-century attitudes to history ought not to be regarded as symptomatic of an altogether new and unexpected development, however, but as the outcome of ideas first developed during the second half of the seventeenth century by historians and thinkers concerned with the progress of European history. A figure with an important role in this process was Ludovico Antonio Muratori (1672-1750). Muratori may be considered the founder of critical studies in medieval history in Italy. As a churchman and librarian of the Ambrosiana in Milan and the Estense in Modena, Muratori applied and further developed the scholarly methodology of the Maurists. He was to provide Italy with a corpus of historical sources comparable to other collections already completed or then being compiled by other European nations. Yet Muratori's objective was original in certain respects. Unlike France, in Italy there was no unified state to provide the object or rationale for the writing of national history. Moreover, in Italy academic culture continued to regard ancient civilization not only as the paradigm for every civilization, but also as a cultural tradition particular to Italy.

Muratori distanced himself from such ideas. Despite its lack of political unity, Muratori believed Italy to be the orbit of traditions common to all Italians. Furthermore, he maintained that such traditions had been formed not in antiquity, which he considered excessively remote and distinct from the present, but in the Middle Ages. In shaping his thesis, Muratori drew inspiration from the approaches of contemporary historians in other European countries, while his arguments drew their force from his minute knowledge of the written sources. From his reading of these sources, Muratori understood that many of the legal and political institutions of his time were directly related to those of the medieval period. The pursuit of that period appeared to Muratori to be a means to discovering the origins of the modern world.

Moved by these ideas and the conviction that scholarship should serve a public function, Muratori assembled a large number of texts relating to the history of Italy from 500 to 1500. This material formed the basis for the collection entitled *Rerum Italicarum Scriptores* (25 vols, 1723-1751). The project was made possible thanks to Muratori's network of scholarly acquaintances, individuals who assisted by identifying and transcribing records in libraries all over Italy. Muratori subjected the texts to critical and philological scrutiny, applying and further developing the methods of the Maurists.

At the same time, Muratori dedicated himself to the study of the morals, the institutions, the culture and the religion of medieval society. To this end he consulted narrative sources and written records of all kinds, including royal diplomata, administrative documents and literary histories.

Such diverse sources provided Muratori with material for seventy-five dissertations, which he published in six volumes under the title *Antiquitates italicae medii aevi*, between 1738 and 1742. Together, Muratori's dissertations represent a wide-ranging and highly original account of the civilization of medieval Italy. Alongside his own commentary, Muratori included transcriptions of the texts of numerous medieval documents. He was not drawn to the medieval period for its own sake, indiscriminately, however. He certainly considered the period to be one of barbarism, though he never denied that the barbarians had had certain moral and political traditions, such as the simplicity of their mores and fairness in law, which deserved respect. Furthermore, Muratori was aware that the medieval period had not been a uniform continuum. He acknowledged that medieval civilization had made notable progress after 1000, and still more conspicuous advances after the thirteenth century. Confident as he was in the progress of humankind, Muratori interpreted these developments as symptomatic of a progressive purging of barbarism – the beginning of a process that could be seen to culminate in the culture and mores of his own day, with its good taste in literature and its enlightened social values. Moreover, Muratori did not limit his attention to the study of the Middle Ages; as a philosopher and writer, much of his energy was directed to exposing whatever obscurity he found lurking in contemporary society and in the Church. Thus, Muratori's significance is two-fold: firstly, he was the founder of scholarly historical research on the Italian Middle Ages; and, secondly, he was among the first to describe the relationship between the medieval and the modern periods in terms of the progress of a civilization that had its origins in the Middle Ages.

Similar perspectives can be found in the writings of the French scholar, Jean Baptiste de la Curne de Saint Palaye (1697-1781). Among other things, La Curne was director of the Académie des Inscriptions et

Belles Lettres, a prestigious academic institution with an important role in French culture during the first half of the eighteenth century. In this office, La Curne exercised his considerable influence in encouraging academic interest in the study of medieval civilization and medieval documents particularly. He collaborated on the great *Recueil des historiens des Gaules et de la France* (1723), a collection of narrative and other sources for the history of medieval France begun by the Maurist scholar, Martin Bouquet. La Curne undertook a study of a number of medieval chronicles in order to verify their authenticity as historical sources. This he did by reviewing the biographies and the historical context of the medieval chroniclers. However, the most original and significant aspect of La Curne's scholarly work he saved for works of medieval French vernacular literature, writings he considered important evidence for the civilization of medieval France. He planned and in large part completed a *Glossaire de l'ancienne langue françoise*, which was to be the equivalent of Du Cange's Latin *Glossarium*. It incorporated La Curne's own studies of the origins of words and their meaning and usage. Furthermore, La Curne assembled an enormous quantity of material for his *Histoire litteraire des troubadours* (3 vols, 1774), which was long to be the basis of our knowledge of the world of the troubadours.

Later, La Curne applied his remarkable knowledge of the sources to the compilation of the *Dictionnaire des antiquités françaises*, an encyclopaedia of morals, institutions and conditions of life in medieval France. Such was the scale of this project that it was never to be completed, though it would provide La Curne with material for two further monographs of great and lasting success: *Memoires sur l'ancienne chevalerie* (1746-1750), and *Memoires historiques sur la chasse* (1781). In these, La Curne drew a vivid portrait of the medieval nobility and its organization, manners and moral values. The first *Memoires* were translated into various languages, bringing the attention and the interest of educated eighteenth-century society to the characteristically evocative aspects of this side of medieval life. Like Muratori, La Curne adhered to the ethical and cultural values of his time, and was thoroughly convinced of the superiority of contemporary values compared to those of the medieval period. And like Muratori, La Curne saw in the Middle Ages not only the origins of the monarchy and nobility, the political institutions central to the history of France, but also the beginning of his people's national literary tradition. La Curne appreciated the ingenuous and spontaneous air of medieval civilization, though he remained convinced that society enjoyed its greatest achievement only in his own day.

In the eighteenth century, reflection on the medieval past was not restricted to the academies and other circles of scholars. In Enlightenment France, both political philosophers and social commentators frequently referred to the Middle Ages in their attacks against contemporary institutions and the corruptions of feudalism. In this context, a particularly polemical account of the medieval period was issued by Voltaire (the pseudonym of François Marie Arouet) (1694-1778). Among other things Voltaire was the author of a number of ambitious historical works, of which perhaps the most significant is his *Essai sur les moeurs et l'esprit des nations et sur les principaux faits de l'histoire depuis Charlemagne jusqu'à Louis XIII* (1758). For Voltaire, the primary purpose of history was as a source of knowledge 'of the spirit, the use and wonts of the major nations' – knowledge that was to instil awareness of the past mistakes of humankind, thereby facilitating the future progress of society.

The medieval epoch is the subject of the greater part of Voltaire's *Essai*, though it is not regarded as a distinct historical period. The barbarian invasions together with the political power of the Christian Church had put an end to classical civilization. An epoch began in which barbarism and violence, poverty and superstition were to dominate European society. Voltaire compared this process with other ancient civilizations, such as those of India and China, and in some respects also Islam. In his opinion these civilizations were able to preserve wise governance of society. The gravest responsibility for the corruption of society in Europe fell to the Christian Church, which had transformed religion into a tool for domination and oppression. This situation had extended beyond the Middle Ages, well into modern times. Only in the last fifty years, thought Voltaire, had European society begun to free itself from the ties of the past and embrace reason and justice in its organization.

Voltaire's *Essai* was intended as a warning about the damage that violence and superstition could inflict on society. There was evidence that conditions of life had improved; from the thirteenth and fourteenth centuries towns and commerce revived; kings endeavoured to find efficient forms of government; artists and writers produced a few masterpieces. But intolerance and oppression still lay in wait, and society was not strong enough to oppose them.

Certain aspects of the past, such as aristocratic privilege and the authority of the Church, were still to be overcome in Voltaire's time, and his circumstances do much to explain his historiographical perspective. He was reasonably well-informed about past facts and events; he made clever use of scholarly works by Muratori, La Curne and the Maurists. However, he was not concerned with representing the past objectively; instead, he aimed to present a polemical account, one that was intended to demonstrate the need for rational reformation of government and customs. Entirely missing is any effort to understand the nature and functions of medieval institutions and habits. Historical reconstruction is made to provoke indignation against a system which appeared dominated by the abuse of power and superstition.

In Voltaire's *Essai* the Middle Ages is not dealt with as a distinct period, but merged with the rest of European history. That said, Voltaire's view of the period profoundly influenced the attitudes of cultured people in the eighteenth century.

However, there were voices that did not consider the past in such polemical terms. In his *View of the Progress of Society in Europe from the Subversion of the Roman Empire to the Beginning of the XVIth Century* (1771) – an introduction to a history of the empire of Charles V – the Protestant pastor and historian, William Robertson (1721-1793), outlined a version of the medieval history of Europe. Robertson described how the anarchy and barbarism brought on by the invasions had been progressively overcome, and the foundations laid for the superior forms of political, economic and social life in the modern age. Once again, in Robertson's narrative, the barbarian invasions are regarded as the cause of a crisis that was to provoke the downfall of ancient civilization. Even Christianity, to which Robertson gave rather greater consideration than did Voltaire, is seen to degenerate under the influence of the barbarians. Yet from the conditions of barbarism other situations were to emerge, to set the decadence into reverse. Among these were the Crusades. A product of the fanaticism and violence of feudal society, the Crusades are none the less credited with bringing the West into contact with the superior cultures of the Near East. Similarly, the struggle for supremacy between the papacy and the empire created circumstances favourable to the emergence of free communities in the towns of central and northern Italy. And, likewise, the cultural and social predominance of the clergy is shown to have tempered barbarian law through the adoption of ecclesiastical law.

Reasoning in this way, Robertson deduced a logical chain of developments in order to explain how, after the eleventh century, European society had developed progressively more advanced moral and social forms.

In Robertson's account, no significant hiatus breaks the chain of development from the economic, institutional and political systems of the modern period. He did not consider the medieval epoch as a discrete and homogeneous period in history, and nowhere does he speak of it in these terms. Robertson's subject is the development of modern civilization following the violent upheaval of ancient civilization – a development made possible thanks to the recovery of conditions favourable to improved economic and social relations. Once more, the Middle Ages are placed firmly within the framework of European history, not as a backward step in the direction of progress, but as a formative phase in modern history.

Another rather different view of the Middle Ages is presented by *The History of the Decline and Fall of the Roman Empire* (1776-88), the work of the English patrician Edward Gibbon (1737-1794). As a student of classical literature, Gibbon journeyed to Rome in 1764; there, he was struck by the contrast between what he knew of the grandeur of the ancient Roman empire and the pathetic sight of the ruins in the Forum.

Immediately he planned to write a history of the demise of Rome, and to this end he devoted the rest of his life. Taking up an established theme of seventeenth-century historiography, Gibbon considered the Byzantine empire to have been the continuation of the empire of Rome. Consequently, Gibbon's narrative begins with the second century AD, when, in his view, the civilization of the empire reached its zenith, and it ends with the conquest of Constantinople by the Turks in 1453.

Gibbon's account spans the whole of the medieval period. He described the Middle Ages not as a distinct or autonomous period in history, but as part of a much broader process, namely the breakdown of the Roman empire over a period of more than one thousand years. Furthermore, Gibbon's is not an exclusively European perspective, as by far the best part of the events he describes took place in the East. For these reasons, the relationship between the medieval and modern periods is not a central concern. Gibbon was not interested in demonstrating the progress of a civilization; on the contrary, his is a history of the slow decay of a civilization. Once again, the medieval period of European history is made remote from the modern. And in its substance Gibbon's estimation of medieval civilization accords well with the opinions of Voltaire.

All the same, Gibbon's work offers some novel perspectives. Most original is its focus on civilization in decline. Gibbon's preoccupation with this subject was utterly opposed to Enlightenment optimism and confidence in progress. Moreover, in the lengthy course of Rome's demise, Gibbon found room for a diversity of prominent phenomena, and particularly the appearance of other cultures, such as the Germanic peoples, the Arabs and the Turks. Similarly, much attention is given to episodes that unsettled established socio-political structures, such as the invasions, the Crusades, and the appearance of new religious movements. These Gibbon describes with a subtle sensitivity for cultural difference and primitive value systems. A talented narrator, Gibbon engages the reader, urging her or him to meditate on the scale and variety of the events described, without reducing them to single, rational line of development. Gibbon's image of the Middle Ages is the image of a period with its own particular historical experience – one with values different to those of modern civilization – a period of significance vastly beyond barbarism.

While Gibbon was writing, other unusual approaches to aspects of medieval civilization were being developed in England. The Anglican bishop Richard Hurd (1720-1808) published a volume of *Letters on Chivalry and Romance* (1762). Inspired by the chivalric *Memoires* of Le Curne de Sainte Palaye, and based on literary sources, Hurd's text is an idealized celebration of the moral and sentimental values of medieval chivalry. A similar nostalgia for the lost world of the medieval past is expressed by the collection of *Reliques of Ancient Poetry* (1765) by Thomas Percy (1729-1811), and by the *History of English Poetry* (1774-

81) by Thomas Warton (1729-1790). This nostalgic turn found literary expression in the songs of Ossian composed by James Macpherson (1736-1796) and published between 1760 and 1763. Macpherson's poetry was inspired by his reading of ancient Gaelic poetry. Also at this time there emerged in England a taste for medieval ruins, especially the remains of abbeys and castles in the landscape. Such monuments were seen as particularly evocative symbols of national heritage. The vogue gave way to the Gothic Revival, a central movement in European culture and taste that began at the end of the eighteenth century and lasted for much of the nineteenth.

The myth of the Middle Ages in German culture

Above all it was in Germany, from the end of the eighteenth century, that the Enlightenment concept of the Middle Ages was openly put up for discussion. In this context, previously established notions were supplanted in favour of a novel interpretation of the medieval period and its significance for the history of the peoples of Europe.

During the eighteenth century, Germany witnessed a cultural revival brought on in part by the Enlightenment. This revival produced very particular responses, chief among which was a preoccupation with the cultural and moral characteristics particular to the German people. These characteristics were to be used to build a sense of national consciousness, which was to take the place of the non-existent unity of the state.

One example of the use of history to this end can be found in the work of Justus Möser (1720-1794). Möser wrote a history of the German people, from the oldest accounts in the writings of Caesar and Tacitus to the end of the Middle Ages. Contrary to the attitude expressed by French Enlightenment writers, for whom the difference between national groups was no more than the product of climate and juridical institutions, Möser maintained that all peoples are unique, historically constituted entities characterized by a spiritual heritage expressed in language, customs and in law. All peoples aspire to a position of honour in their political dealings with others, and this honour is defended through the force of arms. In Möser's interpretation, the peculiarity of the German people was derived from their ability to combine individuality and collective solidarity in the organization of society, economy and the state. This capacity characterized the institutions of the earliest German peoples, before reaching its height in the age of Charlemagne. Thereafter, ancient German society disintegrated, and with it the honour of the German people. For Möser, the end of the old order was brought about by the growth of the economic and political authority of the great landowners, by the disappearance of the rank of freemen under the yoke of feudal dependence, and by the introduction of a monetary economy and new institutions of state. For Möser, then, the medieval period is crucial to the German national consciousness.

The idea of the 'national spirit' – that is, the spiritual, political or cultural essence of a people – was greatly influential in Germany in the last years of the eighteenth century, thanks partly to the mystical philosophy of Johann Gottfried Herder (1744-1803), a seminal figure in the period of transition between the Enlightenment and the growth of the cult of Romanticism. The idea of the national spirit was used not only to distinguish German cultural traditions from those of Enlightenment France, but also to provide a basis for political opposition to the occupation of Germany by Napoleon. In any event, it nurtured curiosity for Germanic and medieval antiquities. In this context, Adam Müller (1779-1829) made a study of feudalism, a medieval phenomenon Müller interpreted as a form of social organization and political life based on the spiritual principles of loyalty, protection and free service. For Müller the principles of feudalism were the ethical foundations of social cohesion and economic production, in contrast to the mechanicism and utilitarianism of social relations brought on by bourgeois individualism. In his reconstruction, medieval Christianity gave spiritual significance to social cohesion and the authority of the nation's heads.

At first this reflection on the distinctiveness of the German people had no explicitly nationalistic implications. In fact, writing of this kind is often accompanied by an enthusiastic vindication of Germany's place in European civilization. But when thinking of European civilzation, German writers were engaging different sets of values to those implied by Enlightenment commentators elsewhere in Europe. Thus, in a short piece entitled *Die Christenheit oder Europa* (1799), the poet, Friedrich von Hardenberg (1772-1801) (otherwise known as Novalis) exalted the period prior to the Protestant Reformation as a time when all Europe had been a single spiritual community united in the Catholic faith. According to the poet, medieval society was connected by simple but profound sentiments and bound in mystic solidarity. Earlier, in his lectures on history given at Jena in 1790, the poet and dramatist Friedrich Schiller (1759-1805) referred to the Middle Ages as a period in which freedom had been the foundation of society and civilization, if in rather disorganized and sometimes tumultuous forms, and in contrast to the despotism and slavery of the Roman empire. At this time, too, Friedrich Schlegel (1772-1829), teaching at Cologne in 1805-6, devised a theory of universal history in seven epochs, with the Middle Ages at its centre. Schlegel described the medieval age as one of order and spiritual peace, beginning with the incarnation of the Son of God and continuing with the diffusion of Christianity and its message of love. Subsequently, while teaching at Vienna in 1810, Schlegel formulated an appreciation of the medieval period as an age of poetry. He taught that medieval poetry expresses sentiments of vitality, grandeur and beauty, which more than make up for the poetry's rudeness of form or the poets' poor taste. Moreover, Schlegel overcame the prejudice against medieval culture spread by Renaissance and Enlightenment discourse; this he did by claiming that the medieval period had preserved the heritage of classical culture before enriching it with the influence of Christianity, and transmitting it to the modern world.

A variety of spiritual themes can be seen to underlie these assessments of the Middle Ages. The period is perceived in positive terms and even attributed with exemplary values. Implicit in the texts is the authors' yearning for a way of life (and a way of spiritual life) removed from or even opposed to the values of the present. This quest encouraged the making of a myth – the myth of a better time now lost in the past. Although they did succumb to nostalgia and polemic, the exponents of this myth were expressing their faith in the potential for future progress once lost values had been restored.

Such idealistic theories were the work of writers and thinkers who had little to do with scholarly research in historical studies. In Germany in the early nineteenth century, the writing of history proper adhered to the narrative tradition, and, above all, to the model set by Gibbon. This production was given fresh impetus by a growing interest in patriotic and nationalistic themes. The Swiss historian Johannes von Müller (1752-1809) told the glorious history of his people and its rise to political autonomy during the medieval period in his *Geschichte der Schweizerischen Eidgenossenschaft* (1786-1808), a history of the Swiss confederation in five volumes. The same topic inspired Schiller's famous play, *William Tell* (1804). Swiss independence, as expressed in the cantonal constitution, was to be a favourite theme of Romantic and liberal political culture.

In Germany, in his *Allgemeine Geschichte der Völker und Staaten des Mittelalters* (3 vols, 1814-22), and above all in his *Geschichte des deutschen Volkes* (1809), Heinrich Luden (1778-1847) looked fondly upon the ancient origins of the Germanic peoples. By their virtue and love of freedom, these people had prevailed in their supremacy. This kind of national history was intended to provide modern Germans with instruction in the principles of freedom and responsibility – principles that were considered indispensable if German society was to organize itself into a state and assume its role in the community of nations.

Soon interest began to build in other areas of Germany's medieval history. Friedrich von Raumer (1781-1873), in his *Geschichte der Hohenstaufen und ihrer Zeit* (6 vols, 1823-5), described the age of the Swabian emperors as one of glorious affirmation of the German people and its place in Europe. It was in that era, so the historian claimed, that the German people came to be possessed of an original, universal civilization based on the fusion of Germanic, Roman and Christian traditions.

An understanding of the complex and diverse character of medieval civilization animates the great works of legal history written in the first half of the nineteenth century. The pursuit of legal history signals a new approach to the study of the past. Previously, Johann Gottfried Herder had taught that law was among the key components of the nation's cultural patrimony. Karl Friedrich Eichhorn (1781-1854), professor of law at the universities of Göttingen and Berlin, developed this idea in his *Deutsche Staats- und Rechtsgeschichte* (4 vols, 1808-23). In this work, Eichhorn reconstructed the original forms of German law, revealing how the same forms had remained constant throughout subsequent historical developments. Eichhorn's colleague at Berlin, Friedrich Karl von Savigny (1779-1861), applied the same conception of the organic nature of law to his *Geschichte des römischen Rechts im Mittelalter* (6 vols, 1815-31). Von Savigny maintained that Roman law had survived the barbarian invasions, as by that time it had been so thoroughly incorporated into the lives and practices of people. After the invasions Roman law met barbarian traditions in a fruitful union that produced a novel juridical civilization in Europe. Like others of his time, von Savigny regarded the Middle Ages as an era of complex exchange between diverse cultural traditions.

It could be said that, in the first thirty years of the nineteenth century, German culture approached medieval history as a testing ground for concepts about German identity and the nation's role in European civilization. As the movement developed, writers and commentators sought to broaden their knowledge of the period by developing more reliable and broadly based approaches to the sources.

An event of enormous importance in this context was the foundation in 1818 of the Gesellschaft für ältere deutsche Geschichtskunde (or the 'Society for the Documentation of ancient German History'). The initiative was sponsored by Baron Karl von Stein, a patrician of Frankfurt, who had been inspired by the Romantic ideals of nation and national tradition. Its purpose was systematically to publish critical editions of sources for medieval German history. The society's motto, *sanctus amor patriae dat animum* ('strength through the blessed love of homeland'), reveals the spirit in which von Stein conceived his project, although the fact that the motto was formulated in Latin, not German, also reveals the humanistic and universalizing tendencies prevalent in contemporary culture.

The scientific and editorial programme was begun in 1824, under the direction of Georg Heinrich Pertz (1795-1876), a young scholar appointed to the task by von Stein. It was to produce a great collection of historical sources: the *Monumenta Germaniae Historica*. The *Monumenta* were divided into five sections, each dedicated to a different type of source: *Scriptores*, *Leges*, *Diplomata*, *Epistolae* and *Antiquitates*. Pertz himself edited the texts of Carolingian chronicles and annals for the first two volumes of the *Scriptores* section published in 1826 and 1829 respectively. Quickly the society commissioned the help of other scholars. Its driving principle was to establish a firm documentary basis for the practice of medieval German history. Compared with the seventeenth- and eighteenth-century collections of medieval sources, the *Monumenta* are characterized by the advanced critical methods of the editors, the equivalent of the methods used in classical philology at that time. The *Monumenta* are the result of exhaustive research and systematic comparison of all known copies of the texts in question. The editors explored libraries and archives right across Europe in order to reconstruct the entire manuscript tradition of particular texts for publication. Thanks to these efforts, vast numbers of medieval documents were made available in print, in a form previously unparalleled for accuracy and completeness. Moreover, the editors did not restrict themselves to German history in the strict sense, as the *Monumenta* were intended to illustrate the Germanic presence wherever it had produced historical records. Hence the *Monumenta* also contain sources relating to European countries in which Germans had had some role, either in the age of the migrations or under the empire.

At the same time, developments were made in the theory and practice of critical interpretation of historical documents. This movement was to establish methodological principles for the writing of history for much of the rest of the nineteenth century. The activity and teaching of Leopold Ranke (1795-1886) is of the greatest importance in this context. Ranke was a professor at Berlin from 1825. It is his achievement that history ceased to be used as material for writers and thinkers, becoming instead the pursuit of trained specialists employed in the universities. Furthermore, Ranke established the principle that objective historical knowledge may only be obtained through contemporary sources. For Ranke and his school, reconstructions and judgements based on second-hand witnesses were to have less or no authority. Ranke devised certain methodological criteria for the interpretation of historical documents. In the first place, sources are to be genuine and close in date to the events they describe. Different kinds of document are to be regarded as representing different levels of significance, depending on the kind of information given and the intentions of the authors. In this way, Ranke developed a hierarchy of sources, attributing greatest significance to official documents produced by institutional bodies, while the least importance was reserved for chronicles and works of literature.

Ranke maintained that the first task of the historian should be to represent the past objectively, or 'as it really was'. In order to achieve this goal, the historian is only to be concerned with information garnered from reliably authenticated sources. Once properly scrutinized, this information is arranged in the correct order or sequence. Following this procedure, the resulting narrative was believed to represent a faithful and objective account of the reality of historical events.

Ranke's long career spans the end of the era of Romanticism and the onset of positivism. He distrusted the ideological and philosophical uses to which history had been put by Romantic thinkers and was a keen defender of the impartiality and professionalism of the true historian.

Despite his claims, however, Ranke's own historical writing reveals a distinct literary bent, as well as betraying the author's attachment to certain Romantic conceptions. For instance, Ranke considered history as a stage set for great actors – both individual personalities and whole peoples – whose roles are inspired by moral and spiritual forces. From the dialogue between the players and their reciprocal exchange, Ranke thought, the historian should be able to isolate the reflex of universal order and harmony. He found an exemplary expression of this harmony in the integration of the Germanic and Roman peoples in European civilization.

As a historian, Ranke was concerned above all with the age of the Reformation and Counter Reformation. He published just one essay on the Middle Ages, an account of the period to the year 962, which appeared in his last great work, *Weltgeschichte* (6 vols, 1880-6). Nevertheless, Ranke is credited with sanctioning the idea that Christian universalism was the crucible from which modern European civilization was subsequently to emerge. The idea was to be enormously influential. It is no surprise, then, to discover that some of Ranke's students at Berlin were to be among the great medievalists of the second half of the nineteenth century. One of these was Georg Waitz (1813-1886), who succeeded Pertz as director of the *Monumenta Germaniae Historica* in 1876. Another was Friedrich Wilhelm Giesebrecht (1814-1889), author of *Geschichte der deutschen Kaiserzeit* (5 vols, 1855-88), a celebration of the medieval empire's role in promoting the German nation and spirit in Europe. Heinrich von Sybel (1817-1895) was a third. As a critic of Giesebrecht's thesis, Sybel carried on a lively debate with the institutional historian, Julius Ficker (1826-1902), on the importance of the medieval empire in the formation of the German nation and state. Sybel maintained that the empire's conquering universalism had hindered the construction of a strong national German state. Ficker took the opposite view, arguing that the same conquering ambition had been the medieval empire's most important attribute, and the means with which the Germanic peoples had influenced the course of European history. This discussion was anything but academic. It was an extension of other debates taking place during the second half of the nineteenth century on the subject of political unification and the role of the German state in Europe.

Romanticism and the medieval in France

Elsewhere in Europe, the culture of Romanticism fostered much interest in the medieval period, though it produced rather different responses to those in Germany.

In France at the time of the Restoration, the Middle Ages were characterized above all as an epoch of religious faith. Couched in peaceful and reassuring terms, this perception was intended as a foil to the instability and violence of the period of the Revolution and the Napoleonic empire, and as a buttress to political legitimacy. Especially important in creating and transmitting this cultural ideology was the work of François René de Chateaubriand (1768-1848). The medieval period was valued for the picturesque aspect of its customs, its literary production, and the forms of its political life. Such a tendency is apparent from a reading of such works as *Histoire des ducs de Bourgogne* by Prosper de Barante (1782-1866), a vivid evocation written in the evocative and poetic tone of the medieval sources.

However, not all treatments of the medieval period were motivated by simple escapism during the first half of the nineteenth century. In the most important cases, reflection on medieval history was conditioned by contemporary concerns over political and social issues. A good example of this may be found in the writing of Simonde de Sismondi (1773-1842), a philosopher and social theorist from Geneva. Strongly influenced by contemporary French culture, Simonde de Sismondi made studies of the political freedoms of the peoples of medieval Europe, interpreting such freedoms as expressions of the people's moral energy. Sismondi recognized that the most striking instance of the inter-relationship between morality, freedom and socio-economic development had occurred in the age of the urban communities of high-medieval Italy. To this subject he dedicated his vast *Histoire des republiques italiennes du Moyen Age* (1807-18). In Sismondi's view, the urban communities were spawned by a drive towards freedom and self-rule; ultimately, they were to lead to the zenith of the economic, social and political life in medieval Italy. At the end of the Middle Ages, with the triumph of tyranny and the Church's meddling in political affairs, the people's moral spark was extinguished and Italy plunged into decadence.

Sismondi's writing is still touched by the philosophical and rationalistic attitudes of much eighteenth-century historiography. Unmistakably Romantic, by contrast, is the work of Augustin Thierry (1795-1856). Thierry turned to the Middle Ages inspired by the novels of Walter Scott. From Scott he borrowed an evocative fictional voice and a sense of the period's dramatic atmosphere. For his subject matter, however, Thierry preferred the conflicts of opposing peoples, and especially the strife engendered by conquest of arms. His first work, *Histoire de la conquête de l'Angleterre par les Normands* (1825), is an epic account of the conflict between the Normans and the Saxons, written with undisguised sympathy for the losing side. In his most famous work, *Récits des temps mérovingiens* (1840), Thierry described the political, cultural and moral state of Gaul under Frankish dominion. He was an active supporter of the socialist movement, and an associate of the philosopher and reformer, Henri de Saint-Simon. Thus Thierry saw the superimposition of one race upon another in the Middle Ages, and the period's legacy of political stratification, as the origin of social problems affecting the subsequent history of Europe. Returning to ideas first formulated in the seventeenth and eighteenth centuries, Thierry considered the Franks to be the ancestors of the nobility, while the Gallo-Romans he regarded as the precursors of the third estate. In his *Essai sur l'histoire de la formation et du progrès du Tiers Etat* (1853), Thierry set out the history of what he considered to be the driving social force in French history, the bourgeoisie, describing the foundation of the medieval communes as a crucial factor in the political progress of modern civilization.

For Thierry, then, the Middle Ages were characterized by dramatic and exemplary actions – and as an epoch of beginnings, if not altogether positive ones.

The period was described in similar terms by François Guizot (1787-1874), a French historian and politician. Guizot was engaged in long-running research into the progress of European civilization. Taking his line from Voltaire, Guizot held that civilization is constructed not only by the actions and affairs of powerful individuals or whole peoples, but is equally the product of economics, morals, social mores and political and juridical institutions. Unlike earlier Enlightenment commentators, Guizot considered civilization not as an abstract concept – the supreme state in the development of humankind – but as a historically constituted and geographically situated reality. Such was the civilization of France, which he regarded as a synthesis of the civilization of all Europe. For Guizot the medieval period was one of formation preceding the fullest achievement of European civilization. In his *Histoire de la civilisation de la France* (1829), Guizot emphasized the singularity of medieval attitudes and sentiments, while condemning the primitive and irregular forms in which they were expressed. Even as he described the strengths of medieval society, Guizot deplored medieval systems of social relationships as hateful. In his *Essai sur l'histoire de France* (1858) he opposed Thierry's idea of irreconcilable racial conflict in the period, arguing instead that the roots of modern Europe were laid by the fusion of Germanic and Roman peoples which, he said, had occurred during the Middle Ages and under the influence of the Christian Church. The logic of this statement notwithstanding, Guizot considered the emergence of modern Europe to post-date the end of the Middle Ages.

After 1830, Guizot was minister for the interior in the government of Orléans. In this office he set out to reorganize the practice of historical research in France. Under King Louis Philippe (reigned 1830-1848), Guizot proposed that a general inspectorate of historic monuments be set up in order to list and protect the country's archaeological heritage, much of which was medieval. Furthermore, he promoted the establishment of the Société de l'histoire de France, for the publication of historical sources. At the same time the government supported the foundation of numerous antiquarian and scholarly societies dedicated to archive research and the publication of historical documents. In 1847, Guizot's successor to the ministry of the interior, the count of Salvandy, reorganized and revived the École des Chartes, first founded in 1821 but inactive due to dire management and financial difficulties. From the second half of the nineteenth century, the École des Chartes was to provide specialist training for palaeographers to further explore the vast heritage of France's national history.

Yet none of these initiatives were to provide the medieval period with a particularly privileged place in contemporary French historiography. This was finally to change with the career of Jules Michelet (1798-1874), one of the most productive and popular French historians of the mid-nineteenth century. Michelet maintained that the aim of the historian should be to comprehensively 'resurrect' the past through its political and religious forms, its economics and its art. In the process, great emphasis was to be given to the most prominent personalities, in whose words and deeds the spirit of the age found its expression. In pursuing his project, Michelet was assisted by a sensitive imagination and a fine literary voice. In his *Introduction à l'histoire universelle* (1831) – and in tune with the attitudes of Romanticism – Michelet claimed that the Middle Ages were a simple and picturesque epoch. Subsequently, in the first six volumes of the *Histoire de France* (1833-44), he attributed the origin and success of the French nation to the medieval period, a process he personified in the figure of Joan of Arc. Michelet's words on Joan of Arc make up some of the book's most affected passages. In the early 1840s, however, Michelet experienced a profound personal and political crisis, which led him to take up a most aggressive stance against the Christian tradition and the history of the Catholic Church. He developed an almost messianic faith in 'the people' as the regenerative force of civilization. He interrupted his work on the *Histoire de France* in order to write a *Histoire de la Révolution* (7 vols, 1847-53), in which he gave vent to his challenge to the Church and the divine right of the monarchy. When he returned to the *Histoire de France* (of which he was to complete a further eleven volumes), Michelet viewed the Middle Ages in a much altered light. Though he did not retract his previous interpretations, he now insisted that they were to be understood as referring to the ideals of the period, with no bearing on its reality. By this time, the Renaissance appeared to Michelet as the supreme period in European history and the birthplace of the modern spirit, and hence he became an enthusiastic narrator of Renaissance history. In another ideologically charged work, *La Bible de l'humanité* (1864), Michelet concluded that it was necessary for society resolutely to turn its back on the Middle Ages, which he perceived as a morbid and unhealthy age still capable of infecting the human spirit.

Michelet's polemics were directed against French Catholics who opposed the secular monarchy of Orléans. At this time, the Catholic movement was seeking to reappraise religious and ecclesiastical life, calling for historians to give greater attention to the role of Church and the Christian faith in the history of Europe. The movement was led by Frédéric Ozanam (1813-1853), a university professor who was among the founders of the St Vincent de Paul Society in 1833. Ozanam was the author of an impassioned meditation on particular episodes from medieval culture, focussing above all on such figures as Dante, St Francis of Assisi and Thomas Aquinas. Ozanam emphasized the importance of Christianity and the Church in creating a civilization permeated by spiritual values. This civilization – medieval civilization – Ozanam held up as the highest achievement of European history. A similar position was taken by Count Charles de Montalembert (1810-1870), a journalist and parliamentarian much credited with safeguarding France's medieval monuments. Montalembert claimed that the medieval Church had been an altogether different institution to the Church under the Ancien Régime. The Christian faith was the source of all the wealth of humanity, passion and greatness he saw in medieval life. De Montalembert was the author of a history of medieval monasticism, *Les moines d'Occident depuis St Benoit jusqu'à St Bernard* (7 vols, 1863-7), with which he set out to defend the cultural and spiritual traditions of monasticism from the contempt in which they were held by liberal historians such as Adolphe Thiers, who had famously referred to monasticism as 'the Christian form of suicide'.

It is in the same context that we meet the figure of Jacques Paul Migne (1800-1875), abbot and historian. Migne was the editor of Catholic journals to which Montalembert contributed. Above all, he is remembered for his great collection of medieval sources, the *Patrologiae cursus completus*. The *Patrologia* contains the works of Greek and Latin ecclesiastical writers, from the Church fathers to Pope Innocent III in the Latin series (217 vols, 1844-55), and up to the year 1439 in the Greek series (162 vols, 1857-66). The aim of Migne's formidable enterprise was to make the entire intellectual heritage of the early Christian and medieval Church available in the most accessible (and affordable) form. To this end Migne set up a publishing house with a purpose-built print-works near Paris. Migne oversaw the whole of his enormous task almost single-handedly. He was trained neither in philology nor history, and so limited himself to resetting old seventeenth- and eighteenth-century editions, without critical reappraisal of the texts in the manner of the *Monumenta Germaniae*. Despite this major shortcoming, the *Patrologia* has been an important vehicle for the dissemination of medieval doctrinal, historiographical and literary texts. It remains in use today, at least as the first reference for less-accessible texts.

Italian Romanticism

In early nineteenth-century Italy, the promotion of medieval history found an exponent of the first order in Alessandro Manzoni. Manzoni's two tragedies, *Il Conte di Carmagnola* (1820) and *Adelchi* (1822), were set in troubled times in the history of medieval Italy. They refer to episodes that must have appeared to Manzoni's contemporaries as recurrent themes of national history – namely, political disharmony and oppression at the hands of foreign invaders. Manzoni was not a historian, though he prepared detailed research in advance of writing. The problems tackled in these literary works – particularly the second, on the conquest and domination of Italy by the Lombards – provoked much discussion and further research. Manzoni followed up the publication of *Adelchi* with a *Discorso sopra alcuni punti della storia longobardica in Italia* (1822). For this he drew on themes developed by Muratori and the Neapolitan historian, Pietro Giannone, and on the recent work of von Savigny and Sismonde de Sismondi. Manzoni identified the Latin population of post-Roman Italy as the ancestors of modern Italians. With the arrival of the Lombards in Italy, the Latins were stripped of their rights and reduced to servitude. Manzoni's statements provoked much lively debate, which reached its height in the years prior to the Risorgimento. Prominent in this context is the figure of Carlo Troya (1784-1858), who was systematically to assemble and edit the written sources relating to the Lombard question.

Unlike France, there was as yet no state institution to provide the framework of national history in Italy, though this circumstance did little to dampen enthusiasm for the great events of Italian history. Muratori had established the understanding that Italian history began with the Middle Ages, in the age of the urban communities – an age of freedom and civility. Besides the communes, particular attention was reserved for the papacy, which was likewise considered the defender of Italian society from foreign oppression. Prior to the mid nineteenth century, history in Italy was the pursuit not of historians but philosophers and political commentators – men poorly versed in the methodical scrutiny of sources. It is for this reason that the most important studies of the Italian communes at this time were the work of German scholars, such as Heinrich Leo (1799-1878), author of *Die Entwickelung der Verfassung der lombardischen Städte* (1824), Moritz von Bethmann Hollweg (1795-1877), author of *Ursprung der lombardischen Städtefreiheit* (1846), and Karl Hegel, son of the famous philosopher, who wrote his *Geschichte der Städteverfassung von Italien* (1847). These works were quickly translated into Italian, further stimulating inquiry and debate in that country.

Historiography in England in the nineteenth century

At the beginning of the nineteenth century English historiography was dominated by political commentators and writers. Of considerable significance was *A View of the State of Europe during the Middle Ages* (1818; further revised editions up to 1848), the work of Henry Hallam (1777-1859). Hallam shared many of Gibbon's attitudes to historical research: wide scope of investigation; attention paid to the legal consti-

tution and the government of the states; keen effort to evaluate past
institutions in relation to the needs and possibilities of their age, instead
of judging them by abstract criteria of rationality as Voltaire often did.
Hallam also shared Gibbon's talents as an absorbing narrator of history.
Yet he differed from Gibbon in that he treated the Middle Ages as a
definite historical period with recognizable chronological limits and
internal coherence. Moreover, he focused his research on the group of
peoples and states that had grown up to constitute modern Europe,
whilst Gibbon had studied the widely flung heterogeneous world that
succeeded the ancient Roman empire.

Hallam maintained that the Middle Ages were important precisely
because the European nations and states had originated in that period
– in spite of the primitive culture that predominated at least until the
eleventh century. Hallam dedicated a chapter to the history of each
European nation – France, England, Spain, Italy – tracing their formation from the barbarian invasions up to the end of the fifteenth century.
He dedicated other chapters to themes relevant to the whole of European society in the Middle Ages, such as the Roman Church, the feudal
system, and the history of commerce, customs and literature.

In the chapter devoted to medieval England, Hallam paid special
attention to the genesis of the English political constitution. This was
an original and almost unique system, based on a balance of power
between the Crown and Parliament. Hallam maintained that in his day
this system was the best in Europe as far as the freedom of the citizen
and political stability were concerned. Consequently, the history of the
English constitution was of general interest not only for the English, but
for 'inquisitive men' of all countries.

The essence of the English constitution lay in the principle that
everyone was to be judged by a court composed of his peers. This
principle of popular sovereignty protected citizens against coercion by
the powerful, whoever they might be. Hallam saw this principle operat-
ing already in the barbarian kingdoms of the Angles and Saxons, during
the early centuries of the Middle Ages; he regarded it as Germanic in its
origins, inspired by the Germanic love of freedom and justice. The
Norman conquest of England put these popular liberties in danger. The
Norman kings were authoritarian and even despotic, but their actions
caused their Norman and Saxon subjects to join together to impose
constitutional restrictions on the monarchy; these were summed up in
Magna Carta, the charter of liberties on which the political rights and
the government of the English people were to rest for centuries.

During the first half of the nineteenth century, the origin of the
nation was a major preoccupation of historical writing in England, as it
was elsewhere in Europe. An echo of this can be found in literary works,
such as the historical novels of Walter Scott. More specifically historical
approaches to the subject paid great attention to the history of the
constitution. This was not by chance, for in the 1830s a lively debate was

taking place in England concerning the role of Parliament in relation to the Crown, as well as the function of Parliament as the bulwark of civil liberties and legislator for a society that was witnessing dramatic changes.

Francis Palgrave (1777-1861) was a lawyer and writer who considered law-giving to be the main task of rulers and regarded investigation of the law as the best approach to discovering a people's national character. With this in mind, he studied the ancient law and government of England in the Saxon age in the essay *Rise and Progress of the English Commonwealth* (1832). Later he extended his research to the Norman period and published *The History of Normandy and England* (1851-64). With these works Palgrave contributed greatly to the general idea that the early medieval period of English history was fundamental in shaping the nation's political traditions. He thought that the Anglo-Saxon state was indebted to its Roman heritage, which had not disappeared in England with the coming of the barbarians. Roman laws had merged with Anglo-Saxon Germanic customs. A strong monarchy thus developed, but one whose powers were tempered by popular institutions of Germanic origin.

Palgrave held that the Roman legacy enabled public institutions to continue to flourish when the Normans replaced the Saxons as governors of the kingdom. Whilst Walter Scott and Augustin Thierry held that irremediable hostility characterized the two peoples and their civilizations, Palgrave maintained that the Normans soon assimilated the Saxon constitution, thanks to its similarities with Norman customs.

In 1838 Palgrave was appointed Deputy Keeper of Records and set about reordering the medieval archives. Collections of documents previously dispersed in many places were transferred to public archives for better preservation and easier consultation. He also edited a series of medieval documents, including many volumes of 'Parliamentary Writs', the legal orders dispatched by medieval Parliaments. Through his activity and publications, Palgrave was very effective in spreading the taste for medieval history and research in England.

John Mitchell Kemble (1807-1857), a philologist and antiquarian, also considered the Saxon age to be the formative period of the English nation. He visited Germany where he attended the courses of the famous German philologist Jacob Grimm. Kemble gained a thorough knowledge of the Saxon language and translated the ancient Saxon poem *Beowulf* into English (1833). Through extensive research in the archives, he also collected historical documents from the Saxon age which he published in a *Codex Diplomaticus Aevi Saxonici* (6 vols, 1839-48). On the basis of this material he wrote *The Saxons in England* (2 vols, 1848), an extensive study of early English history. Contrary to Palgrave, Kemble assumed that the Saxons in England had maintained their original social and political institutions. For this reason, he argued, the English constitution and society were Germanic in origin.

These contrasting standpoints reflected the debate that was taking place on the Continent – above all in Germany – concerning the role of Roman and Germanic traditions in the creation of modern Europe.

The study of the medieval constitutional history of England was to take on more objective methods thanks to William Stubbs (1805-1901), professor of Modern History at the University of Oxford and later bishop of Oxford. Stubbs was an indefatigable editor of medieval historical sources, be they chronicles, biographies, juridical acts or other documents. Most of these were published in the 'Rolls' series, an important collection launched in 1858. Together with A.W. Haddan, Stubbs also edited the proceedings of medieval ecclesiastical councils in both England and Ireland. At the same time he devoted himself to studying English constitutional history on a wider basis than his predecessors. He believed that the constitutional history of the country was an essential factor in the moral and intellectual education of its citizens, and he incorporated the subject into his teaching. The lasting result of his researches was *The Constitutional History of England in its Origins and Development* (3 vols, 1873-8). This analysis stretched from Roman times to the Tudor age and concentrated on the institutional organization of the country – government, justice, taxation. Less attention was paid to diplomatic and military aspects, which Stubbs considered less important in the creation of national identity.

Stubbs agreed with his predecessors' assumption that the English constitutional system had been formed during the Middle Ages, but he differed from them in that he did not consider the Saxon or Norman ages to be the period when political and juridical institutions had taken their characteristic shape. He argued rather that it was in the twelfth century – the age of the Plantagenets – that a developed constitution emerged, one that ensured some form of representation for the political body of the kingdom. This resulted from the integration of the old Saxon principles of popular freedom and local self-government with the techniques of Norman royal government. In the thirteenth century events pushed the system towards a more evolved form; by the end of that century Parliament had taken a definite shape with the three social orders of the kingdom represented. This was the form that was to last as the basis of the English constitution.

Stubbs' work clearly shows the influence of the intellectual and political climate of the Victorian age, above all when he extols the moral superiority of the English political tradition. Nonetheless, his *History* rested on solid learning and enjoyed widespread acclaim even outside England. Once established on a critical basis, English constitutional history became comparable to histories of other nations, while at the same time its specific nature was better appreciated.

By the mid-nineteenth century other scholars in Oxford were devoting themselves to medieval history, following the trail blazed by Stubbs; they were known as the Oxford school of history. Edward Augustus

Freeman (1823-1892), who succeeded Stubbs as professor, wrote a monumental *History of the Norman Conquest*, an extended account of the Norman period in England with particular emphasis on political and military events. The work was based on Freeman's wide knowledge of historical sources as well as on his direct experience of historical sites. Freeman was sympathetic to the Saxons, attributing to them the origins of the popular institutions that were to survive through Norman times and form the basis of the English constitution.

The Middle Ages have special relevance also in *A Short History of the English People* by John Richard Green (1837-1883), a brilliant reconstruction of the whole historical development of the nation and one that enjoyed great success. Religion, culture and law were the main preoccupations of the author. Green did not put dynastic and political events in the foreground, considering that they were not essential to display the national character. Parliament was the expression and safeguard of civil liberties; the unremitting defence of those liberties was the main theme of English history.

It is with Frederic William Maitland (1850-1906) that the history of English law first attains a high level of dispassionate analysis. Maitland was no teacher, but a jurist and a lawyer; he was attracted by the history of the Common Law, that body of customary rules and procedures that formed the basis of English law. In the second half of the nineteenth century, the reform of the Common Law was being debated. Lawyers and politicians were inclined to consider the Common Law as a coherent heritage, which had formed in the past and retained its validity in modern times. By contrast, Maitland maintained that legal history should aim to reconstruct the formation and development of juridical customs, in order to free them from the constraints of the past. Unevenness and shifts in constitutional history could be contemplated without difficulty because the law was a social product that changed with the needs and customs of society. The nature and purpose of the law were to be explained by relating the law to other past social expressions. In this way, history supported reform. Maitland considered anachronism to be the gravest fault of the historian, and he devoted himself to investigating the complex processes by which the body of English law had formed over time.

Acquisition of ever wider documentation was an essential means to this aim. Maitland pointed to the importance of documents relating to the daily practice of jurisdiction and public administration. These revealed not only the technicalities of justice, but also the life of individuals and societies in the past. In 1884 Maitland edited *Pleas of the Crown for the County of Gloucester*; in 1887 he founded the Selden Society, whose purpose was to promote knowledge of English legal sources. He collaborated in the Society's activity by editing various documentary series, among them the 'Year Books', reports of cases debated before the English Parliament in the fourteenth century. Another product of his interest in medieval legal practice is *Bracton's Note Book* (1887), a study of a manuscript containing hundreds of cases discussed before Henry III and accompanied by the comments of the famous thirteenth-century English lawyer Henri de Bracton.

Analytical studies were the foundation of Maitland's great historical surveys. In 1895 he published the *History of the English Law before the Time of Edward I*, written in collaboration with the jurist Frederick Pollock. Here the making of the English law is represented as a complex development, starting from Saxon origins but subject to various later influences, from the Normans to the Catholic Church and the continental law schools. It was not until the end of the thirteenth century that these contrasting influences reached some kind of settlement. Maitland and Pollock rejected the idea that a recognizable nucleus of juridical institutions could have survived intact through the centuries. Rather, they showed how the law formed in connection with social and economic development, though they also paid attention to technical aspects of the law and their evolution. The Crown was credited with an important role in building up the English constitution, whilst the influence of Parliament was thought to have been sometimes overestimated.

In later years Maitland published more essays. *Domesday Book and Beyond* (1897) was a study of the great census carried out under William the Conqueror, which Maitland used as a source for social and economic history. Next came *Township and Boroughs* (1898), which dealt with the origins and legal status of the English medieval town; *Roman Canon Law in the Church of England* (1898) examined the influence of Roman Canon Law over English law through the action of the Church.

Maitland's work was essential in freeing studies of English law from the ideological limitations that had long prevailed during the nineteenth century. He showed that the English legal system was a thoroughly historical product, one with strong specific characteristics but clearly related to the constitutional history of other European nations.

Historiography and positivism

In the second half of the nineteenth century, enthusiasm for uncovering and evaluating historical documents reached a peak all over Europe, as historians determined to represent their subject with total objectivity. What drove them was the expectation that history could achieve the same verifiable certainty that was the mark of the natural sciences.

In Germany, academic history was characterized by scholarly erudition directed towards more and more minutely critical reconstructions of events, particularly in the fields of political and diplomatic history. As such it was propelled by the teaching of Ranke, though German scholars often lost sight of Ranke's wider objectives. A typical example of this is the *Jahrbücher der deutschen Geschichte* (1866-), annals of the deeds of the medieval German emperors, based on all available documentation and motivated by the ideals of accuracy and comprehensiveness.

Alongside the objective tendency in historiography, alternative perspectives developed in the course of the second half of the nineteenth century. The development of these approaches was to be of the utmost importance in broadening and diversifying the practice of history in general and medieval history in particular.

The history of law came to prominence at this time, particularly in relation to the institutional and constitutional structures of nations. German scholars took the lead, as the teachings of Eichhorn and Savigny inspired the formation of what became known as the historical school of law. This group of scholars developed Herder's idea of the organic (non-contractual) nature of law. In this perspective, law is a natural response to the activities, the needs and the character of a given nation. The idea inspired further research into the juridical institutions of the German people, medieval institutions said to have come down from the period of the folk migrations and, still further, from the Germanic peoples described by Caesar and Tacitus. Towards the middle of the nineteenth century, with the spread of liberal movements and the call for new constitutional order among the German states, these studies took on political significance. Studies of this kind responded to the quest to define the particular political vocation of the German people, which observers were keen to identify with the so-called 'Germanic freedom' – a mix of individualism, collective solidarity, personal initiative and central control, which was also to find expression in the constitution of modern Germany. Among the exponents of the historical school of law, particular status was achieved by the so-called Germanists, particularly Jacob Grimm (1785-1863) and Georg Waitz, a former student of Ranke. These men charted the history of German institutional culture, from the ancient Germanic peoples to the political systems of the Middle Ages, based on their extensive and systematic survey of the sources. They attempted to define the nature and characteristics of personal freedoms, and they debated on the existence of the nobility as a juridically distinct class. Moreover, they were concerned with the origins of royal authority and its relation to society, the feudal system and the origins of the private powers of command. Such complex issues they organized into impressive holistic accounts, such as Waitz's *Deutsche Verfassungsgeschichte* (1844-78), a reconstruction of the institutional history of the Germanic peoples from their origins to the twelfth century.

Scholarly research was accompanied by lively discussion of the nature of the German state in the Middle Ages. In particular, attention was focused on the issue of whether the state had been based on powers held by the people at large or on the rule of kings. Along the same lines, observers asked whether the apparatus of powerful institutions was a function of the protection and authority traditionally exercised within

German society, or, alternatively, whether power was imposed by the juridical sovereignty of the state. The question was beaten out between some of the most illustrious scholars of the second half of the nineteenth century, men such as Otto von Gierke (1841-1921), Rudolf Sohm (1841-1917), Heinrich Brunner (1840-1878), and Georg von Below (1858-1927). These men were the authors of lengthy works on the origins and nature of the powers exercised by such institutions as the city-state and trade guilds; on the formal definition of juridical institutes; and on the relation between the political functions of state and the activity of institutions. For the most part, these discussions ended with the conclusion that the institutional framework of medieval Germany had been entirely state-like in nature.

Around the middle of the nineteenth century, the study of economic history was developed in response to other contemporary concerns. The background to this development was a controversy over Germany's political economy, and the search for specifically German principles of political economy in opposition to the values of English liberalism. Particularly influential in this context was *Das National System der politischen Ökonomie* (1841) by Friedrich List (1789-1846). In List's view, the nation is a collective organism with its own particular forms of economic organization. Once again, these are ideas drawn from Herder, the chief architect of the particularist perspective on German culture and history. In turn, List's work spawned the so-called historical school of national economy, and the work of its most important exponents, such as Bruno Hildebrand (1812-1878) and Gustav von Schoenberg (1839-1908). These men were the authors of important works on the urban economy of medieval Germany. Above all, though, the movement is best represented by Theodor von Inama Sternegg (1843-1908), whose weighty *Deutsche Wirtschaftsgeschichte* (3 vols, 1879-1901) was the first text to use the term 'economic history' in its title. This is an enormous work, one conducted in the contemporary spirit of erudite and systematic enquiry, with particular attention reserved for the administrative and juridical sources. Considerable emphasis is given to the political economy of powerful institutions, to the relationship between the juridical status of individuals and their economic activities, and to the institutional organization of economic production. The major economic structures of the medieval period are identified and described, from the landed system of the early Middle Ages to late-medieval capitalist commerce. Inama Sternegg was director of the central office of statistics under the imperial Austrian government. He was eager to employ both statistical as well as ethnographical methods in his analysis, though he was not always able to overcome the limits of the medieval sources. Moreover, he regretted that he was unable to make use of a large body of other, potentially more useful material, such as the records of economic activity, as this material was yet to be published. Despite these shortcomings, Inama established the importance of economic history, history based on technical knowledge of the patterns and processes of economics. Previously, historians of institutions or politics had shown little concern for this side of medieval life.

The theoretical framework for the study of medieval economics was derived from studies of the fundamental types and developmental stages of economic activity. It was Hildebrand who came up with a theory of economic history based on three modes of production, which he claimed are to be observed in all cultures – natural economy, monetary economy, and credit economy. Still greater influence was to be achieved by other theories that established connections between social structures, the organization of production, and patterns of consumption. Karl Bücher (1847-1930) was the author of one such theory, a four-tiered economic model based (in order of complexity) on domestic economy, local or regional economies, and urban and national economies. Hence, he argued, the medieval period was characterized by the prevalence, in successive stages, of certain types of economy. For Bücher, the period is one of interest for what it reveals of the process of transition from one economic type to another. Bücher's theories have a clear affinity with those of Karl Marx (1818-1883) and Friedrich Engels (1820-1895). Marx's and Engels' theories were based on a typology of the basic forms of economic production recognizable in history, not just in Europe but in the rest of the world. These forms are defined in terms of their implications for socio-economic relations; that is, in terms of the social context of the ownership of the means of production. As is well known, Marx identified four modes of production – Asiatic, slave, feudal, and bourgeois-capitalist. Historically, the feudal mode and the first symptoms of capitalism are to be found in medieval Europe. Thus in Marxist theory the Middle Ages may be characterized in terms of coherent and long-term economic systems, though certainly Marx did not maintain that socio-economic change occurs at the same pace among all peoples at all times. Rather, Marx accepted the possibility that different modes of production may co-exist in different contexts contemporaneously.

Marx gave much thought to understanding the context and dynamics of change from one mode of production to another. Of course, this concern was to be the platform for Marx's and Engels' political manifesto and their call for the revolutionary overthrow of capitalism and the institution of socialism. Marx identified a sort of inherent necessity or inevitability in the process of transition from one economic model to the next, one based on conflict between the social classes. At the same time, he underlined the importance of spontaneous, voluntary action in effecting historical change. In the Marxist interpretation of history, social agency is manifested in the actions of the socio-economic classes.

At first, Marxist theory gained but a scarce following among academic historians, prohibited as it was by governments on account of its political implications. Only during the last decade of the nineteenth century, and with the abolition of the anti-socialist legislation of Bismarck, did the influence of Marxist thought show up in historical discourse in Germany, where a group of socialist academics set about tracing the origins of the bourgeoisie and the capitalist system of production to the mercantile and manufacturing economy of medieval towns.

In the practice of medieval history, positivism forsook the fascination for the evocative or idealized-ideological aspects of the medieval period of the kind nurtured by the Enlightenment and Romanticism. Instead, positivism placed fresh emphasis on the socio-economic structures and juridical systems particular to the period. Positivism was concerned with understanding the specific logic of these phenomena, and their general significance in comparative and developmental terms. Hence the concerns of historians were markedly akin to those of the social sciences in the last decades of the nineteenth century. Through the study of European as well as non-European societies both past and present, social scientists were endeavouring to explain the actions and transformation of human cultures with laws similar in kind to the laws observed in physics and chemistry. In this way, positivism set up a determinist view of social agency, in which the initiative of individuals is subject to constraint by race, environment and social relations.

Another historiographical tendency typical of this period is known in German as Kulturgeschichte, 'cultural history'. The goal of cultural history was to represent the organic unity of different expressions of cultural life of a given society in history, including literature, institutions, political activity, economic organization, artistic expression and religion.

Kulturgeschichte found its most impressive advocate in the figure of Jacob Burckhardt (1818-1897). Burckhardt applied the approach not to a people but to a particular period, the Italian Renaissance. For Burckhardt, 'culture' results from the complex sum of politics, art, philosophy, religion, customs and morals; it is not reducible to evolutionary processes or rigid hierarchies, as it is a total, spiritual entity, the significance of which is implicit in the values it expresses. Burckhardt's contribution made it possible to think of other historical periods as entities significant in themselves, without hierarchies or patterns of development. In other work, Burckhardt himself drew attention to certain cultural aspects of the medieval period – Christian learning, the ecclesiastical hierarchy, and the interaction of church and state.

Economic history, social history and cultural history combine in the work of Karl Lamprecht (1856-1915), professor at the universities of Marburg and Leipzig. Lamprecht was both a theoretician and scholar, and an altogether very subtle mind. Lamprecht's work fully expresses the aspirations and the limitations of positivist historiography. He was attracted to the relationship between society and its environment after reading a thesis by the geographer Friedrich Ratzel, who argued for the influence of the environment on the organization and development of societies. Lamprecht was interested in the study of medieval economics, for which he made careful use of documents relating to the ownership and use of land in the period. In interpreting the sources, Lamprecht employed statistical analysis in order to give a quantitative evaluation of the subject. Furthermore, he gave full attention to artistic production and to the attitudes and mores of the medieval mentality. These rich but diverse seams of inquiry Lamprecht combined in his first great work, *Deutsches Wirtschaftsleben im Mittelalter* (4 vols, 1885-), an analysis of the social, economic and institutional organization of society in a particular region of medieval Germany, the Meuse valley. Lamprecht attributed great importance to what he called the 'material culture' of people in the past, including settlement structures and the vital tools of economic production.

Later, Lamprecht broadened this definition of culture still further. He came to consider culture the sum of social production, economy and state institutions – as well as morality, law, art and religion. For Lamprecht, each period has its own particular cultural physiognomy, an appearance that is made manifest through society's collective actions and expressions. Rather minor significance is given to individual actions in this approach.

Fully consistent with the interests of sociological positivism, Lamprecht set out to identify the objective laws that govern the lives of cultures. Firstly, and under the influence of Marxist theory, Lamprecht pursued such laws in the area of economic relations, which he believed to be the scaffolding for all other forms of social life. Lamprecht put these ideas into practice in his monumental *Deutsche Geschichte* (15 vols, 1891-1909), a holistic reconstruction of German history in the medieval and modern periods, which he described in terms of a sequence of successive cultural stages.

Hurriedly prepared and in large part based on secondary information, Lamprecht's audacious statements provoked fiery censure from his contemporaries. In responding to his critics, Lamprecht was moved to substantiate the theoretical foundations of his ideas about cultural stages. In doing so he distanced himself from Marxist theory by taking up the theories of collective psychology which were being put forward at this time by Wilhelm Wundt, the founder of experimental and social psychology, and Lamprecht's colleague at Leipzig. In shifting his ground, Lamprecht maintained that cultural stages are determined and characterized not by economic conditions, but by the transformation of the collective psyche – *Volksseele*. This transformation occurs in a sequence of successive phases. Hence, Lamprecht divided the history of Germany into six phases: the *animist* (pre-medieval) period; the *symbolic* period (up to the tenth century); the *typological* period (from the tenth to the thirteenth centuries); the *conventional* period (thirteenth to fifteenth centuries); the *individualistic* period (fifteenth to eighteenth centuries); and the *subjectivist* period (the nineteenth century). Lamprecht was anxious to defend this model of history by showing it to apply equally to other national cultures. And in doing so he was to propose a theory of cultural morphology, which was taken up in Lamprecht's own lifetime by Kurt Breysig (1866-1940). The theory was later to be given systematic (and largely ahistorical) treatment by Oswald Spengler (1880-1936), who promoted the idea of the natural history of cultures, according to which cultures follow a fixed cycle of origin, apogee, decline and extinction. Spengler developed his theory with reference to particularly prominent episodes in history, though in doing so he gave scant regard to the proper context of his material.

History and the social sciences in France and Italy

In France at the end of the nineteenth century, historical research was characterized by a profoundly positivist approach, and, initially, a lack of concern for social aspects. In 1876, the journal *Revue Historique* was established under the direction of Gabriel Monod. Its agenda was to extend historical research beyond the limits of the subjectively and ideologically motivated historiography of the preceding years. According to the methods prescribed by the editors of the *Revue*, the historian's work was to be rooted in rigorous, first-hand examination of the sources. The historian's every statement was to be documented with a citation from the sources. Furthermore, the historian was to remain completely immune to philosophical and political prejudice, in order to make impartial assessments of personalities and conditions in the past. Such a method was to facilitate the reconstruction of historical veracity in the form of a narrative sequence of cause and effect. More generally, this method was intended to broadcast knowledge of national history. The method was taught in the universities and research institutes, such as the École des Chartes and the École Pratique des Hautes Études. The same method was codified by Charles-Victor Langlois and Charles Seignobos in their *Introduction aux études historiques* (1898), a textbook of positivist methodology for historians. The historian following this method has, in the first place, to identify the sources. Secondly, the sources are to be assessed for authenticity and quality. Once this is done, the historian proceeds by selecting information from the sources and collating these data in order to establish the facts. Thereafter, the facts may be combined so as to reconstruct more general situations, such as natural and environmental conditions, social relations and political institutions. Any attempt further to evaluate or interpret the facts, or to read them for more general historical significance, was considered a threat to the credibility of the historian's statements.

Possibly the most interesting figure at this time was Numa-Denis Fustel de Coulanges (1830-1889) who, in his work on ancient and medieval institutions, broke out of the vice of formalism by interpreting institutions as products of society's responses to its particular exigencies or needs. In his *Cité antique* (1864), his first wide-ranging work, Fustel argued that classical religion, public institutions and forms of social organization together constituted an organic, integrated system. As elements in a compound, historical phenomena may be explained only in terms of their relationship to other phenomena. The study of land-ownership and the agrarian economy of late antiquity led Fustel to consider the impact of the barbarian invasions on Roman institutions and Roman society more widely. He published the results of this research under the title *Histoire des institutions politiques de l'ancienne France* (3 vols, 1875-89; further volumes were published posthumously by the author's pupils). This is a most original thesis, one opposed to the principles of much of nineteenth-century French historiography. Fustel contended that the barbarian invasions did not signal the beginning of a new era, an epoch of ethnic and cultural conflict between Germanic and Roman peoples. The late-antique system of land-ownership was unaffected by the invasion, and so the social structures based on the economics of land-ownership were unaffected by the arrival of the barbarians. Fustel believed that institutions change slowly, in time with the needs and ideas and values of society. He argued that institutional systems distinct from those of antiquity emerged only gradually, as social and political relations were reshaped under the impact of feudal protection and immunity, and as these new relations were adapted into patterns of land-ownership and use. These ideas he explored in *L'alleu et le domain rural pendant l'époque mérovingienne* (1889) and in *Les origines du régime féodal: le bénéfice et le patronat* (1890).

Fustel developed his ideas in relation to the practice of institutional history in Germany. During his lifetime, Fustel was isolated among his colleagues in France, though he was to produce some brilliant students, such as Camille Jullian (1859-1933), who carried on his influence. Meanwhile, further impetus to new historiographical perspectives was exerted by the social sciences, which were coming into their own at this time. The discipline of sociology gained renewed prestige from the work of Émile Durkheim (1858-1917). Durkheim introduced a framework for the practice of sociology in France, with which the discipline was to overcome the limitations of doctrines prescribed by its great patriarch, Auguste Comte (1798-1857). Durkheim reclaimed the close affinity between sociology and history, inviting historians to study forms of social organization in the past, and so to identify, through comparison and generalization, the most general and commonly occurring patterns of social behaviour.

Another original contribution to historical research was made at this time by a geographer, Paul Vidal de la Blache (1845-1918), who steered the study of geography in the direction of the social sciences. In particular he emphasized the importance of the relationship between humankind and the environment, while arguing that geographers and historians should collaborate in the study of the landscape, which Vidal de la Blache regarded both as a natural phenomenon and historical artefact.

Nonetheless, at the end of the nineteenth century, the majority of academic historians in France were unresponsive to such ideas. In fact, most French historians were anxious to distinguish the role of history from that of the human and social sciences, while restating their commitment to the primacy of establishing facts and the autonomy of history as a branch of knowledge.

There was, however, to be one arena for discussion and analysis of the ties between history and the human sciences. This was provided by the *Revue de synthèse historique*. The review first appeared in 1900, under the direction of Henri Berr (1863-1954). Its purpose was to promote history as a discipline embracing all other disciplines dedicated to the comparative study of society – namely, sociology, geography, economics and psychology. That said, the editors did not attempt to overlook the diversity of analytical methods and practices employed by the different disciplines.

Likewise, in Italy, in the second half of the nineteenth century, the study of history was dominated by the universities, by positivist methods, and by minute scrutiny of the sources. Under the influence of contemporary German historiography, growing importance was addressed to the study of juridical institutions. Francesco Schupfer (1833-1925) and Antonio Pertile (1830-1885) – who had been raised respectively in Austria and Germany – traced the origins and development of medieval society in Italy from the institutions of public and private law, with particular emphasis on the role of Germanic and Roman traditions. After the political unification of Italy, the medieval period continued to occupy a prominent position in official state culture, as Italians continued to see the period, and particularly the epoch of the urban communities, as an expression of national spirit. Interest in the Middle Ages was further assured by the importance afforded to the period by literary historians. In the work of such figures as Francesco De Sanctis (1817-1883) and Giosue Carducci (1835-1907), literary history is inseparable from the pursuit of national traditions.

Among the most outstanding exponents of the positivist historiographical tradition in Italy were Pasquale Villari (1826-1917) and Amedeo Crivellucci (1850-1914), professors at the universities of Florence and Pisa respectively. Villari and Crivellucci were responsible for preparing the basis of professional historical research in Italy. Both were concerned with the origins of Italian history in the age between the barbarian invasions and the rise of the communes. Also at this time, the establishment of research institutes and numerous learned societies devoted to national history gave further impulse to archival research and the development of local history.

Towards the end of the nineteenth century, interest in economic and social history took hold in Italy. This development was encouraged by concern over contemporary social issues as well as by the spread of Marxism. In his *I primi due secoli della storia di Firenze* (2 vols, 1893-4), Pasquale Villari abandoned the traditional tendency to interpret conflict in medieval society as a legacy of unresolved conflict between Romans and barbarians, pointing instead to differences between the socio-economic classes. The reference to Marxist theory is still more explicit in the work of Villari's pupil, Gaetano Salvemini (1873-1957). In his *Magnati e popolani in Firenze dal 1280 al 1295* (1899) Salvemini made class conflict the key to his understanding of complex constitutional and social developments in thirteenth-century Florence. Others took similar approaches to studies of the medieval ownership and use of land, and in accounts of the legal condition of the medieval peasantry and rural associations and trade corporations. By analyzing the juridical relations implied by economic production, the aim of these Italian historians was to reconstruct the specific character of medieval Italian society and the origin of the nation. Historians working in this context included Gino Arias (*Il sistema della costituzione economica e sociale italiana nell'età dei comuni*, 1905), Romolo Caggese (*Classi e comuni rurali nel medioevo italiano*, 1906-9), and Giuseppe Salvioli (*Contributi alla storia economica italiana nel medioevo* I: *Sullo stato e la popolazione d'Italia prima e dopo le invasioni barbariche*, 1899, and II: *Città e campagne prima e dopo il Mille*, 1901; *Storia economica d'Italia nell'alto medioevo. Le nostre origini*, 1913).

Collectively these scholars are said to have formed the 'economic-juridical school' of history, though in fact their association was never quite so formal. As historians, their approach to social history was based more on an empirical sensitivity to social dynamics than it was on the theoretically grounded methods of the social sciences. In the first years of the twentieth century, the same movement produced Gioacchino Volpe (1876-1971), author of *Studi sulle instituzioni comunali a Pisa* (1902) and a string of works published between 1904 to 1910, which were later reprinted in a volume entitled *Medioevo italiano* (1923). Initially much influenced by Marxism, Volpe was to be the one who broke furthest away from the principles of the economic-juridical school of Italian history. Volpe's was a wide-ranging and evocative vision of social life in medieval Italy, based on the author's personal, intuitive ability to read the actions of the masses from the texts of documentary sources.

The drive to compose general histories of the medieval period from analysis of economic and social structures (and their associated institutional, political and cultural forms) achieved by far its most original results in the work of the Belgian historian, Henri Pirenne (1862-1935). Pirenne was absorbed with the question of the origin of medieval towns, a question much debated by German historians concerned with modes of economic production and their succession. Pirenne pursued the question in the particular context of the Low Countries. Contrary to established theories, Pirenne recognized the medieval town to have been substantially different to its predecessor in antiquity. For Pirenne, the medieval town was characterized by the presence of a new socio-economic class made up by merchants. By settling at nodal points in the landscape, this group gave rise to permanent settlements in which trading activities were carried on. Pirenne considered the emergence of the merchants to imply revolutionary social change, appearing as if out of nowhere at a particular moment in the Middle Ages, thanks to a coincidence of favourable circumstances. To justify the importance he gave to the mercantile economy, Pirenne carried out a survey of the early-medieval centuries, concluding that the merchant class had not been a feature of that epoch. Pirenne knew that economic historians such as Inama Sternegg had shown that the economy of the early-medieval period had been limited to agricultural production and land-ownership. Pirenne became interested in explaining the background to the predominance of the agrarian economy in the early-medieval period. He returned to the thesis advanced by Fustel de Coulanges, on the continuity of land use between late antiquity and the Merovingian period. As we know, Fustel de Coulanges had argued that the barbarian invasions made little destructive impact on the economic system of the late-antique West. Pirenne now argued that a profound rupture had occurred between the Merovingian and Carolingian epochs, brought on by Islamic expansion in the Mediterranean, which was to lead to the breakdown of trade between the eastern and western provinces of the old Roman empire. This development left the West economically isolated, with the people reduced to the staple economies of the fields.

This is the famous 'Pirenne thesis', a novel interpretation of the transition from the ancient to the medieval world. Pirenne developed the thesis in a number of texts, including *A History of Europe: From the Invasions to the Sixteenth Century* (written 1917, published 1936), *Medieval Cities* (1925), and *Mohammed and Charlemagne* (1937). Together, these works make up Pirenne's theory of economic change in late antiquity and the Middle Ages. With them, Pirenne proposed a novel view of the chronological limits of the medieval period, while reinterpreting the period's significance in relation to the origins of modern Europe.

The importance of the role given to economics in determining the transition from one economic system to another recalls the theories of Engels and Marx. Yet Pirenne was no Marxist. He considered that the forces behind economic change are to be found not in the mechanisms implied by the social organization of production, but in the wilful actions of individuals and groups prompted by religious or moral ideals. At certain moments in history, such agency had led to revolutionary change. Moreover, the emphasis given to commerce in cementing the economic structures of medieval civilization reveals the markedly liberal bent of Pirenne's personal politics. His thesis was noisily received and widely rejected. Nevertheless, it has been greatly influential in provoking a reconsideration of the processes that accompanied the transition from the ancient to the medieval world, by setting forth an interpretation of the origins of the medieval economy which has nothing to do with the presumed characteristic mores of the Germanic peoples.

Historiography in the twentieth century

In spite of the important results achieved by economic and social history, for much of the first half of the twentieth century historiography was restricted to narrative treatments, usually in the field of political history and usually based on the scrupulous weighing of the written evidence. This kind of history became known as 'histoire historisante' or 'histoire événementielle' in French, expressions that refer to the descriptive and narrative preoccupations of its exponents. The positivists had dreamt of turning history into a tool for the study of human behaviour; for this purpose, the aims and methods of history were to be those of the natural and social sciences. With the turn of the century the dream was disturbed by historicism. Historicism is a philosophical and historiographical position, one that makes a clear distinction between the 'natural' sciences and those of the 'spirit'. Historicism implies that, as these two branches of science have entirely different subjects, they must therefore make use of entirely different analytical methods. By building on some of Ranke's ideas, advocates of historicism underlined the originality and uniqueness of historical facts, thus dismissing any attempt to identify constants in history. It follows, then, that historical events, figures and movements must be seen within their particular context if their proper significance is to be understood. To this end, the work of the historian was not to be motivated by outside interests or presuppositions of any kind. For historicism, history is history for its own sake. That said, historicism gave special importance to moral, political and religious contexts, and it promoted the study of ideas as a way of approaching the past.

But it was not without its critics. How, the critics asked, was the historian to gain access to history when, as the historicists supposed, the past is a closed book, a distant and unrepeatable phenomenon? Other questions were asked regarding the ethical relativism implicit in the systematic historicization of values.

The severity of its critics notwithstanding, historicism mobilized considerable followings in Germany and Italy, where it influenced a good part of the most important historiographical production in the early decades of the twentieth century. Yet it was to have nothing to do with the most influential contributions at this time in the field of medieval history. These were the work of scholars who cannot be ascribed to particular movements or schools, though all were touched by the irrationalism that gripped European culture in the aftermath of the First World War, as previously established values were cast into doubt. Occasionally, writers of the inter-war period found in the Middle Ages a repertory of cultural conditions and personalities and symbols with which to illustrate their experiences and concerns.

Exemplary in this context is *The Waning of the Middle Ages* (1919), by the Dutch historian and philosopher, Johan Huizinga (1872-1945). Influenced by Lamprecht's theory of culture, Huizinga described the civilization of late-medieval Flanders not in terms of psychology, but rather as a state of mind. He chose the season of autumn as a metaphor of that state of mind, in order to evoke the sense of a twilight age, of time drawing to a close, when comfort was sought in the ceremony and ritual and the games that Huizinga considered the supreme expression of cultural achievement. Huizinga's history is manifestly inspired by the author's experience of living in what was seen as the twilight of European civilization, in the enormous social and cultural upheaval that followed the First World War.

Another significant book in this context is *Frederick II*, by the German historian, Ernst H. Kantorowicz (1895-1964). Published in 1927, Kantorowicz's biography of the medieval emperor presents its subject as a historical model for a superior type of man, one endowed with an innate yen for creation and dominance. Such an interpretation was inspired by the ideals of an élite circle of writers associated with the German poets Stephan George and Hugo von Hofmannstahl. Kantorowicz was working outside the university system when his book appeared, and he was duly criticized for his lack of respect for academic convention. He returned fire with a second volume in which he set out the scholarly, documentary basis of his work, and for this he was rewarded with a university appointment. His political career was to be more controversial still. In 1933, as the Nazis attempted to appropriate *Frederick II* as an expression of Nazi ideology, Kantorowicz cleared his desk and later fled to the United States. In America, he settled to the study of medieval political doctrine and ritual, which he saw as most intense and self-conscious expressions of medieval culture.

The turn to irrationalism is evident in works by other German historians who developed an interest in medieval authority as the pre-eminent expression of morality and culture. Of these, the best known is Percy Ernst Schramm (1894-1970), author of comprehensive and systematic research on kingship forms in medieval Europe, and their juridical, political and spiritual values. Schramm was also interested in the insignia of medieval military and political powers, and the juridical and symbolic significance of this display. The result is a comprehensive evocation of the ritual and emotive aspects of political power.

During the 1930s, new prominence was gained by studies in the history of religious spirituality. The trend was anticipated by the work of Ernst Troeltsch (1865-1923), a historian, sociologist and historian of religion. In his 1912 study, *Soziallehren der christlichen Kirchen und Gruppen*, Troeltsch investigated the organization and the doctrines of social groups based on religious petitions. Studies in the history of spirituality (or Geistesgeschichte in German) were less concerned with the cultural and theological life of the organized Church than with spontaneous expressions of religiosity by individuals and groups, which were regarded as a creative force in social life. Alongside the age of the Reformation, the medieval period was given special attention by historians active in this area of research. Rich in popular and heretical religious movements, the medieval period offered an abundant field for studies of the social context of religion, and the relations between spontaneous and institutionalized forms of religiosity. A leading exponent of this brand of history writing in Germany was Herbert Grundmann (1902-1970).

The approach attracted much support in Italy, too, where it was nourished by the anxiety of Catholic culture in the face of 'Modernism'. In Italy, Modernists were calling for a reinterpretation of Christianity's sacred texts to take account of the historical and philological advances of the nineteenth century. They were also critical of the centralization and bureaucracy of the Catholic Church. In his history of Christianity (*Storia del Cristianesimo*, 1946-51) and in other works (such as *Studi su Gioacchino da Fiore,* 1931), Ernesto Buonaiuti (1881-1946) identified various aspects of early-Christian and medieval religion which seemed to correspond with the contemporary yen for more spontaneous and intense forms of faith. Buonaiuti was a priest as well as a historian, though he was barred from teaching on account of his modernist leanings. Buonaiuti's contribution none the less attracted Raffaello Morghen (1896-1983) who, in such works as his *Medioevo Cristiano*, delivered a thoroughgoing reinterpretation of the period in terms of the spiritual life of medieval civilization.

A number of different approaches to the study of constitutional history were developed in the inter-war period, with the intention of challenging the rigid formalism of late-nineteenth- and early-twentieth-century studies of Germanic and medieval institutions. This was the 'Neue Lehre' (or 'new doctrine') propounded by Austrian Otto Brunner (1898-1982). Brunner proclaimed that the use of modern juridical principles to interpret medieval institutions was by nature erroneous and inadequate. Returning to theories first developed in the context of the long-running discussion on the nature of the medieval German state, Brunner credited medieval juridical concepts with a degree of originality that previous historians had failed to recognize. The key to Brunner's thesis was his understanding that the nature and function of juridical institutions are contingent upon the social context of struggles for power. In this, Brunner recognized that characteristic ideological and cultural conditions frequently do not require social or other relations to be formalized in juridical terms.

In the wide and varied panorama of early-twentieth-century writing on the Middle Ages, a prominent place is occupied by two French historians, Lucien Febvre (1878-1956) and Marc Bloch (1886-1944). These men set out to revive the ideals of the *Revue de synthèse historique* and to give them fresh purpose. In 1929, Bloch and Febvre set up a journal, the *Annales d'histoire économique et social*, which was to beat new paths in historical research. Their agenda was to develop the pursuit of social history in relation to the study of economics and mentalities. Simultaneously, they encouraged collaboration with geography, ethnology and folklore, iconography and archaeology, in order to overcome the limitations of written sources.

Febvre dedicated the greater part of his research to the sixteenth century; Bloch, though, was a medievalist. In his first significant publication, *Les rois thaumaturges* (1923), Bloch focused on the supernatural or sacral character attributed to kings in the medieval period, though not in terms of the mystic power that had so appealed to German historians. Instead, Bloch regarded this perception of medieval kings as a function of collective psychology, one that was to be understood and explained using the tools of ethnology and folklore, as well as in terms of contemporary circumstances or political agendas.

In his *Caractères originaux de l'histoire rurale en France* (1931) Bloch interpreted the characteristic forms of the landscape of rural France through analysis of settlement, land-ownership and use, and the juridical customs of the rural world between the eleventh and the eighteenth centuries. Different disciplines converge in this account, including geography, toponymy and legal history, to produce a holistic treatment of the formation of the landscape of modern France. By far Bloch's best-known and most sophisticated work, however, is his two-volume study of feudal society (*La société féodale*, 1939-40). This brings together a number of Bloch's earlier studies to provide a comprehensive treatment of French society from the ninth to the thirteenth centuries, in terms of the bonds of solidarity and dependency between men, and the forms of social organization and attitudes which shaped feudal society. A mass of original insights, Bloch's work was to enliven and give renewed scope to the study of the juridical and political institutions of the feudal world.

The example of Febvre and Bloch has been of huge significance in demonstrating the potential for innovation in the methods of social history. That potential was widely realized only after the end of the Second World War, as European historians grew frustrated at political history, abandoning historicism and expressing their distrust of the objectives of histories of religion and power. In this context, and as positivism had led them to do one hundred years before, historians once more turned to social history. This movement came to strength during the 1960s, though now it was to amount to rather more than a simple return to the positions of nineteenth-century positivism. Instead, historians rejected the traditional requirement to identify universal laws governing historical development. They are sceptical of the purpose of reducing the organization and the experiences of people in the past to immutable, ahistorical principles such as race, environment and inalterable social mechanisms. In this way the theory of historicism has been important, but not as important as the progress of the social sciences, which, now more empirical and experimental, offer a vital contribution to historical research.

In this way, and since the mid-twentieth century, the attention of historians has been trained on social, economic and cultural forms, which are often considered within the scope of particular geographical limits as well as chronological ones, in order to understand their internal make-up (or 'structure'), their functions and transformation. In this context, historians have made much use of the analytical methods of the social and economic sciences. And they have drawn considerable influence from the work of Fernand Braudel (1902-1985) and his studies of the relations between social history and its environmental context, socio-cultural structures and the place of regional economies in global systems. An important reference for social historians is provided by the journal *Past and Present*, founded in England in 1952 by a group of historians with the aim of applying Marxist theories to the interpretation of dynamics in social history. Inspired by the founding principles of *Annales d'histoire économique et social*, the editors of *Past and Present* have fostered history's close co-operation with the disciplines of sociology, demography, economics and anthropology.

Another journal dedicated to the promotion of social history is *Annales*. Following the deaths of Bloch and Febvre, and under the direction of Braudel and other eminent French historians, *Annales* has encouraged historians to make use of the principles of sociology, psychology and anthropology in the analysis of collective mentalities – the principles, in other words, of the human rather than the social sciences. *Annales* has made an enormous impact on the orientation of contemporary historiography both in and out of France. Among the most illustrious representatives of this trend of French historical studies are two medievalists: Georges Duby and Jacques Le Goff.

Recently a new theoretical approach, known as deconstruction, has influenced historical studies, especially in the United States. This approach, influenced by developments in linguistics and literary criticism, denies that an objective knowledge of the past can ever be attained through study of the sources. In its most extreme form, this approach appears to ignore all the debates that have taken place over the last two centuries concerning source criticism and the nature of historical knowledge.

Many of the most significant developments in the practice of history in the last few decades have been made in the area of medieval studies.

Medieval history has been taken up from all manner of novel and unusual perspectives. That said, it should not imply that recent readings in medieval history necessarily produce radical or even more accurate interpretations of the period. Frequently, the more innovative approaches simply present anomalous, aberrant or exotic aspects of the period in unusually sharp focus. The popularity of approaches of this kind now appears to be on the decline, while lively interest and prominence continues to be accorded to studies of the economic and institutional mechanisms of medieval society, studies made from the perspective of political and economic theory and anthropology. In the meantime, consideration of the moral or ethical dimension of medieval experience remains in the background of current debates, though this would seem to be the path to beat if we are to appreciate what the period means in relation to the historical consciousness of the contemporary world.

The problem of periodization

A coherent or disparate age?

In the previous chapter we described the principal ways in which the idea of the Middle Ages has been constructed in modern historiography. Now let us consider the Middle Ages as a period of history, and what the basis and limits of this approach may be. The business of breaking down periods from the continuous flow of history, and the use of these periods as frameworks of historical knowledge, is not an entirely arbitrary process, neither is it merely a response to practical necessity, one intended to provide manageable units for courses of study, say, or convenient chapter-headings for general history books. Rather, periodization requires us to make judgements about the past, and to identify salient characteristics in the organization and life of past societies. When these characteristics extend over long spans of time, they can be used to distinguish a given period from other periods in which the same features are less significant or even absent.

Periodization therefore requires the historian's intellectual effort in identifying and retracing the general contours of past experience, and the incidence and rhythm of change. Periodization implies that, underlying the continuous flux of everyday life, there are more or less resilient structures.

It is not by chance that this definition of periodization is given in the most general terms. There is no such thing as a prescribed formula for working out and classifying periods in history. The historian who accepts this method of approach must make her or his own selection and assessment of criteria that, in the historian's opinion, best represent the period under investigation. The historian must explain her or his choice by analyzing the historical circumstances behind the emergence and continuation of the criteria chosen. It should be said that such an exercise is not a primary or even a necessary aim of the historian's work; on the contrary, historians will often be heard to express reservations about this subject, and to complain about the inherent arbitrariness of conceptually subdividing the continuous passage of time. Historians know that in the past, as in the present, individuals and societies' lives rarely involve definitive caesuras. They also know that the application of a single framework of periods can be misleading, as the incidence and timing of change do not always coincide across the full range of human endeavour. Political institutions and economic systems, intellectual culture and settlement patterns – all may be subject to diverse rhythms of change, thus presenting a variety of over-lapping or unrelated periods. What is more, it may not always be possible to integrate such diversity within a single general scheme for the periodization of history 'as a whole'.

In describing the organization and the actions of societies in the past, therefore, it has become customary to acknowledge the existence of different levels of experience or endeavour, and to consider that these levels change and develop according to different rhythms. Certain aspects of social life are conditioned by our surroundings and natural environment. Before the advent of modern technology, these ways changed extremely slowly; hence, certain traditional cultural forms survived through periods of hundreds of years or more. In such cases, change may occur only under the impact of deep but sporadic crises. Then there are those aspects of the life of societies that develop in shorter spans of time, from a decade or so to a lifetime – cycles of economic productivity, for instance. In cases such as these, progress and change occur in response to particular circumstances determined by collective action and the behaviour of individuals. Together, such strands of long- and medium-term change make up a skeleton of 'structures' and 'cycles'. Overlying them is an endless variety of unconnected events, the ever-changing fabric of activities, situations and relationships engendered in the course of everyday life through the agency of individuals. How to inter-relate the diverse levels and sequences of historical experience is another obstacle to periodization. Where are we to look in identifying the significant moments of change in history? Implicit in this question is the understanding that history is not a uniform continuum. Historical development *is* punctuated by cycles and crises, on the basis of which it can be broken down into periods, and these periods characterized by their most distinctive and long-standing features.

Theoretical reservations do not diminish the value of periodization. The recognition of homogeneous and significant stages in the course of history is of much use, for the straightforward purposes of categorizing and pigeonholing historical phenomena, and for a fuller comprehension of the inter-relatedness of the actions of societies in the past. Without designated periods it would be impossible to plot the long-, medium- and short-term patterns that have shaped civilization, and so to understand the reasons underlying change and its timing. The kinds of misgivings aired above place stringent conditions on this kind of analysis, ensuring that such analysis is supported by general concepts relating to the nature and workings of societies. Studies of this kind can produce important and valuable results. Almost despite themselves, it seems, critical approaches to periodization have positive effects on historians' perception of progress and change in the past. With these problems in mind, then, let us consider to what extent it is still possible (or acceptable) to make use of the medieval concept as a historical period. Firstly, what are the terms in which this period may be defined and characterized?

We have seen that the idea of the Middle Ages was spawned by a tradition of historiographical thought beginning in the fifteenth century. In a sense, our period is a product of European cultural history. The period, and its significance, does not come to us firsthand, and so the question must be: to what extent is this concept still relevant or useful for the interpretation of history? For instance, are the chronological limits traditionally assigned to the period still significant? From the Italian humanists to the time of Christopher Keller, the beginning and end of the period were set in relation to major upturns in civilization and political events of a decisive and momentous sort. Now, though, the positions of Renaissance and early-modern historians may be reconsidered, and the limits and nature of the period redefined.

Clearly, it is no longer possible to pinpoint precise dates for the beginning and end of the medieval period, and neither is it acceptable to privilege one category of phenomena over another in attempting to explain why a period begins or ends. Both the dawn of the Middle Ages and their twilight extended over broad spans of time measurable in centuries, in the course of which the symptoms of profoundest change slowly intensified, welling up in many fields of human experience.

The beginning of the Middle Ages can now be assigned to a period of at least three centuries, from the beginning of the fourth century to the end of the seventh. This period witnessed the institution of the Christian Church and its integration with the Roman empire; the barbarian invasions and the birth of a mixed, Germano-Roman society within the borders of the empire; and the end of the imperial economic system, which had been characterized by state control of production and the commercial union of provinces bordering the Mediterranean. However, the period between the fourth and the seventh centuries does not yet display distinctly 'medieval' characteristics. For the most part, it is best considered as a phase of antiquity, the last ebb of the ancient world – a period now known as 'late antiquity'. This period used to be referred to in rather pejorative terms; now it is celebrated as an era rich in novelty, a product of the still-strong heartbeat of Roman society as that society continued to thrive in altered, unfamiliar conditions. Steadily, as the institutions of the Roman empire continued to decline, that which was 'late antique' little by little became 'medieval'. From this point of view, the year 476, the date traditionally chosen to signal the end of the ancient world, is of no great moment. The overthrow of a puppet emperor did not precipitate any grave political crisis, nor did it bring about much tangible change in the economic, institutional and social life of the late fifth century. The event did not cause particular concern to contemporaries; indeed, some fifth-century writers recognized the significance of a more painful rupture about a quarter of a century earlier, around the middle of the fifth century, when the eastern and western parts of the empire were separated on moral and political grounds. At that time, the consequences of the seemingly unbreachable tide of barbarian invasion were made clear to those in the West by the sack of Rome by Vandals in 455.

Similarly, the end of the Middle Ages may be described in terms of a heterogeneous jumble of occurrences, which, over the course of a couple of centuries, took on such consistency as to alter the overall course of historical development. In describing the end of the Middle Ages, and before one can speak of the consequences of technological innovations and geographical discoveries made in the fifteenth century, one must consider the impact of a long series of economic crises over a period of more than 150 years, crises that resulted in deep economic depression for many regions of western Europe. In addition to these factors, we should be aware of the demise of the institutions responsible for upholding political order and social cohesion in the preceding period – namely, the papacy, the empire and the orders of chivalry. We must also take account of the spread of new ethical and religious values and concepts of truth. Seen in this way, the end of the medieval period and the coming of the early-modern period appear to overlap. How the two periods may be split apart varies according to the particular criteria we use to distinguish them. However, it is probably safe to say that the transition from medieval to early-modern times was rather less drastic than the other transition, that which brought the Middle Ages into being. Social and cultural forms certainly changed with the end of our period, but they were not overturned. In the areas of economics and politics, many forms and practices continued unaltered into the early-modern world. Such continuity can be observed for state institutions, for instance, which developed without interruption between the end of the thirteenth and the beginning of the sixteenth century. Similarly, in economic terms, the system based on the balance of agricultural production and commercial capitalism survived essentially unchanged from the thirteenth to the sixteenth century, despite continued crises. As soon as we begin to look in detail, the late-medieval period appears to be rather less distinct from the early-modern period than traditional histories would have us believe.

Once we are clear about the terms in which the medieval period may be distinguished from the periods before and after it, it remains for us to consider the problem of the period's nature in itself. It is not enough to regard a period simply as the length of time lapsing between incidences of epoch-making significance. Instead, it must be possible to recognize a period for its principal and most long-standing characteristics. Such diagnostic traits might include economic structures, ideologies, mentalities, political systems and forms of cultural production – features that define the nature and integrity of a period. If we were to consider the traits previously used to characterize the beginning and end of the medieval period, we might find that they are so disparate that the period seems not to be a homogeneous unity at all. For example, barbarian kingdoms of the early Middle Ages had little in common (and much at odds) with the monarchies of late-medieval Europe. Likewise, there is no discernible line of descent between early-medieval economies, dominated by the great estate owners, and the commercial capitalism of the late-medieval period, based on the exchange of manufactured commodities. Seen from these perspectives, the profile of the period is altogether variable and disparate.

Let us not forget that the idea of the Middle Ages was born from the polemics of Renaissance and later commentators. It is not the product of dispassionate research into the course of history. As a consistent and homogeneous historical period, the Middle Ages was the creation of certain observers who were concerned with the corruption of standards in literary culture, customs and institutions, a corruption that was supposed to have gone on throughout the period. In this humanistic and Enlightenment conception, the same negative characterization is applied to the period in its entirety. Later commentators were to overturn this view, only to replace it with another broad and all-encompassing characterization, one that emphasized the devotion of medieval society to Christian values, or the supposedly cohesive nature of medieval economics. Such generic (and largely ahistorical) perceptions of the Middle Ages assisted in promoting the idea that the period is straightforwardly consistent and invariable from beginning to end.

With the development of modern historical research and the pursuit of more objective, less ideologically motivated readings of the past, the medieval period has been newly conceived as one of 1000 years and more of change and diversity. This change in attitude towards the era began in the eighteenth century, when critics began to distinguish new and unexpected light amidst the gloom of medieval barbarism. Voltaire, for example, called attention to the medieval origins of the bourgeoisie and the state. More significantly, Robertson divided the medieval period in two halves, each with its own distinct appearance: the first dominated by barbarism, both in cultural terms and in the institutions of economic and public life; the second, a more dynamic age, when European society set about the formation of new institutions, administrative and legal practices and economic systems, and in doing so prepared the way for the emergence of the modern world.

The idea that the earlier and later stages of the medieval period were significantly different in kind was accepted and elaborated by historians throughout the nineteenth and twentieth centuries. Above all, the period's first phase was marked out as a coherent epoch in itself, an age characterized by the settlement of Germanic peoples within the Roman empire and the predominance of a warrior élite, the economics of land ownership, and the first fusion of Germanic, Christian and Roman traditions. The early period was not separated from the rest of the Middle Ages, however, as many of its characteristics remained current through successive centuries. Nevertheless, the early period was perceived as having a distinctive appearance all its own. This distinction was recognized by referring to the first medieval centuries as the 'early'-medieval period, or 'early' Middle Ages. Similarly, attention was given to traits considered to exemplify the final centuries of the medieval period, such as the growing division of society into distinct and often competing classes, the crisis of Catholic unity and its cultural as well as ecclesiastical consequences, and the profound economic crisis that followed the bubonic plague. The centuries in which these characteristics manifest themselves, from the second half of the thirteenth century to the early fourteenth, broadly speaking, are together labelled the 'late' Middle Ages.

It will be clear that between the earlier and later phases of the medieval period there is another time-span of some three or four hundred years, from the eleventh or even the tenth century to the middle of the thirteenth. The prominent aspects of this period cannot be made to square tidily with the characteristics of either the earlier or later phases of medieval history. Rather, the interim shows up a number of the same features as the preceding medieval centuries, though now these features are progressively cleansed of their barbarian associations through the achievement of economic prosperity, and with the appearance of new social groups, such as merchants and clerks. Further impetus to development was provided by the incorporation of Christian values in secular life, and the revival of ancient learning and science – as well as the accumulation of wealth across an ever-wider section of society. At the height of the period is the twelfth century, when European civilization appears to have been impressively self-confident and harmonious in all aspects of social life, in government as in the economy, and in culture and literature as in architecture and the arts. It is not by chance that the twelfth century has been considered the first 'renaissance' in European history.

The central centuries of the medieval period have been credited with a degree of autonomy and coherence equal to that of the preceding and subsequent phases. Therefore it is customary to regard the medieval period as being divided into three phases. Among English- and German-speaking historians, the three phases are known as the 'early', 'high' and 'late' Middle Ages (in German, 'früh', 'hoch' and 'spät Mittelalter'). Here, the adjective 'high' is attributed to the central centuries of the period, implying that those centuries were the apex or apogee of the Middle Ages. In Italian, only the adjectives 'alto' and 'basso' (as in 'alto medio-evo') are used to refer to the early and later periods respectively, as the use of an adjective term for the intervening period has not been established. At the end of the nineteenth century, Italian historians referred to the central Middle Ages as the 'età comunale', after the Italian communes, though obviously such a designation has limited relevance elsewhere in medieval Europe. Likewise in French there is no widely agreed term in use to indicate the central part of our period. The closest approximation refers to the 'époque féodale' or 'feudal age' of that country's history, and is therefore largely redundant in any other context.

Are we to conclude, then, that the familiar uniformity of the medieval period has been altogether eroded by the speculations of modern historians? Is it the case, in fact, that the period of time separating the end of the ancient world and the arrival of the modern period can no longer be considered a proper 'period' in history? Perhaps this would be going too far. Although they are recognizably different each from the others, the three phases of the medieval period may be considered the origin, apex and decline of one and the same historical development. Together they imply a complex of multitudinous social factors, economic systems and cultural traditions, all of which went through continuous change and development before succumbing to the novel and imposing transformations brought on by the advent of the modern era.

The uniformity of the medieval period must be sought not in the inalterable nature of certain key characteristics, but in their coherent development. This progress may be likened to the curve of a graph, arching from points low on the vertical axis (the sixth and seventh centuries), rising steadily upwards and reaching an apex (the twelfth and thirteenth centuries) before changing course and tending downwards, though never returning to its lowest levels. Finally, the direction of our curve anticipates another upturn sometime around the end of the fifteenth century. The curve is not semicircular; its general trajectory points up, thus explaining why, in many respects, the relation between medieval and modern appears to be one of continuity.

The Middle Ages and European history

Having considered the medieval period as a concept (and construct) of modern historical discourse, and considering the variety of attitudes and positions taken towards the period, it follows that an alternative position be proposed.

The medieval period may be considered remote and at an end. It may be viewed with fascination or repulsion, depending on the interests and values of the observer. In any event, it may be accepted as an historical experience with its own significance, its own values and ways of life. Alternatively, it may be considered an integral part of a longer process of development, one that produced familiar practices and ideals, and which has contributed to the making of a distinctly European cultural identity.

To see the medieval period as a remote and unfamiliar age is to regard it as a distinct civilization. Such an approach places particular emphasis on the achievements of medieval people in the fields of economics and politics, and in literary, artistic and religious spheres above all. Such achievements are vividly apparent in the still-impressive evidence of medieval monuments, which inspire wonder even today. From this perspective, it makes no sense to place the medieval period in relation to other periods of history, either in comparative or developmental terms. The medieval period is complete in itself, and so need not be described as the background to later, more sophisticated developments.

A less rigid extension of this way of thinking about the medieval past is represented by anthropological approaches to the period made in the last thirty or forty years. From this perspective, attention focuses not on the most prominent aspects of cultural or intellectual endeavour, but on the most repetitive and unreflexive phenomena. These might include collective attitudes (or mentalities) and social practices – as well as the customs and rituals that societies use to regulate the actions and needs of their members, and to ensure their very survival. In approaches of this kind, it is seldom necessary (if it is ever possible) to link medieval cultural systems with others in the modern period.

The opposing idea – that the medieval legacy is a vital component of modern European civilization – derives from a concern with the origins of contemporary culture, its premises and their implications. This approach risks treating the medieval period as a period of mere beginnings – a period in which certain important conditions took on a primary (read: immature) form. Seen in this way, the medieval world bears witness to the antiquity and venerability of familiar aspects of modern life, though in their present form those aspects are usually the products of more recent developments.

Before we attempt to confront these difficulties, one further consideration. Whatever position we take up, we must accept that the medieval period makes sense exclusively in the context of European history. Any extension of the concept to other societies and other parts of the world is based solely on the chronological relationship of events with others in medieval Europe. Even the Marxist definition of the Middle Ages as a period characterized by a particular 'mode of production' cannot be applied to all the countries of the world during the European Middle Ages. Rather, the Marxist theory applies only to those situations that may be compared with the patterns of ownership and labour peculiar to medieval Europe, whatever its chronological limits.

Thus, to speak of 'medieval' China or India is simply a custom of modern discourse, and a mostly meaningless one at that. Some legitimacy may be claimed for the concept when it is applied to cultures or societies that were engaged in reciprocal exchange with medieval Europe, such as the Islamic world, though this relationship is one of straightforward proximity and contemporaneity. The 'medieval' Arab world has its own characteristic order that marks it out as a civilization apart from that of medieval Europe.

It is precisely because the medieval period is unique to the history of Europe that Europeans are unable to regard it with indifference or neutrality. For this reason, the contrasting historiographical approaches described in this chapter can be taken together to produce a richer and more profound appreciation of the role of the medieval experience in the making of European history. The medieval period is certainly the initial phase in the formation of Europe, but as such it is a whole in itself, a civilization of its own that was not lost entirely during the subsequent course of history – rather the contrary: the medieval legacy continued to exercise an influence, both in the life of European society and in the formation of European cultural consciousness. To take a somewhat abstruse phrase, one could say that what is medieval is simultaneously the deeply buried base and a dynamic element in the structure of European civilization. On this basis, the discussion may now turn to a consideration of certain key themes in medieval history, topics that illustrate some of the fundamental experiences of life in the Middle Ages. In post-medieval times, these themes have been afforded the status of constants in European history and thought.

Some general themes in medieval history

Invasions, barbarians, Germans

The appearance of barbarian peoples within the frontiers of the Roman empire, and the imposition of barbarian rule on Roman society; the end of the ancient world and the decadence of ancient culture, customs and ways of life – the medieval period begins with the discomforting realization that even the most complex and developed civilization may be easily and irreversibly overwhelmed.

Modern European society has held on to anxious memories of this experience, fearful, at successive turns, of once more falling prey to the prospect of violent invasion, while historians have endeavoured to temper the role of violence in the course of civilization, looking to long-running internal causes to explain the end of antiquity. However, there can be no denying that the barbarian invasions introduced a novel and thoroughly unprecedented set of circumstances. Previously, the Roman and barbarian worlds had been in every sense separate. The Roman empire was a political organization, the aim of which was to embrace the limits of the civilized world. Beyond its confines were the barbarians. Following the invasions the two worlds lived cheek by jowl within a shared environment. This collision was to determine the direction of much of the subsequent history of the Middle Ages. One long-standing tradition considered barbarity to be a moral rather than a cultural condition, one that was qualitatively inferior and therefore necessarily doomed to fail on contact with superior forms of civilization, such as those represented at the beginning of our period by Christianity and the classical heritage. Seen from this perspective, the origins of European civilization may be described in terms of the exhaustive but necessary victory of the principles of civilization. However, the role of the barbarians in this process was not always merely one of passive acceptance or even recalcitrance in the face of civilization. So much is clear from their awareness and recognition of the values of civilization, their reception and pursuit of the traditions of ancient culture, and the efforts made to stem the very sources of barbarism. Thus, the conflict instigated by the barbarian invasions was eventually resolved with the prevalence among the new society of medieval Europe of a system of values and norms which was substantially that of the ancient world, albeit somewhat adapted and updated. In this case there would seem to have been a significant degree of continuity between classical civilization and that of modern Europe, to judge from the apparent affinity of the system of values prevalent in both periods.

That said, such an interpretation begins to seem less convincing if we replace the concept of barbarity with that of Germanism – that is, when we attribute the barbarians not with defective forms of civilization, but with a different civilization altogether, one that was perhaps simpler than its classical counterpart, but which was likewise possessed of values meaningful in their own right. As we saw in Chapter 1, this somersault in historical perspective took place at the end of the eighteenth century, particularly in Germany, and it has been upheld by most subsequent historiography.

Hence it is no longer acceptable to speak of the formation of European civilization in terms of the progressive disappearance of barbarian cultures before the superior traditions of the vanquished Romans. Better now to speak of the symbiotic exchange between classical and Mediterranean traditions embodied by imperial Roman culture on the one hand, and Germanic traditions on the other – a process of reciprocal influence and mutation through which both are transformed and neither predominates. Hence the equilibrium achieved in a given context or territory, or among a particular people, may not be the same in all contexts in which the process took place. In certain circumstances, Roman traditions retained prominence, while in others Germanic traditions came to the fore. Thus European culture took on its uneven, variegated structure, whose base elements may be glimpsed in the continent's major linguistic groups and the cultural forms particular to them. This way of thinking gained particular prominence in modern German culture, on account of that country's preoccupation with its own distinctiveness, especially vis-à-vis the models of civilization proposed in the French and English traditions, and the drive to define Germany's role within European civilization as a whole. Such a way of thinking has general purchase, however, as the problem concerns all Europe, not just the Germans. It would seem that the barbarian invasions introduced a duality of cultural values to the dynamic of European civilization, which resurfaces, in diverse but inter-related ways, throughout the course of European history.

Of course, this observation has assumed menacing significance on such occasions when definitions of Germanism have ceased to make reference to values compatible with those of the ancient and Christian tradition, calling instead upon particular barbarian traditions based on myths of strength and blood and destiny and death. Such myths were in fact the products of the decadent culture of mid- to late-nineteenth-century Europe, trawled from diverse civilizations and remote epochs. Although the subjects of such myths were often regarded with suspicion in the original context, in the nineteenth century they were presented as symptomatic of perennial values once more of relevance to modern man.

When these ideas showed up in political discourse, at the end of the nineteenth century and during the two World Wars, the conception of German particularism was renewed, and seemingly inextricably linked to that people's barbarian heritage, as an irreducible element in the development of European civilization. However, this way of thinking was devoid of any firm historical backing, as it failed to take into account either the complex evolution of Germanic culture from the Middle Ages to the modern era, or the inherent cultural differences between German-speaking peoples. German as well as other historians are even now working on dismantling the very concept of a special 'barbarian' culture as opposed to late-antique imperial culture. All the same, the idea of the double origin retains its significance as a means to interpreting the common characteristics of European civilization. The same idea retains a certain significance, too, in the interpretation of modern Germany.

Christianity and the Church

The Middle Ages are often described as the 'age of faith' – a time when Christianity and the Catholic Church guided minds and souls, moulding society and culture without competition. In this way, the medieval centuries have sometimes appeared to modern observers as a blissful epoch of certainty and spiritual cohesion, albeit one when reason and criticism were lost to simple faith. In contrast, the modern era is characterized by its attachment to the spirit of critical inquiry, and its recognition of the faculty of reason as the only measure of truth, as an age when absolute truths are lost to lonely individualism.

This perception of the period is easily explained. The Christian faith provided the institutional and ideological framework for much of medieval life. The Christian belief in the Creation and original sin, and in the redemption made possible through Christ's Passion on the cross – and, above all, the belief in heavenly salvation as the supreme goal of humankind – provided the basis of intellectual and moral activity throughout the period. Christian concepts determined medieval interpretations of the physical world as well as social order and political power. Likewise, medieval ideas about history and its meaning were Christian ideas. Christianity also determined the key moral and sentimental ideals of medieval society. At the heart of Christian morality is charity, the Christian conception of which goes far beyond pity and almsgiving. The Gospels advocate Christ's teaching to love one's neighbour. For the followers of Christ, all people are the children of God, and all are equal in the love of Christ. This conception is profoundly at odds with the virtues of justice and philanthropy promoted by classical ethics, insofar as Christian teaching presupposes an unconditional, compassionate disposition in respect of one's neighbour, as exemplified by God's love of his children. The Christian ethos is still further removed from the values of honour and supremacy fostered among the ancient Germanic peoples. The medieval Church set out to broadcast the principle of Christian charity. The same principle was, at least in theory, to inform the customs and values of medieval society, and to guide the actions and intentions of medieval institutions.

That said, we would be mistaken in thinking that the Christian life was an altogether easy or consoling experience in the Middle Ages. Religious observance, the life of the Church, and the scale of investment made in pursuit of Christian ideals and salvation – all led to the emergence of diverse (and competing) interpretations of the Christian message. The story of medieval Christianity is a tormented one of high and frequently disastrous drama.

How to live according to Jesus' teaching in the Gospels posed a problem from Christianity's earliest days. Monasticism was one response. Early monastic founders advocated detachment from the secular world and adhesion to strict rules of conduct as prerequisites for the successful pursuit of a Christian vocation. Monasticism was progressively to take on a variety of forms, gradually abandoning its early insistence on ascetic solitude in favour of rules of monastic life based on community, humility and penance. Nevertheless, the monastic tradition remained committed to the belief that the secular world was, by and large, not conducive to truly Christian ways of life. The history of medieval monasticism is characterized by the institution's continual and uneasy introspection. There was much controversy surrounding the proper routes to the realization of monastic ideals. This produced successive reforms of the Benedictine Rule, fostering the innovation of new forms of ascetic or spiritual life, and prompting much discussion on the subject of the monk's place within Christian society. Conversely, in the Christian tradition, the pursuit of spiritual values is not in itself a means to salvation. An indispensable complement is provided by the sacraments – ritual acts through which the faithful receive the Holy Spirit and are blessed with divine grace. What is more, the sacraments may only be imparted and performed by persons who have received special consecration (itself a sacrament) as mediators of the Holy Spirit. The indispensable nature of the sacraments led to the development of the clergy, a body of specially anointed men charged with imparting the sacraments and the Word of God to the faithful. Through the sacraments the Christian clergy exerts its authority over the faithful, as it has the power to withhold the sacraments from reprobates and sinners.

The sacramental function of the clergy was to be the source of a good deal of trouble for the medieval Church. Questions hung over the capacity of the priesthood to dispense the sacraments, in response to which candidates for the clergy were expected to live a life of purity and doctrinal learning. Later, critics of the institutionalized Church grew sceptical of the very necessity of the clergy in preaching the Gospels and administering the sacraments, when independent, private observation of the precepts of the Gospels was considered by some the ideal route to realization of the Christian life. Extreme positions tended to deny the role of the sacraments in the salvation of souls. By no means was the Church oblivious to these problems; there was much debate among the clergy regarding the nature and the workings of the sacraments. Outside its ranks, however, the Church condemned its critics as heretics and set about persecuting them. Heretical movements were, however, symptomatic of deeper problems, which were to remain in the shadows until such time as social change forced them into the open – problems regarding the place of secular society in the Church, and the relative status afforded to laypeople and the clergy in the eyes of God. Was it possible for laypeople fully to achieve perfection or redemption? Moreover, should the laity be allowed to participate in preaching the Christian faith? And was the layman the agent of his own salvation? Similar questions were posed concerning the condition and role of lay women.

As doubts about its roles and powers mounted during the central Middle Ages, the Church sought to consolidate its position. It organized itself into a tightly closed juridical, political, economic and cultural institution, aloof from the run of Christian society upon which the Church nevertheless exercised its firm ideological grasp. Moreover, the Church claimed a pre-eminent role for itself in the political and social as well as the spiritual activities of its subjects, thus providing a solution to the problem of Christian life in the world. Salvation could be achieved through adherence and submission to the institution of the Church, which was the source of all knowledge and sanctity. Of course, such claims to absolute power led the medieval Church into conflict with secular authorities. Political institutions were understandably anxious not to see their temporal powers compromised by the clergy. The Church met with further resistance from its very flock. More and more, Christians became attracted to informal, personal forms of devotion, for which they sought within and even beyond the margins of the institutionalized Church. New forms of religious devotion grew up in the space between monasticism and the traditional patterns of secular life. Calls were made for the Church to limit its activities to spiritual instruction. And at this time, too, a radical reform of the very nature of the Church was proposed. The Church was to be reconceived in terms of the body of the faithful. The theological infallibility of the clergy was to be revoked, and the key religious texts were to be made available to all, thus rendering obsolete the mediations of the clergy.

Even the system of Christian doctrine was troubled by criticism. Critics of the Church took strength from a revival of interest in aspects of Greek philosophy, particularly as regards nature, the world and man. This resulted in a system of universal knowledge distinct from the Christian one. The Church went to the greatest lengths in order to minimize the potential for conflict, attempting to appropriate contrasting beliefs to its own by Christianizing them. Still, such concepts held on to their heteronomous character and their potential for philosophical and scientific speculation, in many cases giving way to a peculiar doctrine of double truth, one based on reason and the other on faith. This was not always a straightforward exercise in expediency, intended to curtail scepticism or dissent. Instead, it was an explicit acknowledgement of the existence of two parallel systems of knowledge. By their nature, these systems are irreconcilable; but they are equal in validity. Such a doctrine was to place the integrity of Christian philosophy in some jeopardy.

To describe the Middle Ages as an age of faith and religious fervour is justifiable, therefore, so long as we accept that the history of medieval Christianity is one of constant crisis and change, in which both Church and faithful struggled to perfect their pursuit of the Christian life, without ever achieving a definitive end or satisfactory institutional solutions.

Power and the limits of power

The medieval period was an epoch in which European society experimented with various forms and degrees of political power, which remain the basis of western political culture. There can be no doubt that medieval society was profoundly hierarchical in structure, though this observation should not imply that the principle of authority was beyond question. Medieval political history is characterized by the opposition of two very different conceptions of power – one Roman, the other Germanic. Under the late Roman empire, absolute political power lay with the emperor, as the jurisdictional and legislative functions of late-Roman society depended from him. In this context, Roman citizens were subjects, with little if any opportunity to influence the administration of government. Both in pagan and Christian times, imperial authority was considered to be sacred.

In the Germanic tradition, by contrast, power was a function of common assent exercised through assemblies of freemen and warriors, which deferred to the king for leadership in military operations. This type of government is rather less complicated than the highly complex system of rule of the late-Roman empire. In fact, almost as soon as the successor kingdoms were established within former Roman territories, the meeting of great assemblies dwindled. Popular rule was replaced by restricted groups of military leaders and lords, while kings attempted to imitate as best they could the pattern of imperial authority. However, certain Germanic concepts of power and authority were to survive the period of transition, reappearing in the novel configurations of later medieval institutions. And it was from the dialectical relation between affirmation of the prerogatives of power and the right to govern, on the one hand, and control of and resistance to this authority, on the other, that the dynamic of medieval political culture was to spring.

One idea close to the heart of many medieval claims to power was derived from Biblical precedent and the understanding that power is divinely sanctioned and thus requires no consensus to take effect, as emperors, kings and other leaders must answer only to God. The anointing of sovereigns, which began in the middle of the seventh century, gave confirmation and foundation to this idea, as it came to be considered as a sort of sacrament, setting the anointed above all other members of political society. Yet by no means did the practice put kings and emperors beyond all accountability, for if their authority was made legitimate by the grace bestowed by sacrament, it followed that the Church had jurisdiction in the political as well as spiritual lives of kings. Hence, the Church commanded kings to conform to models of Christian virtue in order to be worthy of their office. Alternatively, sovereigns were to be subject, in common with every other Christian soul, to spiritual sanction. In the Carolingian era, this was the ecclesiastical version of the right of control exercised over political authorities – and a very particular version it is too, given that control was exercised not by the political body in its entirety, but by the clergy in an autonomous role as mediator between kings and their subjects. In due course the idea was developed that kings should exercise their powers upon the instructions and under the guidance of the clergy.

The rights of the political community were upheld against royal authority by other institutional forms of Germanic origin. Under the Carolingians and the later kingdoms there existed a powerful lay class, the landed and martial aristocracy; these men collaborated in the political actions of the kings, to whom they were tied under oaths of allegiance. This relationship between kings and their powerful allies implies inter-dependency and the conferral of certain rights and responsibilities on both sides. In effect, the exercise of rule and the defence of the realm were jointly shared by the king and this noble class; it was therefore possible for nobles to withdraw allegiance from an unworthy or unfaithful monarch. Outside this privileged and powerful class, other groups had little say. In the ninth and tenth centuries and subsequently, the political class was a narrow one; prevailing economic and social structures effectively excluded much of the rural population, while in the cities there were as yet no autonomous systems of political representation.

In practice the lay political class was made up of the feudal class of the kingdom, and as such it exercised its right to participate in and control the administration of royal power. But this is not all there is to medieval political culture, not by any means. From the twelfth century onwards, new and increasingly authoritative forms of royal power were developed, based on a renewed conception of the power of kings, on might and coercion, and on the assumption that society at large is practically incapable of regulating itself when not forcibly compelled to do so. Men such as Henry II of England, Frederick Barbarossa and Roger II of Sicily bowed neither to the clergy nor to the ties of the feudal contract, elevating themselves beyond the reach of all other orders, as rulers with orders only from God. In these circumstances, the king and only the king had the power to write laws.

These developments raised the question of whether or not the king himself was subject to his own law. On this issue, the monarchic and authoritarian position maintained that the king was the very incarnation of the law, and as such was not to be bound by it. Such claims met keen opposition, fuelled by the experience of feudalism, changing cultural perspectives, and the twelfth-century rebirth of logic and philosophy. Opponents of the absolute rule of kings argued that the king ought, in fact, to be bound by law, as the law depends on universal principles of equity, which precede and are superior to every act of legislation. The classical concept of tyranny was reintroduced to bring to book any king who sought to put himself above the law by demanding subjection – not by consent or co-operation but by terror. In theory, in the twelfth and thirteenth centuries, the right to oppose tyranny was extended to all subjects. Although it had little impact in practice, the potential for dissent was consistent with an expanding society in which new classes and novel social and political relations were emerging. In this context, John of Salisbury, one of the most brilliant thinkers of the twelfth century, went as far as to justify tyrannicide.

In practical terms, the effects of this limitation on the range of royal power were given political and constitutional substance above all in England. In medieval England it was established that sovereignty was properly the possession of the *communitas regni* – a community made up of the king, lay and ecclesiastical barons, and the people, all in association. Law-giving was the prerogative of the crown and the barons together. In addition, monarchs were bound by the law of the land, which was regarded as a tradition common throughout the realm, as a guarantee that established norms could not be undermined by the royal will. The new political order was worked out in the *Magna Carta*, signed by King John in 1215, and put into practice with the institution of parliament.

No such restriction was given to the reach of royal authority in other parts of Europe at this time, though the functions of fiscal and political administration assumed by the *cortes* of the kingdoms of Spain, for instance, and the consolidation of electoral colleges of princes under the German empire, are two instances of the widening participation in the exercise of power. Only in France did specifically monarchic developments emerge, based on juridical doctrines of Roman origin, and giving way to a constitution in which the political orders of the kingdom had not the means to participate in the sovereignty of the state.

The debates on the limits of power extended to the theocratic theories promulgated by the Church in the last centuries of the Middle Ages in order to give a theological and juridical footing to the institution's desire for control and ability to intervene in all the affairs of the world, political ones included. According to such theories, states had limited sovereignty, depending on the hierarchy of the Church for final verification of the legitimacy of their political powers. Once again, one is dealing here with a theoretical position, one that had little chance of leaving a lasting impact on political realities. Ecclesiastical theories were rebuffed by defenders of the autonomy of the state, which was defined as a natural society in pursuit of its own ends, and intent on improving the conditions of life for all its members. This branch of thought is associated with a revival of interest in Aristotelian philosophy in the thirteenth century. From it, fourteenth-century political theorists, such as Marsilius of Padua, were to develop theories with revolutionary consequences for the state and the exercise of sovereignty. Indeed, they claimed that the state was constituted by the citizenry, each member of which holds important rights and responsibilities, while no political prerogative is extended to the privileged upper orders or the clergy; the Church, they argued, was to be deprived of any role in the life of the state. Sovereignty rests with the community of citizens, and is exercised predominantly in two ways – through the creation of laws, and in the delegation of executive powers to freely chosen governing bodies, which are bound by the will of the community and accountable to it.

Thus, at the end of the Middle Ages, the doctrine of popular rule was theoretically established, even if it received little endorsement in practice. Occasionally it was adopted by the empire, now a fragmented and ineffective institution, which used the doctrine as a juridical bulwark against the theocratic pretensions of the papacy. But it also spawned developments which were to have practical relevance, such as the concept of majority – essential in determining the validity of deliberations among a political body made up of a sum of individuals – and the principle according to which rulings were to be approved by those to whom they were directed before coming into effect.

The most significant use of these theories was made by the institution of the Church itself, on the occasion of the fifteenth-century synods that put an end to the Great Schism, and which were a sort of parliament of Christianity, inspired by the principle of the superiority of community, the faithful in this case, over the monarch, represented by the pope, even in matters of faith. These councils did not become permanent institutions within the Church, however, just as the doctrines of popular sovereignty were not to provide the juridical basis of the late-medieval states. The conflict between authoritarian and participative conceptions was to continue beyond the Middle Ages. In many ways, it remains a key problem of political culture even today.

Nations

Nations are a structural component of the cultural and political physiognomy of Europe, with their origins in the Middle Ages. Classical antiquity recognized no such thing as nations. Though certainly the inhabitants of the Roman empire represented a variety of cultures within the empire's borders, the empire did not recognize the political relevance of cultural identities, nor did it grant them separate institutional forms. Rather, Rome sought to appropriate and absorb difference; it was to be a universal empire, its aim being to embrace the limits of civilization. It is to the Middle Ages that we must look for an understanding of Europe's make-up of nations. It was in the Middle Ages that the modern concept of the nation was conceived, in contrasting, antithetical ways, assuming forms that retain powerful relevance to this day. In one way, nations may be regarded as groups characterized by their own particular histories, and by the nature of their communication and exchange with other, analogous groups. From a different perspective, the nation is an isolated entity convinced of its superiority, and tending to hostility in its dealings with neighbours.

The latter definition is one that obtains at the outset of the early Middle Ages. In the migration period, each of the Germanic peoples considered itself a chosen people, supreme among others in dignity, honour and war. The cohesive, collective identity of each group was explained in terms of the members' common ethnic origins. Most commonly, politico-cultural bonds were regarded as the bonds of blood. Among the Germanic peoples it was claimed that all members of the group shared a common ancestry, and prior to the conversion to Christianity, the mythical ancestors were acknowledged as divinities or demigods. Furthermore, divine or mythological origins were attributed to a people's laws, its constitution, and its core customs and beliefs. Ethnic identity was regarded as a primordial factor, one carried on in the people's traditional habits and customs. It is easy to see how this kind of difference has lent itself so readily to nationalist movements in the modern era. If we were to accept such a simple characterization, the idea of the nation could be regarded as a barbarian legacy put in place during the course of the Middle Ages and passed on to more recent times.

As a concept, however, the nation was not always regarded as a closed or exclusive (and outwardly aggressive) entity. In the nineteenth-century cult of Romanticism, the idea of ties of blood was done away with. Instead, thinkers and philosophers considered the nation in an organic, spiritual context, with which the actions and customs of individuals are always consistent. However, even the Romantic conception was suspended between a recognition of the dignity of all nations, as products of civilization, and the tendency to establish hierarchies in order to legitimate national or state egoism, thus returning to the tribal concepts of the age of migrations.

After the end of the Second World War, historical research was directed to analyses of migration-period peoples. The results of this work were to cast considerable doubt on the concept of nations as organic entities. It emerged that groups once considered to have been ethnically homogeneous were, in fact, the products of intercourse among groups of diverse ethnic origins. In this context, the creation of common origin myths was a strategy to reduce ethnic diversity and to promote solidarity and a sense of common purpose. Such strategies were not always successful in achieving lasting unity; new peoples could split apart again; weaker groups might be entirely effaced from the political scene as a result of military defeat. As the more stable and coherent groups became stronger, they absorbed and accommodated other ethnic groups, as in the case of the Franks, who assimilated at least part of the Gallo-Roman population. Likewise, the Lombards periodically released slaves to swell the ranks of their people in Italy.

Consequently, the cultural traditions represented by the laws, morals and armaments particular to each group, were subject to much cross-fertilization and change. In contrast to the coherence and stability previously claimed on their behalf, the peoples of early-medieval Europe appear now as rather fluid groupings in continual transition – a process known to historians as ethnogenesis. Stability is in short supply before the institution of Carolingian administration. The Carolingians set out conditions that favoured amalgamation of groups settled within restricted territories. Despite this, the same process of continual formation can be detected in peoples that became the basis of European monarchies during the central Middle Ages.

Although these peoples have been regarded as national bodies, well-defined in their make-up and territory, in fact, in the central Middle Ages, national communities were built up from small political units, frequently Carolingian or post-Carolingian in origin. In the course of the twelfth and thirteenth centuries, kings began to extend the reach of their territorial powers beyond the limits of the post-Carolingian system, and aided by their military followers and men of culture of different kinds – churchmen, historians, jurists, poets – they sought to instil novel ethical, religious and sentimental values, so inspiring the ideals of assent, consensus and pride among the populations encompassed within their newly-broadened dominions. The process has been analysed in much detail in the case of France. The consecrated king enjoyed the protection of St Denis, the special patron of the monarchy. Miracles were said to occur during the royal consecration, and the king himself was believed to have the power to perform certain miraculous deeds. The French monarchy was considered heir to and perpetuator of the tradition of Charlemagne and his battle against unbelievers. Jesters' tales, sermons and royal letters were the media through which these ideas were transmitted within the royal domains. Thus all the king's subjects enjoyed a share of the honour of the monarchy, and the protection of St Denis. The king's land was France, par excellence, and thus the 'French' were to be all those who inhabited those lands, regardless of ethnic origin. This ideology was of greater importance than language in consolidating the identity of the realm, as the French language was common to other, neighbouring peoples not subject to the French crown. Also central to the success of the project was history. A number of histories of the kingdom of France were written by churchmen in the service of the monarchy at this time. Court historians were concerned with presenting the French past as a unified and continuous business, with the king as the defender of the people.

Similarly in England, Germany and Spain, the cultural and political élites in the service of the monarchs were active in presenting the kingdom as a homogeneous and unified entity possessed of a common history. The belief in shared history was to have greater purchase than the old belief in ties of blood. All the same, legends telling of the remotest origins of the nation were preserved, though they were now little more than scholarly curiosities.

Even at the height of the Middle Ages, the nations of Europe were still in the process of formation. This process was much influenced by state powers. Medieval history does everything but confirm concepts of the remote ethnic origins of national communities. Instead, history reveals the nation to be an artefact shaped by historical development and by cultural and political strategies. In the European tradition it is nevertheless true that sovereign institutions tend to refer to groupings of national kinds, groups that claim a distinct cultural identity and ethnic cohesiveness. This situation is a long-term consequence of the survival of primitive political concepts introduced into the Roman territories by Germanic invaders.

The demographic cycle

Initially, interest in the Middle Ages was stimulated by the cultural aspects of the period, its literature, morals and customs, and political and social orders. Subsequently, this interest was extended to medieval economics. As historians widened the parameters of their studies, they realized that the history of the population of Europe, as a biological entity, had proceeded in step with the very same chronologies recognized by historians of medieval culture and politics. The beginning of the Middle Ages (between the fifth and the seventh centuries) coincides with a startling decline in population. Early-medieval commentators wrote lamentingly of the destitution of society and the desertion of the countryside. Their despair is confirmed by archaeological data. Countless settlements that had flourished in the second and third centuries were abandoned by the fifth and sixth centuries; many towns disappeared; and everywhere the extent of forestation and uncultivated land increased. It is estimated that the entire population of seventh-century Europe stood somewhere between fifteen and twenty-seven million. To put the size of the early-medieval population in perspective, in 1900 the population of Europe consisted of 400 million people, rising to 680 million or more in the 1980s.

Subsequently the population slowly began to climb. Population growth may be measured from levels of expansion in the area of land under cultivation, and from the resumption of trade. The recovery was at first halting and sporadic. But by the tenth century economic growth was widespread and sustained, opening the way to the foundation of new settlements, and heralding the economic and social dynamism of urban populations. Thanks to new forms of administrative and fiscal record-keeping developed in certain countries, it can be estimated that the population of Europe experienced continued growth until the second half of the thirteenth century – by which time the number of people may have increased by as much as 100 per cent to approximately 70 million. This level of growth was maintained only briefly before renewed decline set in. Around the mid-fourteenth century the decline in population accelerated rapidly, a consequence of the Black Death which, by 1350, seems to have done away with about a third of the population of Europe. Long after the disease abated, in many areas the population failed to make good its losses; in others, the population went into ever-deeper decline, plummeting to less than 50 per cent of the levels reached at the end of the thirteenth century. The slump went on into the mid-fifteenth century, when it was set in reverse by a wave of expansion that was to bring on the development of early-modern European society.

Thus, in terms of the chronological limits traditionally assigned to it, the medieval period corresponds to a demographic cycle that consists of three phases – depression, growth, and further depression. The low points of the population curve fall in the seventh century and in the second half of the fourteenth century, while the peak of growth coincides with the middle of the thirteenth century. It should be said that the second low point on our graph is never as low as the first; the population count in the second half of the fourteenth century was probably closer to the levels reached in the eleventh than those of the seventh century. Furthermore, the turn-around at the end of the period was of rather shorter duration than the other transition at the beginning of the period.

The extremes of the medieval demographic cycle can easily be made to relate to the circumstances of economic and cultural life in the period, such as the impoverishment of productive activity and cultural life in the early centuries. This low in turn gives way to a high, and the development of novel technologies in production, the growth in trade and prosperity, and the consequent rise of the town. The boom is accompanied by a surge in cultural production and intellectual activity, and by the development of more sophisticated forms of social relationships and political institutions. Recession returns in due course, at the end of the Middle Ages, and with it disease and famine, social disintegration and ideological crisis. If, as it seems, population dynamics proceed in step with socio-cultural dynamics, what is the nature of this dynamic inter-relationship?

In following up this question, the medieval period presents itself as a testing-ground for the science of demographics. Researchers have been concerned with explaining the background causes of the medieval demographic cycle. In this way, the points of depression at the beginning and the end of the period have been related to plague epidemics, which recurred with ever increasing frequency and virulence. For instance, European society was still in shock over half a century after the worst epidemic of plague in 1348-50. That crisis was preceded and followed by further outbreaks of disease at intervals of about ten years, which further weakened an already exhausted population. Likewise, the period of transition from late antiquity to the early Middle Ages is marked by other scourges of the same kind. Outbreaks of plague are recorded in some parts in the third century. The situation probably worsened in the period from the mid-sixth to the mid-eighth century. Devastating outbreaks of disease occurred in the second half of the sixth century and, later, during the first half of the eighth century. At the zenith of medieval population, by contrast, there were no such frequent or virulent calamities, although disease was by no means unknown.

Therefore, was disease responsible for the ups and downs of the medieval population? In order to be able to say so, it is not enough simply to explain how pestilence impacted on medieval life – we need to understand why these crises are limited to certain periods. In other words, we should beware of implying that disease exists independently from society and that it acts unconditionally of the circumstances of medieval people.

It has been shown that the outbreaks of disease at either end of the medieval period were accompanied by long periods of famine, the results of which were at least as catastrophic as those of the disease itself. The two phenomena are not unrelated: famine depletes an individual's resistance to infection and the physical energy available for work. Famine therefore leads to progressive decline in productivity and health, and so to repeat epidemics.

On this basis it has been proposed that the onset of pestilence at the beginning and end of the Middle Ages was preceded (and promoted) by economic crisis, particularly in agriculture. Some have argued that by the fourteenth century the population had outgrown the resources available to feed it. With no additional land available for crops – and with the stagnation of the rural economy inculcated by peasants' feudal duties to their lords – the population was weakened by malnutrition, falling birth rates and life expectancy, and rising infant mortality.

These factors exposed medieval society to the terrible consequences of disease.

Or so one could argue, at any rate. The difficulty lies in drawing any certainty from our hypotheses, as the evidence is far from adequate. As regards late antiquity there is a great deal of disagreement among scholars concerning population levels. Nevertheless, decline in agricultural productivity and attitudes favourable to birth control can be observed around the time of outbreaks of disease.

Conversely, the growth of the population in the central Middle Ages has been explained as the result of improved productivity made possible by the application of novel forms of agricultural technology and tools. The relationship between technological innovation and social change is a particularly contentious issue among historians. Once again, we need to be clear whether we think that technology leads to social change, or whether social change is necessary to enable change at the technological level. Other factors have been suggested to explain the medieval demographic cycle, such as climate change in Europe and the northern hemisphere. The decline of antiquity and the beginning of the Middle Ages might have coincided with a drop in average temperatures and increased rainfall, leading to flooding and the loss of cultivable land to swamp. These circumstances precipitated the decline of rural economies and health, so provoking outbreaks of famine and disease. By contrast, in the period from the tenth to the thirteenth centuries, this situation was reversed, as rising temperatures and reduced rainfall allowed for the cultivation of vines in parts of England and grain in Greenland.

But not even this explanation can be considered definitive. Despite the formidable advances in its methods, climate history remains a rather inexact science, particularly where the early Middle Ages are concerned, given the inadequacies of the evidence. It is therefore with difficulty that we can point to the causes of the medieval population cycle.

Such difficulties are by no means restricted to the practice of medieval history, however. Even contemporary demographers struggle to offer satisfactory explanations for the direction of change in the global population curve. For now, though, and for our purposes, the evidence for medieval population change would appear to offer some 'hard' quantitative justification for the assumptions of periodization discussed in the previous chapter. Its causes notwithstanding, the medieval demographic curve provides a long-term structural system and framework for the period's most characteristic cultural and social phenomena.

Europe

Throughout this book, the concept of the Middle Ages is tied closely to the concept of Europe. Europe provides the physical geography as well as the socio-cultural framework for the period. The peoples of Europe are characterized not only by the fact that between them they share the

European landmass, but also by their common traditions and inter-relations. It is in this double sense that the concept of Europe was employed at the very beginning of the medieval period by commentators writing in centres north of the Alps, geographically remote from the traditional worldview of ancient Mediterranean culture. In antiquity, Europe was the name given to one of the three parts of the known world, a usage that implied no cultural, political or idealistic connotations. Rather, it was the term *occident* that, in contrast to *orient*, referred to a distinct cultural tradition within the ecumenical world of the Roman empire. However, the western or occidental part of the empire did not fully coincide with the geographical extent of Europe.

The cultural élites of the Christian barbarian successor kingdoms were the first to refer to Europe not only as a landmass but as a community of peoples united by important cultural values. One of the earliest recorded instances of such use of the term is attributed to the Irish monk and missionary, St Columbanus, in around 600. In referring to the many churches of the barbarian kingdoms – churches united in their veneration of St Peter and his successor, the pope – Columbanus spoke of the 'churches of all Europe'. Columbanus seems to have pre-ferred this frame of reference to the concept of *occident*, which in its classical form did not extend to peoples beyond the empire. This concept of Europe was to be greatly successful. During the seventh and eighth centuries it was used to designate the reach of western Christendom subject to the hegemony of the Franks, and it was understood in this way even beyond those borders. The first use of the term *europenses*, Europeans, is found in an eighth-century Spanish chronicle, where it is applied to the Franks in the context of a campaign against the Arabs of Spain, in which Franks appear as the defenders of the Christian world.

This particular use of the term is charged with political and ideologi-cal connotations, while its geographical sense is significantly different to that of ancient usage. The same use is made of the concept of Europe in salutations addressed to Charlemagne, who is variously referred to in the sources as the 'father' and even the 'head' or 'beacon' of Europe. Charlemagne conquered and ruled many barbarian kingdoms in the last quarter of the eighth century. Europe in the sense implied here com-prises that part of the continental landmass subject to Charlemagne's authority, from which an ideal political entity was to emerge. Sub-sequently, the Frankish dominion was declared an empire and Charlemagne its emperor, both titles invoking ancient Mediterranean tradition.

This early-medieval conception of Europe did nothing to damage the understanding that Europe is a whole made up of a variety of distinct parts. This is clear from early-medieval interpretations of a Biblical story concerning the three sons of Noah. Having survived the Flood, the three set out to repopulate the distant reaches of the earth. Church scholars in the barbarian kingdoms attributed the repopulation of

Europe to the efforts of Japheth, Noah's third son. In this interpretation, all the peoples of Europe – and only they – were descended from Japheth. An early Breton source composed around 700 lists twenty generations of Japheth's descendants, followed by twelve persons named after the principal barbarian peoples, as well as one *Romanus* and one *Brito*, therefore including Romans and the non-Germanic races in the family of Europe. Here the myth of common ancestry expressed the affinity of the various peoples of Europe, whilst confirming (and explaining) the autonomy and individuality of each group. The success of the myth was impressive and long-lasting. The story of Japheth was repeated in various forms throughout the Middle Ages, though subsequently the names of his descendent peoples were replaced with those of the repopulated regions. The story served to keep alive the idea of diversity in unity.

Thus the idea of Europe did not assume integrative significance; that is, it was not used to imply an undifferentiated totality, and neither was it intended to deny or efface diversity in favour of a single cultural value. Carolingian culture soon recognized that the kingdoms were the scaffolding of the empire. With the breakdown of the empire, the concept of Europe was applied to the complex of kingdoms and peoples of the post-Carolingian world, with their mutually beneficial political relations and shared cultural and religious values. The Ottonian empire sought to gain mastery over this burgeoning community, though without total success. In this context, Europe lost its unified institutional meaning. The concept of Europe, in post-Carolingian times, represented a particular cultural orbit or sphere, though now this sphere was rather flexible, as it could be extended to accommodate peoples and kingdoms outside the limits of Carolingian imperial authority.

It has been observed that this meaning of Europe seems to alter after the tenth century, as thereafter the term was used to refer to the continental landmass in the physical sense. In practice the term was related to others, such as *christianitas*, *orbis christianus*, *orbis romanus*, and *ecclesia*, terms that express the worldview of official ecclesiastical culture in the wake of the Gregorian reform movement, when the Church sought to extend the limits of the Christian faith and the authority of Rome to the ends of the earth, thereby overwhelming ethnic differences and geographical as well as political borders. With such conquering and hegemonic rhetoric the Church supplanted the very different meanings previously attached to the idea of Europe.

However, even in its prevailing geographic sense, the concept of Europe never lost its power to refer to a community of peoples, a region of Christendom, and a distinct and privileged sector of the universal Church. So much is apparent from the persistent popularity of the myth of Japheth, and from the development of another historical legend concerning the Apostles. According to the latter tradition, when the

Apostles divided among themselves the lands of the earth which were to be converted to the Word of God, Peter and Paul were assigned to what one Carolingian source calls the 'western kingdoms' – or, from the perspective of the twelfth century, Europe.

The memory of Charlemagne continued to nourish an awareness of the political order of the community of Europe. It was not forgotten that Charlemagne had held sway over the 'kingdoms of Europe' – an implicit reference to the continent's political structure. And it was to remain clear that the cultural scope of Europe did not fully correspond with the continent's geographical limits, as beyond the borders of the Christian kingdoms of Europe were to be found barbarian regions as yet unreconciled to the Church, regions extending as far as the islands of the Arctic ocean.

The notion of Europe passed on into the fourteenth century, when it assumed new immediacy as a result of the crisis which struck at the prestige of 'universal' institutions such as the papacy. In response to the erosion of papal authority, the concept of Europe once again served to highlight the organic nature of links between western nations, not only in terms of political and economic affairs, but also in terms of common religious and secular cultural values. This it did without imposing hierarchy or ideological control. Of course, Christianity was to remain the source of faith and religious culture in western Europe, though it was no longer represented by the universalism of the Church of Rome, but by the Churches of the various kingdoms. The national Churches were invested with the traditions and the political organization of their peoples. Therefore the concept of Europe, as it was developed in the last centuries of the Middle Ages (and as it was to be passed on to the early-modern period) is by no means a novel one. In outline, it is much the same as the idea of Europe which was developed at the beginning of our period, though in complexion it shows the signs of a millennium of change. Europe now is a community of peoples possessed of common characteristics and traditions, as well as their own individuality and full political autonomy. The same community does not extend to the limits of the continent as these were defined by ancient geographers, as the eastern frontiers of this community were long to remain imprecise and in dispute. All the same, the politico-cultural structure of Europe enabled the concept to be extended to other peoples and territories as these came to share in Europe's common traditions. In this way, the idea of belonging to Europe spread to the western Slavic states in the fourteenth and fifteenth centuries, becoming a key element of their politico-cultural identity.

One particular precipitating factor was to foster the promotion of a sense of common identity and purpose among the peoples of Europe. This was the Turkish advance on the Balkans. As a result of this development, in the space of little more than a century the two worlds of Europe and Christendom were finally to coincide as never before.

Once Turkish aggression had put paid to the Byzantine empire, western leaders recognized the scale of the threat facing the European states. Alarm led to calls for political unity and co-operation in Europe in the face of a common menace, though nothing was to come of the drive to unity – a circumstance that is itself a recurrent theme in European history. In this context the term 'Europeans' resurfaced, not in the restricted sense of the eighth century, but as a term referring to all members of the cultural, political and religious community of Europe regardless of their nationality. Once formulated in rather uncertain form, 'europeic', by Boccaccio, the term was used consciously and quite deliberately by the humanist pope, Pius II (1405-1464) his aim, to pit European unity against the Turkish enemy in the East.

The sources of medieval history

The basis of historical inquiry

History is written from sources. The past may only be known and represented on the basis of the surviving evidence. This evidence can occur in a variety of forms, which are the sources of all knowledge of history.

Axiomatic though this statement may be, it deserves some explanation. First and foremost, it eliminates a common misconception concerning the nature of the sources: modern history books are *not* sources of historical evidence, despite the custom of English-speaking historians to regard them as 'secondary sources'. Secondary sources are modern writings derived from 'primary' sources, but only the latter are true sources of history. The essential quality of any historical source stems from its proximity to the subject. This proximity may be measured in chronological terms; that is, a given source may be said to be 'close' to particular events if it can be said that the source was produced during or soon after those events were actually taking place. But that is not all. Certain types of records may be deemed to be 'closer' to particular historical phenomena than others. For example, the records most closely related to the business of an assembly are the proceedings, directives and other documents produced and approved by the assembly itself. Less formal eyewitness accounts made after the event by individuals present at the assembly are sources at one remove from a direct correlation with events. A third level of information may be provided by the records of individuals who were not present but whom nevertheless we may judge to be more or less reliably informed. By contrast, a description of the same assembly by a modern historian cannot and will not contain any information that is not already present in (or deducible from) the primary sources. On the other hand, the modern historian, by drawing on a multitude of different sources, is in a position to suggest a historical context for individual events, though this significance may not be at all apparent from even the closest primary sources.

Once a source has been adjudged to be close to the circumstances to which it refers, it is the historian's task to assess the source for reliability. In other words: what kind of information can we draw from a given source? And how far is that information going to be accurate or reliable?

It was in order to provide answers to questions such as these that historians began to develop analytical methods of source analysis. To this day the methods we take to the sources continue to be improved and their merits refined.

Perhaps the most significant development in this area came in the nineteenth century, with the development of objective critical methods intended to ascertain the reality of events and the nature of institutional relations. In this context, particular attention was paid to verifying the reliability of information contained in written records, in order to distinguish authoritative texts from questionable or even plainly false records. This was done by examining the nature of a given document, the condition and context of the author, and the historical circumstances in which the document came into being.

Official documents and others of a legal nature were regarded as the most reliable sources by the pioneers of analysis of medieval records. In contrast, the accounts of chroniclers and private memoirs were reckoned most liable to fraud or error. Critical analysis of medieval sources exposed the extent of falsifications also to be found in legal documents. It was soon acknowledged that large numbers of medieval documents had been falsified in part or in whole, and that many texts seemingly intended for the information of contemporaries or later generations had been distorted by the interests or ambitions of particular groups or institutions, if not by the very ignorance of the authors themselves.

Written sources are not the only sources, however. Scholars of classical antiquity have long considered and made use of antiquarian material, particularly inscriptions and coins, partly to make up for the dearth of written evidence from the period. In the course of the nineteenth century, the volume of this class of evidence gained ever greater substance thanks to advances made in classical archaeology.

Among the sources, a distinction was drawn between *evidence* – that is, information explicitly set down as a record of actions or events in the form of verbal messages transmitted in writing – and *remains* – artefactual remains of the material environment of past societies, which were deposited and preserved once they ceased to be used. In terms of the intrinsic reliability of these sources as evidence for history, a further distinction was made between 'intentional' sources, the origin and purpose of which was to transmit information of certain kinds, and 'preterintentional' sources, the historical potential of which is independent from the object's original function. Broadly speaking, this is the distinction between written records and archaeological remains. Archaeological or artefactual evidence was generally accepted to be more reliable than other forms of evidence, as by its nature the material record is less susceptible to falsification by self-interested authors. All the same, 'intentional' records are without equal when it comes to reconstructing the narrative plot of events. The significance of material evidence is usually less overt, and requires specialized methods of analysis and interpretation in order to yield explicit, informational readings.

The systematic and critical classification of historical documents was intended to determine the informative potential of the sources and to develop the most appropriate techniques for extracting accurate and reliable information from them. This approach lay at the heart of the widely ranging and thoroughgoing accounts of medieval political and institutional history carried out in the nineteenth century.

As time went on, analytical methods were further refined and applied to more complex and subtle readings of the sources. This coincided with the broadening of the very notion of historical evidence and its forms, a development brought on by the increased diversity of analytical perspectives.

While much effort was invested in exposing false records, it has long been accepted that even a false record is, so to speak, a genuine one. By themselves, false documents are reliable evidence of particular circumstances and exigencies in response to which such documents were brought into being. In the same way, even the most obviously fantastic and incredible chronicles are expressions of the ideas and ideals of their authors. As the range and scope of research interests has widened, so the aims and methods of documentary analysis have been transformed. The requirement simply to verify the reliability of particular categories of information encoded in texts has been supplemented with methods aimed at reconstructing broader cultural impulses. A fundamentally important advance was made relatively recently, with the understanding that no 'intentional' source can be so carefully constructed as to exclude even the most implicit traces of 'preterintentional' evidence. In other words, historical sources can be made to yield information that the author did not intend to give or was unaware of giving, information regarding the author's opinions and ideas, as well as her or his attitudes or beliefs and linguistic and cultural contexts. The value of written sources lies not only in what they say, but in what they give away by saying it, unconsciously. For this reason, the association of written and 'intentional' sources implied above loses much of its immediacy. Likewise, it would be misleading to say that all archaeological evidence is preterintentional. On the contrary: a very large part of the material record was intended by the makers to perform an emphatically informative function. This is particularly true of monuments of various kinds. Monuments may be defined in a very broad sense, to include commemorative statues or effigies of public figures and (in the Middle Ages) cathedrals and monasteries, palaces and castles – as well as the more or less humble funerary monuments of individuals. In numerous instances, a monument's message – or the religious, social and political values which underlie it and which determine its significance in the original context – was made clear by texts written on the monument itself, in the form of inscriptions, if not by references to or descriptions of monuments in literary or written sources. Analyses of this category of written evidence should follow the same precautions long familiar to documentary historians. That said, monuments are mostly meaningful without the mediation of the written word. Any monument represents the ideas, values and needs of the social group that made and used it. This group comprises the patron, the craftsmen and the public. Thus even the information provided by a monument is intentional, revealing as it does the intentions of those who made it and the circumstances of this production.

Archaeological material can also be read as an 'unintentional' source; that is, as a source of information that the makers did not consciously intend to impart – information regarding construction or production techniques, for example, and the availability of formal exemplars or models and the provenance of primary materials. The same kind of involuntary clues are also to be found within sources of written evidence. Documents, too, have their material aspect, and therefore can be categorized as historical remains. Medieval chronicles, and written texts in general, were preserved in codices, volumes that are not infrequently contemporary with the texts they contain. When a manuscript is known to have been written by the author of the text (and not by a later copyist), it is known as the 'autograph' manuscript. The material complexion of a given codex is an abundant source of evidence, from the quality of the parchment and the arrangement and layout of pages, to the kinds of scripts used in writing the text and the occurrence of decoration or illustrations. Add to this the inter-relations between texts in the same codex, and an idea emerges of the complex of information and meaning bound up in medieval books – information relating not only to the techniques of medieval book production, but also (in the case of autograph manuscripts) to the progress and timing of the composition of works, their audience and social context. This is evidence beyond the evidence of the words themselves. A reading of this evidence may lead to a fuller understanding of the text.

Administrative and juridical documents, both in original form and as copies, are another particularly rich source of information of this kind for the medieval historian. Their form was conditioned not only by the organization of the offices of notaries and others, but also by the political and cultural strategies of the issuing authorities. The authorities expressed their status through official formulae and titles given in the text, and through the material (and visual) semblance of documents; that is, through the choices of script and inks, and the use of seals and other signs of authentication. Furthermore, the material complexion of original documents may reveal much of the working methods of scribes in writing and validating texts, processes that were often long and laborious. Furthermore, the organization of archives and registers – the repositories of original documents and transcriptions from juridical documents, respectively – is evidence of the significance in which they were held by beneficiaries.

The material form of documents and the circumstances of their transmission, therefore, make up an integral part of the information-bearing capacity of written records.

These considerations go a long way to diminish the value of the theoretical distinctions imposed between different categories of evidence, and with them the positivist idea that different kinds of sources provide different kinds of information. To sum up, it is possible to think of the sources of history, without typological distinction, as fragments of the past. These fragments come to us divorced from the complex web of experience and practice within which they were made and used and meaningful; together with other materials lost in the course of time, these fragments were once components of the whole cultural universe of a society. The nature of the sources demands the historian's analytical effort in constructing a mental picture of that whole, through analysis of the many channels of information inherent in each type of source. To this end, such analysis will need to be as exhaustive and flexible as possible, if it is to exploit the maximum informational potential of a given source, while relating this information to evidence drawn from other sources. By such means the complex web of actions and experience within which such sources were made and which give them their meaning can be reconstructed.

The 'typology' of sources

Despite what has been said regarding the theoretical aspects and methodological principles of documentary analysis, the fact remains that a typological classification of sources, based on the prevalent kinds of information they contain or the use for which they were made, retains much practical utility. Such a typology of sources is of use in directing the researcher to the kinds of sources likely to yield information of a particular nature, while making clear the kinds of information one can normally expect from sources of a given type. On this basis, analytical techniques appropriate to particular types of source material have been developed; these techniques provide a firm and effective basis for the full assessment of the sources.

Given, then, that the typological classification of sources has an essentially practical value, the remainder of this chapter is taken up with an explanatory list of the principal types of source traditionally recognized in historical research.

Written sources

These consist of a range of documents in which information of various kinds occurs in the form of a verbal message given in writing.

Narrative sources

Narrative sources comprise texts describing historical events in more or less straightforward, discursive fashion. Usually the primary purpose of writings of this kind was to witness and provide a record of the actions or events described. They occur in a wide range of forms, from simple registers of important events listed annually ('annals') to 'histories' recounting the deeds of a king or events in the life of a particular city, kingdom or monastery; and, finally, the typically vast 'universal histories', conceived as repositories of all available knowledge and inspired by contemplation of the moral or Christian significance of the history of humankind. Narrative sources also include biographies and commemorative eulogies and panegyrics. The following chapter contains an extended analysis of the production of narrative sources and histories in the Middle Ages.

Documentary sources

This category incorporates documents of a juridical nature intended to validate and record the rights, privileges and obligations conferred upon institutions and individuals in legally valid and binding form. Examples of documents of this kind are diplomata, privileges and bulls issued by a public, secular or ecclesiastical authority in favour of a stated beneficiary. Other such sources are the records of agreements, contracts and settlements between private individuals. Chapter 6 presents a fuller account of this category of material and the approaches to it.

Decrees and legislative sources

These include not only the law codes drawn up by medieval rulers and the statutes of urban communities, but also documents produced during the routine administration of government, such as the Carolingian capitularies, imperial and royal constitutions, and the day-to-day deliberations of feudal diets or parliaments and public assemblies, as well as ecclesiastical law-giving such as papal decrees, resolutions of councils and collections of canons.

Judicial, administrative and fiscal documentation

In the interests of convenience, the above is a rather loose heading intended to cover a variety of documents pertaining to the functions of public bodies and the institutions of state and other courts under aristocratic, feudal and ecclesiastical jurisdiction. The same category includes the proceedings of tribunals and courts of justice, and mandates issued by medieval sovereigns and their instructions to local officers and functionaries – as well as records of fiscal censors and assessments of tax due from households and private revenues, such as the Florentine *catasti* of the fifteenth century. Of particular importance for ecclesiastical and secular administration are the detailed inventories of properties and revenues drawn up in various forms from the Carolingian period to the end of the Middle Ages. Though properly they do not belong under this heading, we refer here in passing to the extensive lists of the names of individuals inscribed in so-called books or rolls of the dead (*libri* or *rotuli mortuorum*) used in the liturgy of commemoration by monks. These, like university matriculation rolls and the registers of members of guilds and confraternities, are important sources for demographic and social studies.

Official and private correspondence

Collections of letters – usually letters drafted or received by members of one or other socio-cultural élite – present a unique source of information regarding the exchange and interpretation of news, the condition of interpersonal relationships, and the articulation of individual attitudes and opinions. Of particular prominence in this category are the letters of Pope Gregory the Great, and the records of Charlemagne's correspondence with later pontiffs – as well as the letters that circulated between the members of an élite circle of Carolingian scholars and intellectuals in the eighth and ninth centuries. During the central and later Middle Ages the volume of this material increases as members of other social groups (such as the crusaders and university students) began to exchange forms of written communication. Also belonging to this category are records of diplomatic correspondence, important evidence for the condition of political relations, and evidence, too, of the ideological positions and the self-image of leaders.

Hagiographical sources

This category comprises biographies of saints and other forms of evidence relating to the cults of the saints and their posthumous miracles, the rediscovery and translation of relics, and descriptions of the building of dedicated churches. Such sources are mid-way between history and legend, though this condition does not discount the value of the material. On the contrary, hagiographical writings are sources rich in medieval attitudes towards sanctity and the holy, religiosity and collective mentalities, often with an eye to the culture of social classes that left no trace in other types of records.

Liturgical texts

This category consists mostly of texts used during the celebration of the rites and offices of the Church: prayers, readings and the order of various liturgies. They include lectionaries (anthologies of Biblical and Gospel readings), sacramentaries (manuals for the administration of the sacraments), *ordines* (the orders for the solemn ceremonies of the liturgical year) and pontificals (containing the order of rites celebrated by bishops). While essentially these are concerned with the life of the Church, they have implications for the history of medieval culture, in so far as ecclesiastical ceremonies went through complex development and significant change. Moreover, special liturgies were practised in honour of sovereigns and states, which are the source of much important evidence about political and religious doctrines and ideas.

Literary and doctrinal sources

In general, all the texts written in the Middle Ages, even those that were not intended to witness or record particular events, make individual but nonetheless essential contributions to our understanding of medieval culture and civilization. For this reason, the typology of historical source material may be extended to include literary works (poems and romances) and doctrinal writings (in the form of theological, juridical and political treatises) produced in the medieval period. The significance of this category of evidence is for the most part indirect; such sources may be used to build up a picture of medieval culture through the mores and mentalities implicit in such texts. Though the study of medieval literary and doctrinal production is a specialist pursuit, some knowledge of this class of evidence is nevertheless essential for an understanding of the spirit of the age.

Material sources

Material or artefactual sources are those which provide information above all through their form, context and function. They may or may not comprise verbal compositions or text.

Archaeological evidence

Archaeological sources include all manner of artefacts produced in order to meet the needs of individuals and social groups in the past. They include an enormous variety of materials, such as the grave goods found in barbarian burial contexts, as well as everyday domestic implements such as pottery vessels and other instruments. The same category includes the by-products and waste from the activity of production (such as glass- and metal-working, for example). Material evidence comprises the remains of houses and settlements, and monumental buildings such as (in the Middle Ages) churches and castles. This category of evidence is described in greater detail below, in Chapter 8.

Numismatic evidence

For our purposes, numismatic evidence is the evidence presented by metal coins struck and issued in the Middle Ages. An analytical excursus on their characteristics and the history of medieval coinage is to be found in Chapter 7.

Seals and insignia

This category refers to the wide range of figurative and symbolic emblems used to identify both secular and ecclesiastical authorities throughout the period. It is interesting from a number of different points of view. The figurative images found on seals were very carefully constructed according to very precise norms. As such, they make up an interesting and evocative repertoire of the ritual costumes and gestures adopted by medieval powers. Even the very material, form and dimensions of a seal are significant indexes of the relative status of the authority to which the seal belongs. Different sorts of seals were used by the same authority in issuing different sorts of documents. Most often the visual form of seals consists of image and text. Insignia and heraldry make use of a complex symbolic language based on abstract forms and colours. These forms are material for the study of family history and the development of lordship and aristocratic alliances.

Epigraphs

Naturally, epigraphs or inscriptions are of interest as much for their material form as for their documentary significance. They are written statements or formulae, though a good part of their significance derives from the formal characteristics of the inscribed object, such as its size, material and the type of script used. Significance is also inherent in the context or the location for which the object was intended. Medieval inscriptions are found in funerary contexts and on monuments commemorating the deceased, as well as those applied to monumental buildings in celebration of the builder's (but more often the patron's) achievement. Painted inscriptions were employed to refer to and describe religious and other scenes in wall paintings.

Artistic sources

Like medieval works of literature, medieval works of art are another source of interest for the historian. The historical value of artworks derives as much from their formal qualities, which are the proper concern of specialists in the field of art history, as it does from the programmes underlying the realization of a work of art and the conceptual meanings expressed. Moreover, artists often depicted the environment and the surroundings of medieval life and contemporary customs, fashions, dress and pastimes. On the other hand, medieval art is a vehicle of medieval beliefs and concepts and ideals. The iconography of medieval art – the conceptual or symbolic meanings encoded in pictorial conventions – provides a bridge between the history of the arts and more general historical reconstruction.

This concludes our summary of the principal types of source material available to medieval historians. Typologies of this kind seldom exhaust the seemingly endless range of available evidence. One could distinguish other categories based not on the types of evidence but on individual characteristics common to one or more types, such as the particular formulae used by juridical documents, or decorative motifs applied to ceramic vessels or tableware. Over the course of twenty years, one contemporary academic enterprise aimed at establishing the typology of medieval sources has come up with some sixty-seven categories or 'types' of evidence. The project continues; it is as yet unclear what the final number will be. The proliferation of potential sources is not merely the result of the development of more and more subtle interpretative strategies and their effect of breaking down diverse streams of evidence from larger bodies once considered in their entirety. It is the result, moreover, of the pursuit of history in fields disregarded or inadequately represented heretofore. One such field is that of landscape studies. The study of the medieval landscape involves the analysis of administrative documents and tax registers and a wide assortment of other evidence from medieval and modern periods alike. Historians of the medieval landscape must therefore make use of modern documentary sources – another 'type' of source, and one with its own proper methods of analysis and interpretation.

The language of medieval sources

The great proportion of medieval documents, of whatever kind, was written in Latin. This is not because Latin continued to be spoken in the Middle Ages. Even in the regions most influenced by Roman tradition – and even at the very beginning of the medieval period – the language of everyday oral discourse moved progressively away from ancient Latin, taking on original phonetic, lexical and syntactical characteristics. This process gave rise to the Romance and neo-Latin languages, languages that are significantly different from the common language from which they are descended. The change began as early as the third century. Come the seventh century, and following the barbarian invasions, it was well advanced.

All the same, Latin was to remain as the language of written communication in all parts of medieval Europe, even in regions such as

Germany and England where the spoken language was altogether unrelated to Latin. This situation obtained through to the end of the eleventh century. In the twelfth century, the vernacular (or vulgar) tongue was given written form. At first, this was restricted to poetry, which took the forms of its expression from oral tradition. Thereafter, from the thirteenth century, the spoken language was used in the writing of texts of many other kinds. However, Latin was long to remain the language of the Church and the language of scholars. In general terms Latin is the language of 'high' medieval culture.

In order to make a direct approach to the written sources of medieval history, therefore, some degree of familiarity with Latin is essential. However, it should be said that medieval Latin is different from classical Latin. During the course of the medieval period, classical Latin was progressively transformed into a contrived language remote from everyday discourse. This notwithstanding, the transformation was a positive, incremental one, thanks to which medieval Latin was more than adequately empowered to perform the roles for which it was engaged by medieval writers.

In the first medieval centuries, in the time of the Romano-barbarian kingdoms, the career of written Latin language is characterized by the rapid and sometimes irretrievable loss of classical and late-Roman forms. Between the sixth and eighth centuries, the corruption of the language in Roman territories was assisted by developments in spoken language, which now moved markedly away from 'good' Latin. Simultaneously, the collapse of scholastic institutions put paid to any hope that the practice of good written language might arrest further corruption. Among peoples whose linguistic traditions were unrelated to Latin, as in England and Ireland, Latin was imported as the language of the Church. Isolated and incongruous, in these contexts Latin usage went impoverished, unsustained as it was by the efforts of expert teachers.

The principal characteristics of barbarian Latin are: the reduction of declensions to one or two cases; the loss of many synthetic verbal forms and their replacement with periphrastic expressions; changes in vocabulary, with the importation of words and meanings from the spoken vernacular; the appearance of words of Germanic origin; and increased variety and inconsistency in orthography (spelling) caused by change in sounding of vowels and consonants, and by the attempts of poorly trained writers to transcribe new sounds. Furthermore, barbarian Latin is marked by the writers' inability to construct complex sentences. This had already come about in the early Middle Ages, when some of the most popular literary models were provided by late-antique ecclesiastical sources, the authors of which had purposely chosen an unmannered colloquial style of writing in order to put over their message in the most comprehensible terms. The Latin of barbarian texts seems terribly impoverished and incorrect when compared with the classical canon. (As with any rule there are notable exceptions, of course. In the early period continuity was ensured by the sporadic survival, at local or regional level, of effective centres of learning, such as those of Visigothic Spain.)

This rather desperate situation began to change in the first half of the eighth century, when, in certain urban and monastic centres such as those in Italy and in England, schools were established for the pursuit of learned and literary studies. This innovation gained in strength when Charlemagne made it his policy to see that the clergy and the administrators of his kingdom were adequately schooled in grammar and literature. To this end, grammar manuals and vocabularies were composed and the rules of good Latin revived by the study of works by ancient pagan and Christian writers. The results were not always perfect, as scholars experienced difficulty in reconstituting classical forms – and as the uses of oral discourse continued to press upon the language of scholars and writers. In the Carolingian period, however, Latin language was corrected and reformed into an effective vehicle for communication, whether it be for the purpose of writing a theological treatise or a historical account or chronicle. At the same time, Latin ceased to be the spoken language in the Romance countries, increasingly becoming the affected and artificial language of scholars. Latin was thus reserved to particular groups and particular uses. When compared to the condition of the Latin language in orbits unaffected by Carolingian influence, it is clear that the extent of the Carolingian achievement is impressive. In southern Italy, for instance, written language continued to feel the very powerful influence of the spoken tongue, gaining in vivacity what it lost in correctness.

However artificial or contrived it may sometimes seem, medieval Latin was not a dead language based only on the rote repetition of scholars. Rather the contrary – medieval Latin was continually elaborated by writers and adapted to a diverse selection of expressive and functional requirements, to the extent that writers developed forms unknown in antiquity. For example, in the Carolingian age religious hymns were composed based on the tonal accents of the words, resulting in original and unusual rhythms unparalleled by classical forms but specifically adapted to the cadence of contemporary music.

From the eleventh century the burgeoning of cultural and learned activity – not to mention the greater frequency of contact among scholars – led to an ever more confident and refined control of Latin. On the one hand, greater concentration on the classics of ancient literature saw the recovery of a wealth and subtlety of expression that had previously been lost, while on the other, the capacity of the language to serve modern uses was increased. New words were created which respected classical linguistic patterns while aspiring to a novel expressiveness. In the same context, the style of written Latin becomes incredibly refined and affected. Much use is made of alliteration, rhyming and the rhythmic sequences of voices. In the twelfth century, the versatility of written Latin is perhaps best displayed in poetry, as poets developed new and virtuoso metrical arrangements. The same developments can be seen in prose writing, too, which now adopted the *cursus*; that is, the practice of bringing periods or constructions to an end with a string of words or clauses, the sounds of which follow and repeat certain rhythms. Subsequently, in the thirteenth century, the uses of Latin changed in different ways in response to the widespread adoption of the vulgar tongue as a medium for literary production. In this way, Latin became the language of science, law and theology. Its forms were simplified in order to express logical arguments more clearly. Once more reformed, Latin became the language of medieval scientific thought. New words were created to refer to the abstract concepts of philosophy and law, sometimes derived from Greek, sometimes from Arabic. And at once the language lost its splendour, its syntax becoming simplified and its style progressively monotone and turgid. The result was that form of scholastic Latin that, in the fourteenth and fifteenth centuries, was to attract the censure of men who called for the revival of the classical Latin of the ancients. Despite the tirades of the precursors of early-modern humanism, however, it should be said that even the scholastic Latin language of the late Middle Ages was more than effective as a vehicle for philosophy and science. Even at the end of the period, the language retained its status as a universal language, used by students and scholars throughout Europe as a vehicle for learning and communication, at a remove from the diversity of spoken languages.

The writing of history in the Middle Ages

The writing of history was a constant concern in the Middle Ages. By writing history, medieval historians sought to find the meaning of human actions and events in relation to the truths of the Christian faith, while others sought to illustrate and celebrate the traditions of ethnic groups and political institutions, or to preserve the memory of the extraordinary, marvellous and tragic deeds of men. Almost all were anxious to draw moral and religious lessons from history. In short, the writing of history played a particularly complex and important role in medieval culture, one that goes well beyond the simple recording of prominent events. What is more, medieval attitudes to history did not undervalue the story of humankind in favour of the transcendental values of the Christian faith.

So much is clear from the fact that the rate of production of historical works is fairly high by the standards of the period. These were works conceived in a variety of often very refined literary forms. The significance of historiography as medieval cultural production is still more apparent from the fact that medieval historians sought to make sense of events, and explore the role of individual agency, chance and fortune in shaping history. In different ways throughout the period, medieval historians proposed different solutions to the problematic relationship between the will of men and the will of God in the making of history.

Not all of medieval historiography is so ambitious, however. Alongside texts in which such problems are developed and explored, in the Middle Ages, as in most other periods, more simple forms of historical writing were produced. These include incidental and unstructured records of events, as well as studied or otherwise pedantic compilations derived from earlier works. Yet with these kinds of histories we are far from qualifying the complexity of medieval historiography, either in its range or cultural ambition.

Given the aims and the ambition of medieval historians, it is no longer appropriate to regard medieval histories as straightforward registers of information or facts about the period – sources to be broken down, and their details tested for authenticity, following positivist methodologies for the interpretation of 'narrative sources'. As well as describing more or less accurate or impartial accounts of events, medieval histories bear witness to a diversity of attitudes, beliefs, ideas, sentiments and mentalities; as such, they are vital expressions of many aspects of medieval culture. An assessment of cultural context is essential if we are to understand the deepest significance of medieval events and the meaning of their documentation.

This chapter presents an account of medieval historiography. In this discussion, the various texts are not classified and described typologically, according to the various types or genres of narrative writing produced in the Middle Ages. Although we shall list works, authors and the kinds of information they provide, the aim of this chapter is above all to give an idea of the development of historical culture in the period.

The origins of medieval historiography

The origin of medieval historiography may be associated with the *Historiae adversus paganos* by the Spanish priest, Paulus Orosius (b. 380/5; d. after 418). Orosius' text opens with a description of the creation of the world, and it ends with an account of events in the author's own lifetime. In its progress it combines the two great historical traditions embraced by the culture of the late Roman Empire – the Graeco-Roman tradition and the Biblical story of Israel. In Orosius, Old Testament history continues with the incarnation of Jesus Christ and the origin of the Apostolic Church. Writers had sought to reconcile these diverse traditions ever since the recognition of Christianity as a lawful religion in the Roman empire. One such writer was Bishop Eusebius of Caesarea (*c.*260-339/40), a close advisor to the emperor Constantine. In his *Chronica*, Eusebius worked out a synoptic universal chronology by combining chronological systems from a variety of traditions, particularly those of the eastern empires and Greece and Rome. Eusebius' work was translated into Latin by St Jerome, who extended it to include the period up to 378. Orosius made use of this and numerous other works in composing his integrated account of 'universal' history, though his intention was not simply to compile a historical encyclopaedia. Instead, he was concerned to highlight the progress of humankind, and to recommend the potential for conciliation between the pagan and Christian traditions.

Pagan writers claimed that Christianity had weakened the Roman empire, and was responsible for the catastrophic barbarian invasions that began at precisely the same time as Orosius began work on his history. Orosius drew from the two greatest Christian philosophers known in his day, St Ambrose and St Jerome, and from their meditations on history. Building on this legacy, Orosius proposed a complex interpretation of the progress of history and its diverse themes. He was determined to show that, if Christianity had not banished all evil from the world, it had at least markedly improved conditions of life on earth

– an improvement that was to advance further with the spread of evangelization. For its part, the Roman empire is not represented as antagonistic to the mission of Christianity; since the first century BC, from the time of Pompeius Trogus, pagan philosophers and historians had regarded the empire as an ecumenical institution, one with the potential to unify diverse peoples with its universal culture. For Orosius, the unity of the empire created conditions vital for the universal dissemination of Christianity. By referring to the prophecies of the Old Testament book of Daniel, according to which a succession of four universal kingdoms were to hold sway one after the other until the end of time, Orosius claimed the fourth and final empire to be that of Rome itself. Once it had embraced Christianity and the barbarian peoples, the empire was to endure eternally.

Orosius' work had enormous and lasting influence. Throughout the medieval period up to the time of Dante, the *Historiae* were a prime source of knowledge of ancient history and its Christian interpretation.

Barbarian histories

The success of Orosius' *Historiae* notwithstanding, the writing of history subsequently took a variety of directions as the interest of historians was drawn to the great upheavals brought on by the end of imperial government in the West and the installation of the barbarian kingdoms. Under Rome's successor kingdoms, histories were written with the barbarian kings and their peoples as principal protagonists. Such writings include accounts of the experience of migration and settlement within the former western empire. Their authors were not barbarians but Romans, educated exponents of late-Roman civilization, who took up positions of authority under the new regimes.

The first text of this kind is the *Historia Gothorum* by Cassiodorus (*c*.485-*c*.580). Cassiodorus was a Roman senator and a close advisor to Theodoric, the Ostrogothic king of Italy. The full text of his history does not survive; it is known from a later adaptation by the Gothic notary, Jordanes (*De origine actibusque Getarum*, or the *Getica*).

Other prominent works of the second half of the sixth century include: the *Chronica* of the Visigothic kingdom by the Spanish bishop John of Biclaro (d. after 591); and the *Historiae Francorum* by Gregory, bishop of Tours (b. 538/9; d. after 4 July 593). These were followed in the early seventh century by the *Historiola*, an account of Lombard rule in Italy, by Secundus of Non, a northern-Italian monk. Again, the text of the *Historiola* is lost, though it was later to be used extensively by the historian Paul the Deacon, whose work survives. From the same period we have the *Historia* or *Origo Gothorum* by the Spanish bishop Isidore of Seville (*c*.560-636). Common to all histories conceived at this time is a positive interpretation of the influence of barbarian rule in reshaping the political life of the post-Roman world. The perspectives and the interests of those Roman historians are profoundly influenced by these individuals' attachment to their native soil. At the same time, the empire slowly ceases to provoke strong feelings of devotion; in fact, Cassiodorus was to be the last to attempt to combine allegiance to the empire with support for the local Ostrogothic kingdom. The new attitudes are expressed most clearly by Isidore of Seville, who concluded his history of the Visigoths with an impassioned eulogy to Spain and the beauty and fertility of his native land under good Visigothic government. In another of his historical works, a universal history, Isidore neglects the scheme of the four successive kingdoms based on the Old Testament, making use instead of a scheme of Judaic origin previously revived by St Augustine, based on the six ages of man, to distinguish periods in the history of humankind. In so doing, Isidore robbed the history of the Roman empire of the religious significance with which it had been charged by Orosius' great *Histories*.

The Roman writers were also concerned with recording the national traditions of the barbarian peoples reigning in Rome's former provinces. Writing of this kind was intended to establish the identity of the new kingdoms. In this context, glorious traditions were set down as proof of the kingdoms' legitimacy and prestige. However, the barbarian kings are celebrated above all for their commitment to the Christian faith, and as protectors of the Church. Gregory of Tours regarded history as proof of God's presence in the world and the ultimate salvation of humankind. He gave no special religious interpretation to the history of the Frankish kingdom, instead reserving his greatest attention to the career of the Church and its clergy under the Franks. Moreover, writers of the sixth and early seventh centuries continued to consider their own epoch to be linked in some way to the past, a circumstance that best explains the enduring appeal of the universal history both as a learned pursuit and as a record of events vital to the understanding of the present, such as the succession of the ancient kingdoms, the coming of Christ and the foundation of the earthly Church. Thus, the chronicles of John of Biclaro and Gregory of Tours begin with accounts of the Creation; and both Cassiodorus and Isidore of Seville produced versions of universal history. The final expression of this tendency in early-medieval historiography is represented by the so-called *Chronicle of Fredegar*, a complex work probably composed by more than one author. The first half of the *Chronicle* is dedicated to episodes from ancient history, while the second half gives a history of the Franks to the year 642, for which the author(s) relied heavily on Gregory of Tours. The text illustrates the continued determination to produce written history in Frankish Gaul well into the seventh century, while pointing to a decline in literary standards and the quest for historical accuracy. Furthermore, the *Chronicle of Fredegar* reveals how the influence of Roman traditions had begun to tail off, a process that was to continue into the eighth century, to judge from the few historical works written after about 650 which offer original perspectives and structures. Eighth-century histories are the work of individuals who associated themselves wholeheartedly with the traditions of the Germanic peoples from which they descended. Works of this kind were intended to represent the character, the successes and the values of these peoples, and so to foster consciousness of national identity. In keeping with the aims of this project, historians gave up their preoccupation with universal history in favour of straightforward narrative accounts entirely dedicated to single groups or kingdoms.

This is the tendency represented by the *Liber Historiae Francorum*, a short work written around 726 or 727, charting the mythical ancestry of the Frankish people from the Trojans, with accounts of the Franks' legendary deeds at the time of the Roman empire. The narrative becomes progressively more detailed in its account of the rise of the mayors of the palace under the last, impotent Merovingian kings, and the subsequent emergence of the Carolingian dynasty led by Pippin the Short. The sympathies of the anonymous author are explicit. The ideological theme that underlies the work is the supremacy of the Franks over other peoples – a hegemony anticipated by the Franks' early skirmishes with the Romans. Rather more subtle and reasoned accounts of national histories are to be found in the two principal historiographical texts of the eighth century: the *Historia ecclesiastica gentis Anglorum* by Bede (673/4-735); and the *Historia Langobardorum* by the Lombard historian Paul the Deacon (*c*.720-*c*.797). Both authors were educated and cultured men; in literary terms, their works are far superior to those of their barbarian predecessors. Both are products of a revival in learning and culture which was taking place in England and Italy at this time. For Bede, the progress of the national history of the Angles and the Saxons was driven by the progressive Christian conversion of minds and manners, and by the foundation of the national Church as an expression of the unity and identity of the English people. For Paul the Deacon, the sources of Lombard national history were provided by tales of warrior exploits, and the virtues of the Lombard kings and their people, from the period of the great migrations to the height of Lombard authority in Italy. The prestige of the Lombard kingdom is expressed not in its hegemony over other peoples, but in its heroic defence of national sovereignty. For both writers, the function of history was to define the moral strength and identity of their peoples, the significance of which is greater even than the experience of military and political history in fostering a sense of national unity.

With his historical works, Bede succeeded in resolving certain technical difficulties relating to the chronological sequence and timing of events in history. In Bede's day there was no single system of absolute dating in general use, and no system that was simultaneously valid for use in the past and in the present. The chronological reckoning developed by Eusebius of Caesarea and continued by St Jerome was intended to coordinate the variety of chronographic systems used in antiquity, though this scheme had resisted all successive attempts to integrate it with the chronologies of the barbarian kingdoms, and was therefore useless in establishing the chronological relationship of events in more recent history. Bede's concern with the accurate measurement of time resulted from urgent liturgical concerns rather than strictly historical problems. Churchmen needed to be able accurately to calculate the date of Easter. Easter is a moveable feast, the date of which is based on the concordance of cycles of the moon and sun; the feast of Easter falls now on the first Sunday after the full moon following the spring equinox.

In order to compose accurate Easter calendars, and to ensure that the feast was celebrated at the same time throughout the Christian world, complicated astronomical calculations were required, and with them a system for numbering successive years. To be of use, and in order to give the precise date of the Easter feast in all places and at all times, this system of dating had to be universally valid and acceptable.

The problem had been tackled and a solution proposed by the Scythian monk, Dionysius Exiguus, at Rome in the year 525. Dionysius took the year of Christ's birth as the starting point for his chronology. The key date for the beginning of the Christian era Dionysius placed 754 years after the foundation of Rome. From this, he worked out the Easter cycle for the period AD 1 to 532, subsequently bringing his calculations forward to the year 626. Bede took up Dionysius' tables, and from them he worked out a second great Easter cycle for the period between 532 and 1063. When he came to write the history of the English Church and people, Bede used this Christian calendar to provide the history's chronological structure. In so doing, Bede introduced the system of reckoning years in relation to the year of Christ's birth (Anno Domini, or AD), which remains in use to this day.

Carolingian historiography

Use of the system spread rapidly. Indirectly, it influenced the formation of a new genre of medieval history writing, one that would have been inconceivable without the development of just such a system.

The Anglo-Saxon missionaries who brought the word of God to the continent in the eighth century carried with them chronological tables giving the dates of Easter for future years. These 'Easter tables' (*tabulae paschales*) were to provide the chronological framework for the composition of annual records detailing significant events affecting the lives of a number of Frankish monasteries. In some cases, such annual records were made directly on to and alongside imported Easter tables. Subsequently, annual records were made independently of Easter tables, thus becoming a distinctive form of early-medieval historiography – or *annals*. This was not an altogether unprecedented development. A similar system had been used in late antiquity, for instance, for calendars recording the succession of consuls. In the early Middle Ages, annals were to be the form most favoured by monastic historians for records of political events in the Frankish realm and the impact of these events on the monasteries. The annalists developed a keen interest in the affairs of the Frankish kingdom, so that the writing of annals seems to have been a particular preoccupation of monasteries closely associated with the ascendant Carolingian dynasty. The writing of annals called for no great literary accomplishment on the part of their compilers. Records were continually altered and updated, and as such are seldom the work of a single chronicler. With time, the arrangement and the format of annals were improved upon, and the chaotic and incoherent style of the earliest examples replaced with a more systematic approach. As monasteries exchanged information and news on contemporary events, so written annals were lent and borrowed, and their contents compared and integrated, thus giving rise to families of annals bearing ever richer and more detailed stocks of information.

Between 788 and 793, Charlemagne ordered that an annual record of the affairs of the Frankish realm be drawn up by ecclesiastical scholars in the service of the court. In this way, the annals now known as the *Royal Frankish Annals* were begun – the *Annales Regni Francorum*, sometimes also referred to as *Annales Laurissenses maiores*, after the monastery of Lorsch, where the oldest manuscript was found.

The Carolingian court was a centre of history writing in other forms and for other purposes, above all during the reign of Charlemagne's successor, Louis the Pious. Political strife both within and without the imperial family gave court historians the motivation to record and interpret important characters and occurrences. The biography was one literary form sometimes chosen in this context, though as a genre it had not been widely used since the end of antiquity. The royal biography was revived by Einhard (*c*.770-840), a key figure in political and cultural life at the court of Charlemagne. At the beginning of the 830s, Einhard conceived his eulogy to the late emperor, the *Vita Karoli Magni*, in the form of a biography. This he illustrated not only with accounts of the emperor's military successes, but also with details of Charlemagne's personal attitudes and anecdotes from his private life. As his model, Einhard turned to the *Lives of the Twelve Caesars* by Suetonius. Not only did Suetonius' text lend itself as a prestigious literary prototype – the reference to Suetonius' imperial biographies implied Charlemagne's succession from the emperors of ancient Rome. The exemplary figure conjured by Einhard's biography was intended as a model for Charlemagne's successors.

The troubled reign of Louis the Pious furnished material for two biographies: one written in Louis' lifetime by the German bishop Thegan (d. after 840), the *Vita Hludowici imperatoris*; the other – also the *Vita Hludowici imperatoris* – composed shortly after his death by an anonymous court scholar known to modern scholars as the 'Astronomer' on account of the attention he paid to astronomical phenomena.

An almost unique example of a biography produced for a subject other than a king is the *Vita Walae*, written by the monk Paschasius Radbertus (d. *c*.860) to commemorate (and so to vindicate) the political career of one of Charlemagne's cousins. Wala played a prominent role in the chaos brought on after Louis had ascended to the imperial throne. Wala's *Life* is unique in its form, as it makes no apparent use of ancient models. In fact, it is composed in the form of a dialogue between two monks. Between them, the speakers' words paint a portrait of Wala and his character, while interpreting the significance of his conduct in political affairs.

The classical tendencies of Carolingian court culture reappear with the *Historiae*, written after 841 by Nithard (d. 844), a nephew of Charlemagne. Though he was a layman, Nithard was an educated man of letters. His *Historiae* are a record of the bickering between Louis' successors over the division of the empire. Both the structure of the text and the intentions of its author reveal Nithard's debt to ancient historians. Nithard is not reluctant to emphasize the inanity and immorality of the conflict, or to cut through the distortions of court propaganda. The style is dry and the judgement clear-eyed and unaffected. Finally, in his assessment of the course of events, Nithard reintroduces the pagan idea of irrational 'fortune' as the factor that upsets the normal order of things.

With Nithard's *Historiae*, the production of historical works at or for the Carolingian court comes to an end. The writing of history continued in the monasteries and in certain episcopal centres, where the imitation of classical models was put aside in favour of novel and innovative literary forms. Even the writing of royal annals at court was interrupted by the outbreak of internal conflict in 829, though it continued in unofficial form elsewhere. In the western territories, the annals were pursued first by Prudentius, bishop of Troyes, and later by archbishop Hincmar of Rheims. The text of this set of later Frankish annals is known as the *Annales Bertiniani*, after the monastery of St Bertin, in Flanders, where the oldest manuscript was kept. In the east, other records (the *Annales Fuldenses*) were kept by monks of the German monastery of Fulda. Other annals were made in a number of other monasteries, though the concern of the chroniclers rarely extends beyond the limits of local affairs.

Around the mid-ninth century a new mode of historical writing was adopted in certain ecclesiastical centres. This was devoted to the history of particular monasteries or episcopal foundations, and based around the succession of abbots or bishops and the records of their achievements. In this way, ecclesiastical institutions themselves became the object of historical interest. The historians' motive was to safeguard the institutions' traditions of sanctity and their moral and institutional heritage, and to promote awareness of this legacy among the institutions' members, present and future.

The genre was not altogether new. Since the seventh century monastic scribes had composed biographies or lives of their abbots, such as the *Life* of St Columbanus written by his disciple Jonas of Bobbio, and the lives of the abbots of Wearmouth by Bede. As for the episcopal sphere, the most prestigious model was provided by the lives of the bishops of Rome, or the *Liber pontificalis ecclesiae Romanae*. The *Liber pontificalis* is a collection of summary papal biographies beginning with the career of St Peter. It was first composed in the sixth century from earlier records, and continuously updated with details of the offices of successive popes. Entries were added shortly after the death of a pontiff, detailing his most significant achievements in both pastoral and political engagements. Paul the Deacon may have had the *Liber pontificalis* in mind when, as a guest of Charlemagne in the Frankish kingdom, he was commissioned to write the history of the see of Metz (the *Gesta episcoporum Mettensium*) by the royal archchaplain, bishop Angilramn. Earlier in its history, the episcopacy of Metz had been held by St Arnulf, one of the Carolingian dynasty's important ancestors.

Numbers of histories of ecclesiastical institutions were produced in Francia from the mid-ninth century. Of these, perhaps most outstanding in terms of composition, style and historical detail are the *Gesta sanctorum patrum Fontanellensis coenobii*, or *Gesta abbatum Fontanellensium*, a history of the abbots of St Wandrille of Fontanelle, in present-day Normandy; and the *Actus pontificum Cenomannensi in urbe degentium*, on the bishops of Le Mans. A text of similar kind (though peripheral with respect to the Carolingian world) is the *De origine et diversis casibus monasterii sancti Galli*, a history of the monastery of St Gall, begun around 880 by the monk Ratpert. Ratpert's history signals the beginning of a tradition of history writing at St Gall. Further significant developments in this area were made in Italy in the ninth century. At Rome, the *Liber pontificalis* was expanded with the addition of increasingly elaborate and lengthy biographies – and with an unprecedented level of interest in the popes' political dealings. At Ravenna, the cleric Andreas Agnellus (b. *c*.800/5; d. after 846) composed the *Liber pontificalis ecclesiae Ravennatis*, describing the illustrious traditions of the Ravennate Church, with a forceful vindication of the status and privileges of its clergy. At Naples, a similar enterprise, the histories of the bishops of Naples, was begun in the first half of the ninth century, and later enlarged for the period to the end of the century by the deacon, John of Naples (d. after 902) and the monk Guarimpoto (d. early tenth century). In territories of the Lombard kingdom subject to Frankish dominion, in contrast, the writing of history was limited to the transcription and enlargement of Paul the Deacon's history of the Lombards. An isolated example of original ninth-century writing is the brief *Historia* composed by Andreas, a priest of Bergamo. Andreas' text boasts little literary distinction, being in part derived from Paul the Deacon and in part a record of the author's first-hand knowledge of the Carolingian kings of Italy.

In southern Italy, Lombard authority had successfully stood up to Frankish hegemony; Lombard principalities continued to govern at Benevento, Salerno and Capua. In the last years of the ninth century, Erchempert, a monk at the monastery of Monte Cassino, composed a *Historia Langobardorum Beneventi degentium*. For this, Erchempert returned to Paul the Deacon's national history of the Lombards, applying it to the embattled but fiercely resistant Beneventans. In style, Erchempert's writing is unrestrained by his debt to Paul the Deacon. The tone is pessimistic – pessimism being Erchempert's own experience of the fortunes of his people.

In summary, it could be said that in the Carolingian epoch, historiography was closely tied to contemporary politics and the competing interests of rival polities. It may be for this reason that Carolingian historians mostly neglected the tradition of universal history, production of which almost ceased. There is but a single example of a universal history from the ninth century. This was written by Freculph, bishop of Lisieux (*c.*825-852/3), and dedicated to the young Charles the Bald. Despite the tendency away from universal history, Freculph's text demonstrates that knowledge of the prominent episodes of ancient history was not lost. The account ends in the sixth century, with the establishment of Frankish and Lombard control over the best part of the western empire, and with the foundation of a new order, one distinct in kind from the ancient order, which would eventually give way to Carolingian supremacy. Orosius' theory of the continuation of the Roman empire to the end of time is therefore definitively rejected and the status of recent and contemporary institutions affirmed.

The universal history makes one final appearance in the early tenth century, in what may be considered the final product of Carolingian historiography – the *Chronicon* of Regino (d. 915), abbot of Prüm and later head of St Martin of Trier, in Alsace. Despite its form, Regino's chronicle has few of the ideological implications of earlier universal histories. Regino's purpose was to transmit the memory of events in the Frankish and Carolingian epoch, which he set down in the form of annals, counting the years from the birth of Christ. A chronology of the principal religious and secular happenings, from the birth of Christ to the affirmation of Carolingian authority in Francia, precedes Regino's exposition of more recent occurrences, and is presented as a useful source of supplementary information. Regino considered the world that had been dominated by the Franks to be an ideal unity, though he was fully aware that in his day the kingdoms were divided and the various peoples sought to govern themselves.

Tenth-century historiography in France and Italy

The decades following the end of the Carolingian empire are poorly represented in terms of their historiographical output. The few noteworthy texts written at this time are characterized by a distinct narrowing in the authors' horizons. Some of the institutional histories of monasteries and episcopates were carried on, and a small number of projects of this kind begun. Probably the most important of the new works is that of Flodoard of Rheims (*c.*893-966) who, from the year 919 to his death, maintained annual records of events within the kingdom of Francia. Flodoard gave particular emphasis to episodes affecting the life of the archbishopric of Rheims, which at that time was one of the most important dioceses in the kingdom. Flodoard was a canon and for a time the archivist of Rheims; he also composed a history of the see (the *Historia Remensis ecclesiae*) from its origins to the year 948. For this he made abundant and careful use of the cathedral's rich archive, while for more recent events he turned to the records of his own annals.

Slightly earlier than the writings of Flodoard are two narrative accounts rendered in verse. Composed in hexameters, these appear as rather anomalous expressions of an affected and rhetorical style of writing in a scholarly tradition directed to the recording of contemporary history. Firstly, the *Bella Parisiacae urbis* was written around the year 897 by Abbo (d. after 921), a monk of St Germain-des-Près near Paris. Its purpose was to commemorate the defence of Paris from the Normans between 885 and 887. Credit for the safe delivery of the city is divided between count Odo, later king of the western Franks, and the city's patron, St Germain. Likewise, in Italy at the beginning of the tenth century, the deeds of King Berengar I were described in the form of a poem, the *Gesta Berengarii imperatoris*, which was conceived as an apologia for Berengar's actions. The text contains references to Virgil, and clearly the poet had some knowledge of Greek. The poet's agenda is a vindication of the autonomy and unity of the kingdom of Italy under Berengar's reign. Both the Italian poet and Abbo furnished their compositions with glosses explaining the obscurities of the texts, in keeping with the scholarly practice of rhetoric.

In the monasteries of the tenth century, historians composed biographies of prominent figures in the orbit of their institutions, most commonly the abbots. Texts of this kind were intended to edify and inform the community. Particularly significant in this context is the *Vita* of Count Gerard of Aurillac by Oddo, abbot of Cluny (abbot 927-942). This is possibly the first medieval biography of a layperson other than a sovereign. The biographer's interest in the subject was most probably encouraged by Gerard's display of virtues, which were not entirely dissimilar to those expected of monks.

Only after the middle of the tenth century does the writing of history properly recommence in Italy and France. Initially such production was sporadic, resulting in texts that are as diverse in form as in intention. Particularly original for its time is the work of Liutprand (*c.*920-*c.*972), a cleric of Pavia and later bishop of Cremona. Writing around the year 958, Liutprand's purpose was to relate the history and careers of the princes of Europe in his own lifetime, and to demonstrate how God rewards good and punishes evil. Progressively, Liutprand's motives were to become undisguisedly personal. Restricting his frame of reference to Italy, Liutprand was explicit in his intention to give praise to all those who had done him good, and to cast shame on those who had persecuted him. Liutprand's aim is apparent from the very title chosen for his work, *Antapodosis*, a Greek word that in this context implies 'retribution' or 'pay-back'. In one sense, the title may refer to the divine judgement; in another, it announces the author's vendetta against his personal and political enemies.

Liutprand's text is rich in anecdote, insinuation and gossip; sometimes it is ridiculous and on occasion even obscene. It echoes the attitudes and voices of the political factions and professional groups present in Pavia, the capital of the Lombard kingdom. Liutprand raised no pretence over the text's philosophical significance; rather, he considered it an album of frivolous tales or *neniae*. Although the administrative and political offices of the Lombard kingdom continued to function, the kingdom itself did not provoke any strong patriotic sentiment on Liutprand's part. In tenth-century Italy, the use of written history as a vehicle for collective memory and proud sentiments of political independence was restricted to areas beyond the former Lombard kingdom. An example of the use of history in this context is the *Chronicon* composed by an anonymous monk at Salerno around 974, in continuation of the writing of Erchempert. Another is the *Chronicon* of the Venetian writer John the Deacon (active 995-1018), which laid the basis of subsequent histories of Venice by appropriating the tradition established by histories of ecclesiastical institutions and transferring it to a political institution – the city.

In contrast, in Francia national pride and respect for the monarchy are expressed by a number of texts written around the end of the century. At this time, the monk Richer of Rheims (d. *c.*998) composed four books of *Historiae* of Francia, incorporating the annals of Flodoard, his countryman. Richer sought to revive the traditions of classical historiography by adapting them to contemporary circumstances; thus, he chose the monographic form, imitating Caesar and Sallust even in the discourses he places in the mouths of protagonists, and in the descriptions of battles. Nevertheless, the ideology underlying the text is markedly feudal. Though in a context of unstable power relations between the kings and barons, the author glorifies the honour and prestige of the 'Gauls', as he refers to his compatriots – a reference to Francia's ancient inhabitants. This patriotism opened the way for treat-

ment of the national community as a political entity and a legitimate subject for history.

Some decades later, Ademar of Chabannes, a monk of St Cybard of Angoulême (*c*.988-1034) composed the *Historia* or *Chronicon Francorum*. For the most part this is a contemporary history of Francia written from the perspective of the author's day, though much of it is focused on western Francia and the duchy of Aquitaine, where the author lived. The account of recent events opens with a description of the history of the Franks from their mythical Trojan origins. Thereafter, particular attention is given to the reign of Charles the Bald, when, Ademar contends, the kingdom of Francia achieved autonomy within the Carolingian empire. By evoking the distant past, the author emphasized the genesis and development of his subject, a particular political and national entity – the Frankish kingdom.

In the years around 1000, a similar approach was taken by Aimon (b. *c*.965; d. after 1008), a monk of St Benoît-sur-Loire in Fleury, near Orléans. Aimon was charged with writing a history of the Frankish kings and people at the instruction of his abbot, Abbo, who was an advisor to King Robert. Aimon made clever use of earlier sources for his history, the *Gesta regum Francorum* or *Historia Francorum*. The narrative comes to an end at the year 654; it seems Aimon was forced to interrupt his project when Abbot Abbo was cast into disgrace. Nevertheless, the text was to influence the future course of Frankish historiography, as it came to be considered the official history of the origins of the kingdom. Aimon was also the author of a commentary on the miracles of St Benedict, the *Miracula sancti Benedicti*, in which the author's edifying purpose did not deflect his attention from his subject's social and political context. After Aimon, history writing continued at the monastery of Fleury right through the eleventh century and on into the twelfth. Aimon's *Miracula sancti Benedicti* was enlarged by the prior, Andreas (d. *c*.1050), and later by the monks Rodolfus, Tortarius and Ugo – always with a keen eye for contemporary events. Moreover, Aimon and Andreas were the authors of biographies of abbots Abbo and Gozlin, in which much emphasis is given to the subjects' political dealings.

The same motivation to glorify the monarchy while providing religious edification was to influence the *Epitoma vitae Roberti regis*, written by the monk Helgaud (d. *c*.1048) following the death of the king in 1031. The subject is remembered for his exemplary Christian virtue, which is interpreted by the biographer as a model for monks. In this work, the figure of the sovereign was offered for the veneration of the kingdom, and for the first time was attributed the power to perform miraculous cures, using the water in which he washes his hands.

Another history of this kind was written in Burgundy from *c*.1020 by a Cluniac monk, Rodulf Glaber ('the beardless' or 'the bald') (*c*.985-*c*.1047). In writing his commentary on contemporary history, Rodulf

chose to abandon the traditional arrangement of annals or chronicles. Instead, the text takes the form of a didactic treatise with a free and quite original structure. The author's account is a somewhat disorderly mass of information and observation, loaded with moral implications and symbolic significance. His motive is to underline both God's and Satan's presence in the world and the significance of their mysterious ways.

The author's motives clearly informed his choice of material. For this reason, political events alternate with anecdotal and miraculous tales in no strict order; such incoherence is counter-balanced by the consistency of the author's underlying agenda. In France in the first half of the eleventh century, the writing of history was the monopoly of the monasteries, though it reflected a variety of interests. Writings of this kind describe a world teeming with portents; others are dedicated to the lives and deeds of religious figures renowned for their exemplary virtue, while others celebrated the monarchy as a national patrimony shared by all French people.

Historiography in Germany under the Ottonian and Salian emperors

In Germany, too, the second half of the tenth century is marked by the flowering of original history writing, which was animated by the royal and imperial dynasty of Saxony, and by the rebirth in classical studies promoted by the court.

Probably the earliest text of this group is a brief composition by Liutprand of Cremona, describing the condition of Italy and the papacy prior to the intervention of Otto I in Italian affairs in 961; the *Historia Ottonis* defends and legitimizes the king's actions in this context. Around the same time, between 965 and 970, Widukind, a monk of Corvey (d. after 972) composed a history of the Saxons (*Rerum gestarum Saxonicarum libri III*, completed around 968). Also at this same time a history of Otto and his ancestors (*Vita Othonis*) was written by the nun Rosvita of Gandersheim, providing an almost unique example of an early-medieval woman whose writings are concerned with contemporary politics. Then we have the life of Bruno, archbishop of Cologne and the brother of Otto I, written by his friend Ruotger, the clerk of Cologne cathedral (*Vita Brunonis archiepiscopi Coloniensis*, c.966-9). A little later, the emperor Otto II commissioned an anonymous scribe to write an account of the lives of the parents of Otto I. The author may have been a nun of Nordhausen, a monastery which had associations with the royal family. The result was a life of Queen Matilda, the *Vita Matildis antiquior*. The common purpose of these works is to glorify the reigning dynasty together with the whole Saxon people, which is seen as an ethnic and moral community distinct from other Germanic peoples. These motives are particularly apparent in the writing of Widukind,

who turned to models of the old histories of the barbarian peoples in order to recount his people's story from its origins to his own lifetime. The same tendency is represented by Rosvita, whose principal concern was the monarch and his family circle. The new empire provided an imposing set of ideals and values for the dynasty and its chroniclers. The influence of such ideals was even to reverberate through the Church. In the life of Bruno of Cologne, the pastoral offices and the saintly virtue of the subject are appropriated in the interests and to the advantage of the Ottonian *respublica.*

The literary forms of these court texts are varied: Widukind's is a great national history, Rosvita's a short poem in hexameters. The life of Bruno revived the genre of episcopal biography with further inspiration from Sallust, while the life of Matilda is one of the first biographies of a queen to go beyond traditional praise of the subject's Christian virtue to an overt appreciation of her regal qualities.

In Germany, the perspectives of history writers were to widen with the consolidation of the empire, and with the development of its political and religious interests. In the first decades of the eleventh century, Bishop Thietmar of Merseburg (975-1018) prepared a *Chronicon* in which the history of his diocese was integrated with the history of the German empire. In Thietmar's text, local and national interests are fused in an enthusiastic account of the deeds of the Saxon emperors and their promotion of the German nation. The *Chronicon* is elaborate in structure. A single book is dedicated to each successive Saxon king from Henry I to Otto III, while the final five books are given over to an account of Henry II, under whose reign the project was completed.

The Carolingian genre of ecclesiastic local history was revisited by scribes in a number of episcopal centres at this time. Particularly impressive in terms of literary style and abundance of historical detail are the *Gesta Episcoporum Cameracensium*, from the diocese of Lotharingia, which at this time belonged to the empire. It is the work of an anonymous clerk of Cambrai active in the first half of the eleventh century. Also important in this context is the *Gesta Hammaburgensis ecclesiae pontificum*, composed around 1075 by Adam, a canon at Brema (d. 1081/5). Both texts were intended to endorse the bishoprics and their histories while defending their rights and privileges. Moreover, the authors conceived their histories as vehicles for advancing the political ends of the empire in the areas of order, justice and the Christian conversion of pagan peoples on the borders of the empire – areas that were the business of the bishops, and which as such were a central concern for both writers. Even in biographies of individual bishops and abbots – texts produced in some numbers in Germany in the eleventh century – the subjects' actions are characterized by their adherence to the empire's political and religious agenda. Often this condition enabled biographers to overcome the limits of standard eulogies offered up in praise of exceptional austerity and charity, resulting in some startlingly direct and original observations of their subjects. In writings of this kind, particular emphasis is placed on the relation between the subjects' individual actions and personal qualities.

During the eleventh century, the imperial court continued to create demand for histories dedicated to the rulers and the ideals of the empire. Adalbold of Utrecht (d. 1026) drew on Thietmar's *Chronicon* for his life of the emperor Henry II. Significantly, the text is free of references to religious virtues typical of saints. Between 1040 and 1046, the imperial chaplain, Wipo (b. *c.*990; d. after 1046), described the life of the emperor Conrad II in a text dedicated to Conrad's successor, Henry III. Wipo's writing is characterized by his considerable learning; it presents a much-idealized image of the emperor as Christ's vicar on earth, whose glorious dominion brings order and justice to the world. Other biographies of Conrad II and Henry III were made at this time but do not survive.

Around the middle of the eleventh century, scribes in some German monasteries turned once again to the writing of universal histories. One such was Hermannus Contractus, or Hermann the Lame (1013-1054), a monk at Reichenau on Lake Constance, a centre of great cultural and political importance. Hermann earned his nickname from a handicap that impeded his movements, though he was held in considerable esteem for his extraordinary erudition. Beginning in 1045, he compiled an annalistic chronicle from the birth of Christ to the mid-eleventh century. Hermann knew and made use of the *Chronicon* of Regino of Prüm, though his own writing is richer and more detailed. Moreover, Hermann exploited a number of sources unknown to Regino, particularly for the ancient period, and he addressed problems of chronology which Regino had left unresolved. Furthermore, and in contrast to French chroniclers who restricted themselves to Frankish history, Hermann conceived his account of contemporary history in terms of uninterrupted continuity from ancient history after the birth of Christ. In this account, a context for the German empire is provided, which goes well beyond regional or national parameters.

Renewed interest in ancient history is witnessed by other narratives composed in the second half of the eleventh century. These include: the chronicle compiled after 1072 or 1073 by Bernold of Constance (*c.*1054-1100) and much indebted to Hermann the Lame; and the annals prepared by Lampert (*c.*1028-*c.*1081), a monk at Hersfeld, east of the Rhine, writing around 1077-8.

In their descriptions of contemporary events, these German chroniclers of the second half of the eleventh century – as well as the monk Bertold of Reichenau, who continued Hermann's chronicle for the period between 1054 and 1080 – paid a good deal of attention to the conflict between the papacy and the empire over the issue of ecclesiastical investitures. The same issue divided Germany into opposing camps, putting an end to the proud sense of unity instilled by the empire during the first half of the century. These writers conceived their texts in the form of annals, setting down their observations as events unfolded. Nevertheless, these narratives were not rendered in the spare and disorganized manner of some Carolingian annals. Instead, they present complex and detailed accounts in a rational and inquisitive style. Events and facts are marshalled into coherent analyses, references are made to doctrinal ideas, and the evidence of other documents is introduced in order to sustain the authors' arguments. The annals of Lampert of Hersfeld were not even written as reportage but in imitation of Livy, and conceived and composed in a single operation shortly after 1077. Here, the influence of classical models is also apparent in the discourses attributed to protagonists, in the explanation of events in terms of subjective motives, and in the parading of knowledge of events behind-the-scenes, so to speak – most of which are the inferences or inventions of the author himself.

The conflict created by the issue of ecclesiastical investiture in Germany was the motivation behind a number of other texts produced at this time by writers on both sides of the controversy. One such text is the *Carmen de bello Saxonico*, written around 1076 by an anonymous scribe close to the imperial court. It was composed in hexameters, with allusions to Virgil and Lucan, in commemoration of the victory of Henry IV over the rebel Saxons. The role of the king in these events is that of a courageous warrior hero. Some years later, in 1082, the *Liber de bello Saxonico* was written, giving vent to the Saxons' violent contempt for Henry IV. The author was Bruno, probably an ecclesiastic of Magdeburg, and the work dedicated to Werner, the archbishop of that city. Bruno did not shrink from slander and defamation of the emperor, though he employed a rather sophisticated literary form and poetic, clausal prose rich in references to Sallust and Horace. However, perhaps the most original text produced by the reign of Henry IV is a lament written on his death; the *Vita Heinrici IV imperatoris* was conceived in memory of Henry's troubled reign; it celebrates the courageous spirit with which the emperor faced his misfortune. The originality of this work lies in the author's appreciation of the emperor's humanity, without reference to political ideology or to stereotypical models of the sovereign virtues.

History writing in the feudal principalities (eleventh and twelfth centuries)

Beyond the empire, novel forms of historical writing were brought into being by the developing feudal principalities in the second half of the eleventh century. In this context, ruling dynasties made use of history in order to engender memory of their family origins, to rationalize the relationships between various branches of the family, and to record marriage contracts and the basis of dynastic power and its achievement.

In France, this brand of history writing originated with the work of a layman, Fulk le Réchin, the count of Anjou, who prepared a short version of his family history in 1096 (the *Chronica comitum Andegavensium*). The text describes the ascendance of the counts of Anjou, whose success the author attributes to the counts' valour in arms. Another significant and precocious example of this kind of dynastic history was written for the countess Matilda of Canossa, a powerful feudal lady who supported Pope Gregory VII in his fight against the empire over investitures. Matilda promoted literature and doctrinal studies in support of the Church. Among other things she commissioned a biography of Bishop Anselm of Lucca, who had once been her advisor and an important figure in the movement in favour of reform in the Church. Matilda herself was the subject of a biographical poem, *Vita Mathildis seu de principibus Canusinis*, written in hexameters between 1111 and 1114. The author was Donizo of Canossa (b. *c.*1070/2; d. after 1136), a monk of the abbey of Sant'Apollinare of Canossa. The poem is an epic account of the dynasty of Canossa, culminating in the government of Matilda and including much praise for her defence of the Church. It was Donizo's wish that the remains of the ruling family be brought for burial to his monastery, the dynastic mausoleum where the monks prayed for the commemoration of the revered dead. The liturgical commemoration of powerful families by monastic institutions was becoming a custom in many areas of Europe at this time.

Above all, it was in Normandy that the writing of history was valued and promoted by the dukes. Already some years before 1000, Duke Richard I commissioned Dudo, a canon of St Quentin in Vermandois (*c.*960-1026), to write his family's history. Drawing from oral histories transmitted among the members of the court and the ducal family, Dudo composed the *De moribus et actis primorum Normanniae ducum*. This is a record of the great achievements and adventures of the first three dukes rendered in appropriately epic terms. In particular, the dukes are celebrated for ridding their people of barbarian customs, thereby bringing them to civilization and the Christian faith. As court chronicler, Dudo shares his audience's respect for the warrior code; as a churchman, he justifies the warlike actions of his subjects by referring to the spirit of humility and religious devotion which guided them. Such justification was abandoned by the Norman writers of the second half of the eleventh century, who charted the conquests of England and southern Italy almost without scruple.

Contemporary accounts of the actions of William the Conqueror were given by Bishop Guy of Amiens (bishop 1058-1075) and the ducal chaplain, William of Poitiers (b. *c.*1020; d. after 1087). Guy of Amiens set out his version of events in the *Carmen de Hastingae proelio*, in Latin couplets describing the conquest of England in grand style and with unabashed partisan enthusiasm. In form, the text is modelled after Latin classics, though it is probable the author took his inspiration from popular folk songs in the vulgar tongue, through which the memory of these epic events was first transmitted.

In contrast, the *Vita Guillelmi principis* by William of Poitiers is a prose narrative. In it, William the Conqueror is idealized as an exemplary figure, prince and warrior – a man characterized by the virtues of magnanimity, prudence, steadfastness and justice. These virtues explain the duke's dominance over his adversaries, therefore justifying his victory in battle. The ideal religious virtues and spiritual endowments are of little moment in this portrait of a prince, whose faith is typically expressed in the protection he affords the Church and its clergy.

Both Guy of Amiens and William of Poitiers were anxious to emphasize the legitimacy of the Norman conquest of England: in doing so, both refer to mundane motives and constitutional claims; neither interprets the conquest in providential terms, though Guy of Amiens likens the battle of Hastings to the terrible judgement of God. Inspired by the awesome events they describe and driven by political bias, Norman historians accepted that the actions of political figures were to be justified on their own grounds, even though such actions were motivated by mundane ambitions and the quest for power, and seldom (if at all) by religious intent.

The same attitude underlies the historical writing of Gaufredus Malaterra, a Norman monk who moved to southern Italy following its conquest by his countrymen. Gaufredus was employed by Roger I of Sicily to write an account of the conquest of Sicily by the Altavilla dynasty from which Roger was descended. Unable to refer to any legal or moral justification for the extension of Norman power in Sicily, Gaufredus represented the conquerors as warriors of extraordinary audacity and magnanimity, whose very success in arms demonstrated that God's will was in their favour. That their enemies included the Muslim overlords of Sicily provided the author with some supplementary justification with which to interpret the conquest as a battle of faith in defence of the Church, though by no means did he consider the Normans' victories against Christian foes to be any less honourable.

Norman court historians drew on classical models – and on Caesar and Sallust above all – for examples of form and style, and perhaps also in order to endow their royal subjects with characteristics that transcended those traditionally bestowed by monastic historiography. Outside court circles, however, traditional forms remained in use. William of Jumièges (b. *c.*1000; d. after 1070), a monk in Normandy, was the author of the *Historia Normannorum ducum*. William took much from the writings of Dudo of St Quentin, to which he added the biographies of successive dukes up to William the Conqueror, to whom the history was dedicated. As a monk engaged in recording the mundane lives of secular subjects, William of Jumièges was aware of some need to justify his activity. This he did by endowing the former dukes of Normandy with spiritual virtues, as cavaliers of Christ. At the same time, in southern Italy, Amato (d. *c*.1170) of Monte Cassino set out a version of the Norman conquest in Italy in quite epic terms. Despite the immediacy of his narrative, Amato's version of events is firmly situated in a Christian framework, and conceived as a manifestation of the continual presence of God through the deeds of men. Here, victory is a consequence of the deep religious devotion of the victors. Notwithstanding the traditional values serviced by texts of this kind, the Norman achievement fostered certain original developments in the writing of history. This is contemporary history intended to explain the formation of a novel political reality, and motivated by the authors' unfailing adherence to the martial values which had made this new reality possible.

The same attributes are to be found in what is certainly the most complex and sophisticated work of Norman historiography, the *Historia Ecclesiastica* by Orderic Vitalis (1075-1142). It should be said that this was written some decades later, for which reason it is rather more fully developed than texts written in the immediate wake of the conquests. The author, a monk, initially undertook to write the history of his monastery, St Evroul in Normandy, where the text was to be read among the community. As he wrote, his work developed into a history of the entire Norman world, covering France, England and the distant Italian kingdoms. For his project, the author made use of a wealth of information derived from written sources and his contacts across an extensive network of monasteries. Orderic assembled abundant documentation regarding the formation and organization of the Norman world. In the process, he was not to overlook the sources of strife that tore at the unity of the Norman achievement. In particular, the text highlights the conflict that raged between Normans and Anglo-Saxons in England, a circumstance of special significance for the author, as Orderic was himself the son of a Norman father and an English mother. He continued writing until 1141, becoming ever more ambitious in his scope. Subsequently, two further books were added to the beginning of the text, containing a summary of universal history and the lives of the Apostles and popes. A third supplementary book (the seventh in the sequence of the text) charts the history of the Frankish and Anglo-Saxon kingdoms prior to the expansion of Norman dominion. Norman history thus became general, universal history. Although originally intended for the edification of monks, Orderic's ambitious achievement was to find an unusually wide readership among both his contemporaries and later readers.

Another genre of history writing appeared in the feudal world at the end of the eleventh century, in the context of the First Crusade. Many crusaders wrote letters containing news and eyewitness accounts of events. Later, others wrote detailed accounts of their journey, from departure to the final conquest of Jerusalem. Such accounts or memoirs communicate the experiences and impressions of their authors. Perhaps the most frank and vivid account of this kind is to be found in the *Gesta Francorum et aliorum Hierosolymitanorum*, an anonymous account of the deeds of the Franks and their fellow crusaders. This is probably also the earliest work of crusader history, written some time between 1098 and 1101 by a southern Italian knight in the retinue of Bohemond of Altavilla. The author may have been assisted in the task by a cleric, though this circumstance hardly compromised the direct and personal tone of the narrative. More formal, though equally immediate in terms of reportage, is the *Liber* of Raymond of Aguiler, a cleric who joined the crusade in the retinue of Adhemar of Monteil, bishop of Le Puy. In a similar mode is the writing of Peter Tudebod, a Poitevin priest. For his *Historia de Hierosolymitano itinere*, Tudebod made much use of the anonymous *Gesta Francorum*. Then, around 1113, the Norman Radulph of Caen composed the *Gesta Tancredi*, a description of the First Crusade dominated by the author's glorification of one of the princes who took part in the expedition. In this account, the ideal of the unrestrained and magnanimous warrior hero developed by Gaufredus Malaterra lives on.

Subsequently, the events of the First Crusade were revised and represented in less forthright manner. Fulcher of Chartres (1059-1127/8), a learned ecclesiastic and chaplain to Baldwin, king of Jerusalem, was the author of a chronicle with certain literary pretensions, grand in style and containing extracts in verse. Fulcher completed his narrative with a history of the kingdom of Jerusalem to 1127 (*Historia Hierosolymitana*). Still more indicative of a changing mentality (and of the demands of a more varied audience) are a number of re-workings of the history of the First Crusade written around 1107-8. These seem to have been motivated by the authors' conviction that the memory of illustrious deeds done in the service of God ought to be preserved in literary form or in verse, and not left to the lowly language of the original accounts.

In this way, Robert the Monk of Rheims (writing after 1118), Baudri of Bourgueil (d. 1130) and Guibert of Nogent (*c*.1055-*c*.1125) each prepared mannered literary versions of the history of the First Crusade. For these, the authors enlarged the earlier accounts with information reported by veterans and commentaries on the religious and theological significance of events. Demand for literary treatments of this kind was a product of the vibrant cultural climate that characterized the twelfth century. As a result of the widespread diffusion of learning and literacy, the writers of history now reckoned that their audience would no longer tolerate the humble language of earlier renditions.

History and the pursuit of the past in the twelfth century

The twelfth century has been called 'the century of history'. At this time, and in all parts of Europe, the writing of history witnessed spectacular development, as its motives were diversified and forms renewed, while its audience continued to expand.

One of the features that typify the writing of history at this time is the distinction drawn by authors between ancient and more recent history, each of which is assigned rather different functions. The distinction is seldom rigorously applied but is always a factor in the twelfth-century practice of history. In the German empire, ancient history was the stuff of universal histories, and related to the political purposes of the empire. Historians made fresh developments of a scholarly and theoretical nature at this time. Already in the 1080s, Marianus Scottus, an Irish monk who had settled in Mainz, was carrying out painstaking chronological research aimed at calculating the precise date of the birth of Christ. In setting out his conclusions, Scottus claimed that Dionysius Exiguus had miscalculated the date by some 22 years, though in this he was incorrect; nonetheless, Scottus' erroneous calculation formed the basis of his account of universal history.

A little later, the monks Frutolf of Michelsberg (d. 1103), near Bamberg, and Sigebert of Gembloux (c.1030-1112), now in Belgium but then a province of the empire, prepared thoroughgoing and critical re-workings of the traditional universal history. Both men approached the genre with novel ideas regarding its chronological structure, its functions and significance.

Frutolf's version of universal history covers the period from the Creation to the year 1099, making use of much previously neglected source material. The author comments on the interpretations of earlier writers and is not afraid to point out their discrepancies. To the annalistic sequence Frutolf introduces monographic chapters on diverse peoples and important figures; and he confronts problems of comparative chronology. Frutolf revived the doctrine of the four kingdoms, and the old idea that the last of these, the Roman empire, would endure to the end of time. He argues that, after Rome, the empire had migrated to Byzantium, later returning to the West under Charlemagne before passing to the Germans, who held imperial sway in Frutolf's lifetime.

The work of Sigebert of Gembloux is above all an imposing scholarly achievement. Beginning with the year 381 – the last year in the chronology established by Eusebius and St Jerome – Sigebert's annalistic treatment includes all kingdoms for which some historical tradition was available. The most significant events are singled out, with particular attention reserved for the succession of kings. The purpose was to create an integrated universal chronology, one that could be used to verify and interpret the information drawn from other sources such as saints' lives. The chronological sequence is extended to include the author's treatment of events in his own day, without any interruption or change in the style of writing. This is all the more remarkable given the author's first-hand engagement in important contemporary issues such as the controversy over investitures, in which Sigebert took the side of the empire.

Emperor Henry V recognized the commemorative and propagandist potential of written history when he ordered the preparation of an official account of his voyage to Rome in 1110, on which occasion he received the imperial crown. Earlier, in 1106, he instructed Ekkehard of Tegernsee (d. after 1125), the abbot of Aura, near Bamberg, to write a history of the imperial line since the time of Charlemagne. Ekkehard also composed a version of universal history which he dedicated to the emperor. In large part, the latter work was taken from Frutolf of Michelsberg, with much original material in addition. Ekkehard also made considerable use of the chronicle of Sigebert of Gembloux, expanding it for the period up to 1126. For monastic scholars and for the emperor himself, universal history was valued not only as a source of knowledge but also as a means of commemorating the traditions of the German empire and its role in the career of humankind. This conception of history found its most developed expression around the middle of the twelfth century, in the *Historia de duabus civitatibus* by Bishop Otto of Freising (*c*.1112-1158). Otto's history is the product of a political context in which the progress of the empire must have seemed to have taken something of a turn for the worse following the conflict with the papacy, and as a result of internal disintegration brought on by the clash of aristocratic factions over the appointment of the emperors. In this context, Otto of Freising chose the universal history as a vehicle for his interpretation of contemporary circumstances. The result is a deeply pessimistic account of the career of earthly institutions. Returning to the theory of the four kingdoms, Otto interprets the succession of the kingdoms as an expression of the hopeless transience of human destiny. Although Otto considered the Roman empire to have been passed down to the Germans by successive turns, the narrative is peppered with references to momentous catastrophes, the last of which was going on in the author's own lifetime. Moreover, Otto projected his meditation on history into the future – the *Historia* concludes with the reign of the Antichrist, the description of which is derived from a reading of apocalyptic and prophetic literature.

The title of this chronicle reveals the influence its author drew from the treatment of history in the theological writings of St Augustine, especially *The City of God*. However, Otto presents an original interpretation of the nature and relationship of the two cities, describing how upon the death of Christ the mundane and heavenly cities were partially fused in the institution of the earthly Church, and made manifest through the respective functions of the priesthood and the crown. This fusion had been shown to be imperfect by the rift between ecclesiastical and secular spheres (the papacy and the empire) over investitures. For this reason, the celestial city could not to be realized until the end of time; in the meantime, earthly institutions are of necessity precarious and fleeting. Only monks, in their voluntarily separation from the world, could aspire to the stability and serenity of the spirit.

The *Historia* of Otto of Freising signals the apogee of the medieval universal history and its use as a vehicle for theological and moral speculation. In its wake, the genre changed decisively, both in nature and purpose, losing its theoretical connotations in favour of the encyclopaedic registration of vast stocks of historical knowledge. Following the restoration of imperial power under Frederick Barbarossa, Otto partially corrected his text, with concerned to play down its terrible prophecy. Then, in 1157/8, he began to chart the life of the new emperor and the revival of the empire's institutions, and for this he chose a different genre – biography – to express his different intentions.

The scholarly pursuit of the past was not restricted to renditions of universal history at this time. In fact, beyond the borders of imperial authority, the universal history was by and large neglected by writers who preferred a range of other approaches to the past. A particularly significant and original development was hailed by the transformation in the writing of monastic histories in Italy. Most prominent in this regard is the figure of Leo of Marsica (*c*.1050-1115), a monk of Monte Cassino and later bishop of Ostia (and also known as Leo of Ostia). At the end of the eleventh century, Leo was instructed by Oderisius, the abbot of Monte Cassino, to write the *Chronica monasterii Casinensis* from the monastery's foundation to around 1075. In so doing, Leo was to reconstruct the events upon which the fame and prestige of the monastery – the cradle of the Benedictine order – had been based. The result is an imposing text and an exhaustive and detailed account of religious and political developments in the monastery's history. In addition, the text includes a description of the monastery's extensive territorial possessions, properties administered and controlled by the abbots in much the same way as a principality.

At almost the same time, between 1092 and 1099, the monk Gregory of Catino (b. *c*.1060; d. after 1130) undertook a similar project for the central Italian abbey of Farfa. The *Liber gemniagraphus sive cleronomialis ecclesiae Farfensis* (also known as the *Regestum Farfense*) was compiled from documents in the monastery's archive which were considered to be at risk from loss or decay – documents confirming the community's possessions and privileges. Gregory completed the project in 1103, with a collection of abbreviated transcriptions from documents granting concessions on monastic properties – the *Liber largitorius*. Arranged in chronological order, this formidable resource provided the basis for the composition of the *Chronicon* of Farfa between 1107 and 1109, in which Gregory set out the ecclesiastical and the economic history of Farfa in the order of succession of its abbots. Towards the end of his life, Gregory developed his interest in the abbey's lands and records still further, with a topographic register of properties in the abbey's possession – the *Liber floriger*.

This preoccupation with preserving the records of monastic institutions, alongside a drive to safeguard and reorganize monastic patrimony and property, was also to inspire the chronicle of the Italian abbey of

San Vincenzo al Volturno, written by the monk John between 1100 and *c.*1120. The *Chronicon Vulturnense* contains an account of universal history and a chronological list of popes, as well as the texts of documents recording the monastery's foundation, the biographies of the abbots and episodes from the lives of local saints and martyrs. As integral parts of this history of the monastery, the chronicler includes the texts of numerous archival documents associated with the monastery's properties and possessions.

In the same way, the determination to safeguard written records once again provided the occasion for an eager re-writing of the history of the abbey of Monte Cassino in the first half of the twelfth century. Around the year 1138, the monk Peter the Deacon, the monastery's most erudite and unscrupulous archivist, set about reorganizing the monastery's archives and preparing a detailed inventory of all the documents in his care. Peter did not shrink from altering the texts of these documents, particularly in the interests of bolstering the monastery's claims to uncertain or contested rights. On this basis he returned to the chronicle of Leo of Ostia, lately expanded by the monk Guido for the period before 1127. Peter extended Leo's history to his own day, introducing his own falsifications in support of privileges enjoyed by the community of his fellow monks.

The concern to salvage the contents of monastic archives, and in doing so to falsify original documents or copies of medieval texts, is characteristic of a particular moment in the history of the Benedictine order in the first half of the twelfth century. At this time, the wealth and prestige of Benedictine houses were threatened by the emergence of novel political organizations, and by the appearance of new monastic orders. This occurred not only in Italy but also in France and England, and it gave way to a type of historical writing that aspired to juridical and legal validity.

In England in the twelfth century, the aims and methods of historical investigation were transformed, giving rise to a flourishing of historiographical production. After Bede, Anglo-Saxon historians restricted themselves to annual records of singularly important events set down in the *Anglo-Saxon Chronicle*. The *Anglo-Saxon Chronicle* is an almost unique instance of an early-medieval text written in the vernacular; that is, in Saxon rather than Latin. Begun in the late ninth century and continually expanded – firstly in a single, widely transmitted version, and subsequently in local additions made in various monasteries – the *Anglo-Saxon Chronicle* is the only national written record to have been produced in the Anglo-Saxon kingdoms.

In the eleventh century, both before and after the Norman conquest, biographies were written for two royal figures who had occupied central roles during the last years of the Anglo-Saxon state. The first of these is the *Encomium Emmae reginae*, conceived as an apology for Queen Emma; a Norman by birth, Emma was wife or mother to four successive kings of England, two of whom were Danes. The second is the *Vita Aedwardi regis*, a life of King Edward, in which the author deals with the king's life only in the latter part of the text, keeping the opening sections free for a eulogy to Queen Edith and her family, which was among the most powerful of the Saxon nobility. Both texts were the work of continental writers, most probably Flemish monks commissioned by English patrons, and as such they do not represent the views of local society.

The Norman conquest was to provoke a return to history by scholars on the side of the defeated Saxons. In the wake of defeat, Saxon historians contemplated the progress of their people's history in relation to the loss of national sovereignty. The first statement of this kind is found in the work of the monk Eadmer of Christ Church, Canterbury (b. *c.*1060; d. after 1128), an associate and acquaintance of Archbishop Anselm. Eadmer analyzed the consequences of the strict controls imposed on the English Church by William the Conqueror and his successors, to whose authority Anselm was opposed. Eadmer charted the background and progress of this hostility in his *Historia novorum in Anglia* and in his *Vita Anselmi*, a biography of the archbishop and a text rich with the author's affection and esteem. Of course, Eadmer was unable to refer openly to conflict between the two nations. Nevertheless, his writings announce a new conception of history. For Eadmer, history was intended not only to register important events but also to engage the interest of the audience in an issue of burning contemporary relevance.

Some decades later, William, a monk in the abbey of Malmesbury (*c.*1095-1143), set out to relate the history of the English people and kingdom with a still broader perspective and greater breadth of historical knowledge. William of Malmesbury realized that no proper history of his people had been written in the period between the death of Bede and the birth of Eadmer – a period of some 223 years. In the service of patriotism, he endeavoured to make good the deficiency, and for this he drew upon the *Anglo-Saxon Chronicle* and a variety of other sources. He clothed this material in an elaborate literary guise inspired by his close acquaintance with ancient literature. Around the year 1125, William composed two historical works: the *Gesta regum Anglorum*, detailing events surrounding the succession of English kings from the Anglo-Saxon invasions until 1120; and the *Gesta pontificum Anglorum*, on the religious history of England in the same period. In this way, William separated two streams of history which heretofore had been treated as one – as in Bede's history of the English Church *and* people. Nevertheless, William's two texts are united by their shared purpose. On the one hand, William's treatment of political events was intended to demonstrate the merits and defects of the Saxon people, so explaining the Norman conquest as a result of the decadence of English customs; while on the other, he invoked the illustrious traditions of sanctity enjoyed by the English Church, the source of all positive achievement in Saxon history.

In this way, the pursuit of the past became a means of vindicating the vanquished peoples' dignity. The writer did not mythologize the subject. Instead, he sought to establish a balanced relationship with the traditions of the Norman conquerors. The general purpose was unmistakably moral; in fact, in the mind of William of Malmesbury, history was a branch of ethics. William admonishes his readers to pursue good and reject evil through examples drawn from history. Such a strict intent did not exclude that the text could be (and ought to be) interesting and diverting – indeed, William's writing abounds in anecdote, in geographical information and personal portraits, which grow in number and detail as the narrative approaches the author's own lifetime. William chose to break off his account rather than deal with his contemporaries and issues of contemporary relevance. Only later, in the last years of his life, did he set out to chart the events of his own lifetime, though for this he began a separate work, the *Historia novella*. Conceived in the form of annals, this text nevertheless resounds with the author's subtle explication of complicated events, and his skilful dissection of the attitudes, actions and reactions of the protagonists, who are central to the course of events. The tone is drier and rather more objective than that of his earlier writings, though the pace of the narrative is equally lively.

The pursuit of national origins was developed in many ways by other writers. Around 1136, the clerk and later bishop of St Asaph, Geoffrey of Monmouth (d. *c*.1154), composed the *Historia regum Britanniae*. In this work the country's historical tradition is traced back even further than it had been by William of Malmesbury, and placed in an altogether different context. Welsh by birth, Geoffrey based his history on Celtic legends and myths, material that originated in the period prior to the Anglo-Saxon invasion, when the land had been populated and ruled by Britons. Geoffrey approached this material as authentic historical source material, which provided him with a narrative rich in evocative and idealized themes exemplified by the reign of King Arthur and the prophecies of the magician, Merlin, on the future of England. The account ends with the seventh century, when, the author claims, the sovereignty of the Britons was eclipsed.

Geoffrey of Monmouth thus established an alternative to the Anglo-Saxon national tradition. Thanks to the popularity of the legend of King Arthur in the courtly literature of France, Geoffrey was able to attenuate the opposition of Saxon and Norman traditions, while offering a version of insular history that was meaningful to the ruling Anglo-Norman aristocracy. Evidently Geoffrey's history met with huge success, to judge from the enormous number of copies and translations of the text, some 200 of which are still extant.

Another *Historia Anglorum* was written in the same years by Henry, archdeacon of Huntingdon (d. *c*.1154). The account opens with Julius

Caesar and the Roman conquest of Britannia, and it continues into the author's own lifetime. In inspiration it is somewhat less chivalric than the accounts of Geoffrey of Monmouth, being more concerned with political issues than with fantasy or romance. Nevertheless, it reveals the author's sensitivity to narrative qualities in its use of anecdote and a tendency to romanticize. And like its predecessors, Henry's narrative was intended to instruct the reader in the transience of worldly fortune.

An important aspect of these English histories is that, while the authors themselves may have been churchmen, their audience was no longer restricted to the writers' brother monks and other ecclesiastics. The audience for these narratives was increasingly made up of educated laypeople steeped in chivalric culture. For this audience, the history of the kingdom was indistinguishable from the pleasurable pursuit of listening to or reading interesting, absorbing and edifying tales. Although history was not to be confused with romance, it was nevertheless expected to indulge the audience with entertaining renditions of past endeavours.

The importance of the role of lay audiences in fostering demand for writing of this kind becomes apparent around the middle of the twelfth century, when historical writings were conceived in verse and written in the vernacular, usually in a variant of old French known as Anglo-Norman, and probably intended to be read aloud. The earliest example of this kind is the *Histoire des Engleis* by the clerk Geffrei Gaimar, from the first half of the twelfth century. Written in rhyming verse in lines of eight syllables, this is a history of England from 495 to the year 1100, and much indebted to the *Anglo-Saxon Chronicle* and other Latin sources. The court of King Henry II – whose wife, Eleanor of Aquitaine, was a patron of poets and writers – was an important centre for the production of vernacular historical poetry. In this context, Robert Wace (d. after 1171), a Norman cleric, wrote two poems of similar kind: the *Roman de Brut*, which, like the history of Geoffrey of Monmouth, is an account of the ancient and mythical origins of the Britons; and the *Roman de Rou*, a more recent history of the Norman dukes and kings of England up to the time of Henry I.

The dukes of Normandy were the subjects of another historical poem, the *Chronique des Ducs de Normandie*, commissioned by King Henry II from the French cleric Benoît de Sainte-Maure, *c.*1160-70. In writing of this kind, the subjects and their actions are idealized in order to exemplify the values of contemporary court society. These are nevertheless sophisticated works intended to impart information and commentary on the history of the kingdom from the perspective of the new Plantagenet administration. (The Plantagenets set out to bring an end to nationalist squabbling among the descendants of the Saxons and Normans.)

The taste for idealized and romanticized versions of history in the vernacular also developed in Germany at this time, as is represented by the *Kaiserchronik* written some time between 1140 and 1150. Composed in verse form, the *Kaiserchronik* charts the progress of the fourth universal empire; that is, the empire of the Romans later inherited by the Franks and subsequently by the Germans. Much of the text is taken up with sagas and legends, which are presented as evidence of the key role of the German people in forging the success and authority of the Roman empire from earliest times.

In France, a historiographical tradition dedicated to promoting the values of the kingdom had been established since the eleventh century. There was to be no comparable development of narrative writing in connection with the court. In France in the first half of the twelfth century, the most significant historical works, in terms of form and extent, are the *Historia ecclesiastica* (or *Historia Francorum*) and the *Historia moderna* (or *Liber modernorum regum Francorum*). Both texts were the work of Hugh of Fleury (also known as Hugh of Sainte-Marie) (d. 1118/35). Hugh continued the tradition of historical writing developed by the monks of Fleury in the previous century. The first of his two works is a universal history beginning with a studied exposition of Roman history and the career of the Church from the time of Augustus, before setting out the full history of the Franks up to the reign of Louis the Pious. Hugh's second text is a history of the Frankish kingdom from the reign of Charles the Bald, to which the emergence of the kingdom of France within the Carolingian world was traditionally assigned, up to the author's own lifetime. In this way, Hugh's text separates ancient from 'modern' history. In common with William of Malmesbury, Hugh of Fleury implicitly attributes the two parts of history with different degrees of interest and significance.

Hugh's two histories were destined not for the royal court but for two educated princesses: Adèle of Blois, the daughter of William the Conqueror; and Mathilde, daughter of Henry I of England and consort to Emperor Henry V. The author intended the texts to provide his patrons with an awareness of their families' adventures and achievements. In its context and purpose, this writing belongs to a tradition previously cultivated by monastic writers on behalf of courtly patrons, a tradition that typified Norman historiography.

In rather different ways, claims to historical authenticity were made by the writers of numerous *chansons de geste* in twelfth-century France. Written in the vernacular, these epic songs had considerable appeal in the circles of chivalry; most often set in Carolingian times, they represent a sort of legendary evocation of national or dynastic history, one conceived in literary forms consonant with the taste of this audience.

One example of writing of this kind is provided by the *Historia Caroli Magni et Rotholandi*, a version of events during the Carolingian expedition to Spain, culminating with the terrible massacre of the Frankish forces at Roncisvalle. The text was written in Latin sometime around the middle of the twelfth century; it has been attributed to Turpin, an archbishop said to have taken part in the Spanish expedition. Countless vernacular translations were made, as the story enjoyed immense popularity in the courts. It came to be regarded as a historical source, and as such was used to confirm the Capetians' otherwise unsubstantiated claims to Carolingian ancestry. Just a decade or two later in France, the history of the monarchy had taken rather original forms.

Lastly in this context, it is worth noting that the study of ancient history in the twelfth century was added to the scholastic curriculum alongside grammar, rhetoric and dialectic. It became part of programmes of advanced studies. Already in the early years of the century, study manuals and encyclopaedia were composed, such as those by Honorius of Autun. These include the *Summa totius de omnimoda historia*, a general compendium of universal history from the origins of the world to the author's lifetime. In abbreviated form, this work was incorporated by another encyclopaedic work with the evocative title *Imago mundi*, alongside other texts setting out the elementary foundations for the study of geography, astronomy, meteorology and chronography.

Another response to the demand for ordered and systematic historical treatises is represented by the great synthesis of Biblical history written around the year 1170 by Peter (*c.*1100-1187), a canon of Nôtre Dame of Paris, and otherwise known as Peter Comestor ('the devourer') on account of his extraordinary appetite for reading. His work enjoyed such success that it came to be known, antonomastically, as the *Historia scholastica*. Around the same time, the study of history was codified in the work of Hugh, master of the celebrated monastery of St Victor in Paris, a centre of a revival in theological studies at this time. Hugh was the author of a universal history or *Chronicon*, in which he set out his theory according to which history is the foundation of all knowledge, as through history one may comprehend the inherent truth of all things.

Contemporary history in the twelfth century

Alongside the writing of past history, twelfth-century writers were also concerned with recent or contemporary events. In the twelfth century, the writing of contemporary history took a variety of original forms, motivated as it was by the writers' novel and unusual intentions. To take one example, both the form and the significance of the royal biography were revised at this time. Increasingly, biographies were composed during the subjects' lifetime, as the purpose of such writing was no longer to demonstrate that the subject's life conformed to the norms and ideals of exemplary models such as those provided by saints. Instead, biographers determined to illustrate their subjects' idiosyncrasies and individual style of rule. Such an approach was adopted by the author of the *Vita Ludovici Grossi regis*, shortly after the death of Louis VI ('the Fat') of France in 1137. The author was none other than Suger (1081-1151), the king's advisor and minister, and the outstanding abbot of Saint-Denis near Paris. The king is represented as a determined and courageous knight and protector of the Church and the poor – a hero unstinting in his battle against the abuses and aggression of feudal lords.

Still more sophisticated in its approach to history and political ideology is the *Ystoria Rogerii regis* by Alexander (d. before 1143), abbot of the monastery of San Salvatore di Telese in Samnium. Alexander's history was intended as an apology for Roger II, a descendant of the Norman conquerors of southern Italy, who had lately declared himself king of Sicily. The aim of the work was not only to record the bitter conflict brought on by the king's actions, but also to provide them with ideological justification. Such justification is provided by Roger's capacity to enforce peace and justice, the traditional aims of medieval government, through the open use of violence and terror against those who opposed the good benefits of his governance. In practice, reprehensible means of control were justified to this end, even when they inflicted loss and pain. Royal authority is presented as a force founded neither on consensus nor the agreement of subjects, but on the inspired assumption of responsibility through which the hard and ruthless king mysteriously becomes the instrument of God's will.

Similar perspectives are to be found in the most fully developed example of royal biography in the twelfth century, the *Gesta Friderici impertoris* by Otto of Freising. Although the author died before he could finish his ambitious project, as it stands this is a monumental portrait of the new German emperor. The subject is depicted as an unshakeable and resolute defender of justice and imperial prerogative. The emperor upholds order in the political world, while crushing the exponents of fractious political and social movements – the 'unreasoning' opponents of the empire – and their quest for autonomy.

Another royal biography to be written during the subject's lifetime is the *Gesta Stefani*, by an anonymous author writing in England at the time of King Stephen of Blois (reigned 1135-1154). In ideological terms, this is certainly less original than the works referred to above, though like them it was intended to glorify and promote the reign of a most unpopular king. The king appears as the selfless defender of the kingdom, intent on reintroducing peace and justice in place of rampant lawlessness and disorder. Simultaneously, this portrait of Stephen retains the essential traits of a feudal king, a man capable of affability and generosity among friends, and clement in his treatment of subjects and adversaries alike.

These works project idealized images of their subjects; in them, little space is given to aspects unrelated to the exercise of power. Nevertheless, the authors reveal their keen interest in the subject's personality, which is central in determining the outcome of episodes and the progress of the subject's life. This emphasis on human personality is characteristic of twelfth-century culture. It lies behind the first medieval experiments with autobiographical writing, such as the *De vita sua*, or *Monodiae*, of Guibert of Nogent, the historian of the Crusades; the *De rebus in administratione sua gestis* (1145), an account of the administration of the abbey of Saint-Denis by its abbot, Suger; and the *Historia calamitatum* or *Epistola de calamitatibus suis* by the philosopher Peter Abelard (1079-1142), a man whose thought and writing are central to twelfth-century intellectual culture.

Other novel approaches to the writing of contemporary history were inspired by the life of the courts – evolving centres at the heart of new systems of bureaucracy and government – and by the institution of autonomous civic regimes in northern-central Italy.

An exemplary figure in twelfth-century literature and philosophy was John of Salisbury (1115/20-1180), a brilliant and most learned English cleric. John was engaged in the administration of the archbishopric of Canterbury, and to this end he spent much time in Rome attending the papal curia. Between 1153 and 1163/4 he composed the *Historia pontifica*, in which he set out the complex entanglements of European political life between 1148 and 1152, from the point of view of his own privileged station at the papal court. As well as drawing on the accounts of Sigebert of Gembloux and later historians, John made use of the official documents to which he had access,and his own personal records and memories. Yet perhaps the most impressive work of history to be conceived in the atmosphere of the courts – and a text most redolent of its context – is the great *Historia* or *Liber de regno Siciliae*. The work is attributed to Ugo Falcando, although nothing is known of the author's life and even his name is in doubt. The subject is the internal life of the court of Palermo, the centre of the kingdom of Sicily, between 1154 and 1169. The treatment is bitterly pessimistic – the protagonists and their actions are described in unreservedly negative terms, while intrigue, selfishness and duplicity dominate the political workings of the court. This is a most original development, an example of history writing unconstrained by the dominant political ideology. The text describes the triumph of irrationality and corruption, while emphasizing the demise of virtue in political life.

The writing of contemporary history from the point of view of the administration of the kingdoms developed through the second half of the twelfth century, in England above all. In this context, writers adopted the formal, impartial tone of objective reporters, dependent as they were on official government records. One such was Roger of Hoveden (d. 1201/12), a royal functionary with important administrative and diplomatic responsibilities at the court of Henry II. During the last years of his life, Roger looked back upon his career in public office for material for the *Chronica* or *Historia Anglorum sive Saxorum*. This consists of a summary of English history from Bede to the time of King Stephen, followed by a more detailed exposition of events in the fifty years prior to 1201. Roger's analytical account of recent and contemporary history follows that of an earlier text attributed to Benedict of Peterborough for the period before 1192; thereafter, the text is Roger's own. It is peppered with transcriptions from numerous official documents of every kind – diplomatic correspondence, feudal assizes, and the acts of councils and royal charters. Impressively, the narrative does not jettison the literary devices established by historians during the preceding decades, such as the discourses of principal protagonists. This notwithstanding, the purpose of Roger's text is not to retrace the historical identity of the English nation, but to register, in quasi-official form, the acts of central government.

The use of transcriptions from official documents such as legislative texts and fiscal registers characterizes the *Ymagines historiarum* by Ralph de Diceto (d. 1202), a deacon of London Cathedral and an active participant in English government. Conceived in the form of annals, Ralph's text recounts events in the kingdom under the Plantagenet kings. Its purpose was to demonstrate the kings' effective and bounteous rule, particularly under Henry II, notwithstanding their conflict with the Church and the murder of Thomas Beckett. The text is characterized by an unprecedented concern to make its contents clearly accessible to the reader. It is divided into four columns, one each for the author's four principal concerns: the history of kings, military history, ecclesiastical history, and the history of conflict between secular and ecclesiastical powers. In addition, symbols (such as crowns, swords and letters) are placed in the margins, in order to allow the reader to identify the subject of any given passage at a glance. Ralph de Diceto developed this system during the preparation of the *Abbreviationes chronicorum*, a version of universal history from the birth of Christ to the advent of Henry II. The development of textual strategies of this kind was guided by changing attitudes concerning the function of written histories – texts of this kind were now intended to be used as repertories of detailed information on particular subjects, and as such their contents were to be arranged clearly and systematically, in order to enable the reader to locate passages of interest easily and quickly. Ralph's histories anticipate further developments in this direction in the thirteenth century. Another interesting example of this tendency is provided by the manuscript of an Italian monastic chronicle written at the end of the twelfth century. The *Chronicon Casauriense* was composed around 1189 by the monk John of Berardo (d. *c*.1182), in the monastery of Trinità di Casauria, near Pescara. The *Chronicon* belongs to the genre of monastic chronicles replete with transcriptions from archive documents. The folios are arranged with transcriptions in a central text column flanked on either side by two columns taken up with the text of the chronicler's narrative.

Other original developments in twelfth-century historiography are linked to the rise of the Italian communes. Prototypical historical accounts of internal political affairs had been developed already in the second half of the eleventh century at Milan, in the context of the upheaval brought on by the popular Patarene movement. This movement had placed the traditional political and ecclesiastical order of the city in jeopardy. The progress of the movement was recorded by two Milanese writers, Arnulf and Landulf Senior (the latter so-called to distinguish him from another, later Milanese chronicler of the same name). Approaching the subject from rather different points of view, the two men composed accounts of the events that shook the Church and the city of Milan in their lifetime; and both provide wide-ranging commentaries on the historical and political background to these developments. Arnulf (d. after 1077), whose origins are uncertain, was the author of the *Gesta archiepiscoporum Mediolanensium* or *Liber gestorum recentium*. The text recounts events in the Italian kingdom from 925 to the mid-eleventh century. The author's purpose was to celebrate the central role of Milan and its archbishops in Italian affairs. Arnulf considered the city's achievements to be under threat from the subversive Patarene movement, for which he expresses typically aristocratic disdain. Rather more is known about Landulf Senior, the second Milanese historian. Landulf was a priest at Milan. Around 1100 he composed the *Historia Mediolanensis* in which his account of recent events gives way to a panegyric on the venerable traditions of the Milanese Church and its history since the time of St Ambrose. Since antiquity, Landulf reminds his readers, this Church had successfully resisted the persecutions of pseudo-prophets envious of its achievements.

The openly polemical nature of the two texts distinguishes them from earlier histories of episcopal sees. Both the Milanese historians project a sense of civic pride based on local ecclesiastical traditions. As yet, though, writing of this kind makes no claim to political or institutional autonomy on behalf of the city, as it is the Church that provides the platform for Milanese history and civic identity.

A rather different kind of civic consciousness is expressed by a number of historical writings composed at Pisa and Genoa in the first decades of the twelfth century. The literary form of these texts is seemingly as original as their authors' political agenda. At Pisa, this development is represented by a group of texts conceived in proud and jubilant terms, following the success of military operations undertaken in various parts of the Mediterranean to defend the interests of Pisa's maritime economy. In league with Genoa, the Pisans launched a successful raid on the African port of Mahdia in 1087/8. The event was celebrated by the anonymous author of the *Carmen in victoriam Pisanorum*, a verse in 73 stanzas, in which particular emphasis is given to the religious significance of the campaign, and an analogy drawn between modern Pisa and ancient Rome. Later, the victorious war waged by the Pisans against the Arab kingdom of Majorca in 1114-15 was the subject of the *Liber Maiorichinus de gestis Pisanorum illustrium*. This, too, was conceived in verse form, in hexameters of Virgilian inspiration, and probably written by an anonymous Pisan churchman who witnessed the campaign. Around the same time, another anonymous writer composed a brief account of the military successes of the Pisans from the end of the eleventh century, culminating in the victorious campaign against Genoa in 1120 (the *Gesta triumphalia per Pisanos facta*). Numbered among Pisa's most imposing achievements is the city's contribution to the First Crusade, the war with Majorca, and the elevation of the city's episcopacy to the status of archbishopric.

At Genoa, in contrast, the writing of communal history was born from the need to record external achievements, particularly military ones, as well as practical records relating to the institutional workings of civic life. These might include the constitution of the trade colleges and guilds that controlled the government of the city, and the names of consuls and the legal dispositions taken by them. Other records relate to the issue of local coinage. Reports of this kind were begun by Caffaro di Caschifellone (1080/1-1166), a merchant and magistrate who kept records of noteworthy events throughout his life, year by year, from the days of the First Crusade. The result is the *Annali*, a dense and lengthy narrative rendered in straightforward style and untouched by literary pretension. In 1152 Caffaro presented the text of his annals to the consuls and council of Genoa. A ruling was passed ordering the text to be copied at the commune's expense, and the copy deposited in the public archives and continually updated. This is the oldest known form of official communal history. Caffaro himself undertook the business of keeping up the records until 1163.

Civic annals were made in other northern-Italian cities from the twelfth century, though generally with less order than the records of Genoa. At Pisa, public records were maintained by the communal magistrate, Bernardo Maragone (d. 1175/80). Other annals survive from Milan, Cremona, Piacenza, and lists of consuls from Brescia, Parma, Verona and Florence, though it is not known if these are official.

Another historical tradition was developed in the cities of Lombardy during the first decades of the twelfth century, exemplified by a number of literary texts dedicated to the cities' achievements in military and political engagements. The author of one such work was the *magister* Mosè del Brolo (d. *c.*1156), a literary scholar learned in Greek and theology, though probably a layman. Mosè del Brolo composed the *Liber Pergaminus*, a profile of the topography, buildings and legendary ancient history of the city of Bergamo, written in rhyming hexameters. In contrast, contemporary events provided material for the *Poema de bello et excidio urbis Comensis*, or the *Liber Cumanus*, an anonymous lament on the devastation of Como at the end of its long war with Milan (1118-27).

But above all the incentives for the writing of communal history, by far the most urgent was that provided by the expeditions of Frederick Barbarossa against the communes of Lombardy. In this context, Ottone

Morena, a citizen of Lodi and royal justice, wrote the *Historia rerum Laudensium* in the decade after 1151. This is a monographic treatment of Frederick's campaigns through Lombardy, seen from a pro-imperial, anti-Milanese perspective, and intended to heap scorn upon rebels while defending the citizens of Lodi from the overbearing Milanese. Upon Ottone's death, the history was taken up by his son, Acerbo Morena, who continued it for the period up to 1164, without any noticeable shift in perspective. The opposite side of the struggle against the empire is documented by the *Gesta Federici I imperatoris in Lombardia*, the work of an individual known as Sire Raoul or Rodolfo, a citizen of Milan and a communal magistrate there. The text is the fruit of the author's personal experience of the events described. The style is unmannered and without literary flourish, as the author intended the text to serve the didactic purpose of charting the internal affairs of Milan and relations between the communes of Lombardy. This is a particularly lucid and perspicuous account, in which the actions of the empire are reduced to the avidity and arrogance of its leader.

Alongside these works are others of greater literary and ideological complexity, unrestricted to the narrow, local focus of much communal historiography. Of particular significance in this regard is the *Carmen de gestis Frederici I imperatoris in Lombardia*, a verse account in hexameters of the first two expeditions to Lombardy. The text is the work of an unknown writer active after 1160, and is likely to have been written in Bergamo, to judge from the prominence given to that city in the text. The text reveals the author's close familiarity with the forms and values of communal life, though the author's support for the empire is quite explicit. Barbarossa is described as the restorer of imperial majesty and justice in opposition to the ambitions of Milan. Literary art and political commentary converge in this work, which in style is modelled after Virgil's *Aeneid*. The reference to ancient works of literature signals a renewal of interest in the imperial Roman tradition, in which the empire of Barbarossa was to be rooted. It is likely that the author was connected to the imperial court. Classical and Virgilian references are likewise to be found in the *Carmen de destructione civitatis Mediolanensis*, written at about the same time. Once again, this is the work of an anonymous writer, with a refined rhetorical voice and a rather haughty style. The text expresses the author's municipal patriotism, while likening the contemptible enemy to barbarians.

Typical of all the communal historiography of Italy in the twelfth century is the condition of its writers. These were not churchmen but laypeople, and in most cases they were engaged as officers in communal administration; as such, these individuals were educated in literature and law. Their histories are expressions of the political perspectives of government institutions and local society, detached from religious preoccupations. The communal histories are the first appearance of a novel historiographical tradition that was to come to prominence in the thirteenth and fourteenth centuries, not only in Italy but throughout Europe.

Meanwhile, outside Italy, the time for the writing of municipal chronicles and histories had yet to come. Instead, local history was written in the form of chronicles dedicated to princely dynasties, a tradition developed above all in the Low Countries and in Germany.

In Flanders, this genre of history writing had its origins in the written genealogies of counts. One such text is the *Liber floridus* (*c*.1120) by Lambert of St Omer, a medley of historical, geographical and astronomical observations, enriched with numerous miniatures. This preoccupation with genealogy was developed by the *Flandria generosa*, dated just after 1164, the work of an anonymous monk of St Bertin. The *Flandria generosa* is a true history of Flanders based on the succession of its counts. A similar text associated with a local dynasty is the *Historia comitum Ghisnesium* by Lambert of Ardres (d. after 1203), a history of the counts of Guines from their origins to the mid-twelfth century. For this, Lambert made use of oral tradition circulating within and without the court of Guines, together with official documents and epic and hagiographical material, sagas and legends. Another narrative of this kind is the *Chronicon Hanoniense* by Gislebert of Mons (*c*.1150-1224). Gislebert was chaplain and chancellor to Count Baldwin V of Hainaut 1171-95; his chronicle documents the dynasty's growing prestige, recording its illustrious ancestors and their military undertakings. Among this group of texts, particular importance must be given to *De multro, traditione et occisione gloriosi Karoli comitis Flandriae* by Galbert of Bruges, writing in the first half of the twelfth century. Galbert was a priest and notary in the service of the counts of Bruges; his history records the dramatic events that took place in the county of Flanders in 1127-8, following the assassination of Count Charles the Good. This is a private text which does not seem to have been intended for publication. The writing is lively and informed; the text describes a continuous sequence of events recounted month by month and even day by day, as in a diary.

In Germany, too, genealogical, historical and eulogizing texts were turned out in some numbers in the twelfth century. This circumstance reflects the growing political status of a number of noble families active in consolidating territory at this time, thereby creating the principalities that were to make up the political scaffolding of the country following the breakdown of imperial authority. In the German context, perhaps the most representative work of dynastic history is the *Historia Welforum*, written by an anonymous churchman at the court of Duke Welf V of Bavaria sometime between 1167 and 1174. This describes the family's mythical origins and the deeds of the most ancient dukes in epic terms. As the narrative enters the contemporary period, the writing becomes more credible and informed, giving a lucid account of the formation of the principate and the family's authority in Bavaria.

Throughout the twelfth century, under the control of the Staufer dynasty, the empire remained a powerful and dynamic political institution, and it made shrewd use of history as a medium for affirming its status. As already suggested, it seems that certain historians active in Lombardy at this time were writers connected to the imperial court. Between 1180 and 1188, the *Gesta Friderici* of Otto of Freising, together with the continuation adjoined by one Rahewîn, were re-written, possibly by the emperor's archchaplain; the text, in hexameters redolent of Lucan and Virgil, was entitled *Ligurinus* and dedicated to the emperor and his five sons. Barbarossa's successor, Henry VI, was the recipient of historical works written by the imperial chaplain and notary, Godfrey of Viterbo (b. *c*.1125; d. after 1202). Godfrey was active at court from the time of Conrad III. From around 1180 he worked on a number of different versions of a great universal history, from the creation of the world to his own lifetime, entitled *Speculum regum* (1183), *Memoriale saeculorum* or *Liber memorialis* (1185), *Liber universalis* (after 1185), and *Pantheon* (in three versions, between 1185-7 and 1190). Godfrey's stated intention was to provide the sovereign with a complete and compelling account of the history of the world and the affairs of the kingdoms, conceived in the spirit of philosophy and written in a qualified, literary voice (and with frequent interventions in rhyming or assonant verse). He recommended wisdom as one of the virtues becoming to a sovereign; such wisdom derived from an awareness of the episodes of history and the deeds of kings. Together, Godfrey's compositions present a comprehensive vindication of the empire as the supreme form of worldly authority, culminating in the rule of the Hohenstaufen. An entire section of the *Liber universalis* is given over to a verse account of the deeds of Barbarossa. One of the last works of Godfrey of Viterbo may be identified as a short poem on the deeds of Henry VI, which accompanies the *Pantheon* in the surviving manuscripts. Throughout his work, Godfrey defended the reliability of his statements by citing the sources of his information. Despite his claims to careful scholarship, however, Godfrey evidently made much use of legendary traditions, with the result that his histories are rather evocative, fanciful pieces furnished with lists of popes and kings. With Godfrey's writing, universal history becomes a vehicle for entertainment and instruction in a courtly context, and for this reason little emphasis is given to the religious interpretation of past events. Godfrey thus anticipates the developments of the next century. Italian politics under Henry VI – in particular the conquest of the kingdom of Sicily (and the revindication of the legitimate rights of Costanza d'Altavilla) in 1194 – were charted by the Italian writer, Peter of Eboli (d. before 1220), in the *Liber ad honorem Augusti*. Peter's text, written in couplets, combines a rather stylized account of the principal events of the campaign, with satirical attacks on opponents of Henry VI. Throughout, the emperor is the primary object of the author's praise. The original manuscript of the

Liber survives; it is enriched with elegant full-page illuminations illustrating and supplementing the text. The volume was doubtless intended for presentation to the emperor himself. Evidently, in the aulic tradition of historical and encomiastic writing, books were precious or de luxe objects.

The transformation of history in the thirteenth century

In the course of the thirteenth century, historical writing witnessed a transformation in its forms, functions and audience. The nature of this transformation is apparent from the genre of universal history. Universal histories continued to be written in monasteries under the traditional orders, and by the Benedictines above all, at least until the middle of the thirteenth century. All the same, these universal histories lack the two characteristics that had previously provided the very motivation for the writing of texts of this kind – namely, meditation on the theme (and the timing) of salvation, with its theological significance for the overall history of humankind, and the associated tendency to identify a providential institution (usually the empire) as the driving force in history.

The authors of thirteenth-century universal histories tended to take a much wider perspective, and to subject the greater wealth of available material to rigorous and systematic organization. This applies as much to treatments of ancient history as it does to the accounts of more recent events. In this way, thirteenth-century historians applied the techniques first developed by Ralph de Diceto and Godfrey of Viterbo. At the same time, the new writings reveal a return to the sources of ancient history, and the writers' attempt to integrate sacred and profane histories. In particular, there is a drive to acquire more (and more reliable) information regarding the ancient eastern kingdoms. Thirteenth-century historians were concerned with subjecting all available information to careful scrutiny, by comparing statements taken from various sources; once validated in this way, historical information was set within the perfected chronological framework. In other words, the work of the thirteenth-century historian is characterized by an erudite, scholarly tendency, which is itself a characteristic of contemporary European culture. Chroniclers were concerned not merely to reference their sources accurately, but also to attribute each statement with a quotation, and so to distinguish their own observations from others derived from their sources. Particularly when it came to dealing with the recent past, writers found themselves confronted by enormous quantities of material. In the thirteenth century, the interests of historians (and the sources of their information) were not restricted to the confines of the kingdoms in which they happened to find themselves; rather, historians' concern regularly reached to all areas of western Christendom and the Holy Land. Thirteenth-century monastic historians could depend on a multitude of first-hand sources, thanks to the network of monasteries and the personal contacts periodically established during meetings of the general chapters. The resulting texts are rather disorderly on account of the wealth of information they contain, though they were styled after formal literary conventions. Among the most significant examples of this group are: the *Chronicon* of the Premonstratensian canon, Robert of Saint-Marien of Auxerre (1156-1212); the chronicle of Alberic, a monk of the Cistercian monastery of Troisfontaines in the diocese of Chalons-sur-Marne (d. after 1252); and the *Annales* of Alberic of Stade, in Saxony (d. 1265), a Benedictine monk who went on to become a Franciscan. Perhaps the most representative work is the *Chronica* of Matthew Paris (*c.*1200-1259), a monk of St Albans. The *Chronica* are now referred to as the *Chronica maiora*, in order to distinguish them from a later abbreviation prepared by Matthew Paris himself and known as the *Chronica minora*. Both sets of chronicles were written in the period between 1240 and 1259. Matthew Paris' version of ancient history was compiled from earlier historical works composed by monks of St Albans, which had been a centre of historical studies since the twelfth century. Prominent among the sources known to Matthew Paris were the *Chronica* or *Flores Historiarum* by Roger of Wendover (d. 1236), a version of the history of England from the time of Henry II to the author's death; Matthew Paris' own contribution begins with Roger's death in 1236. The writing is characterized by the breadth of the author's interests and his lively narrative style. Although the history of England is the central theme, progressively the text is embroidered with ever more frequent and detailed passages dealing with the situation abroad, in France, Italy, Spain and the Holy Land, and at papal Rome. Despite being arranged in the form of annals, the text follows an explicit narrative structure. Each event is described in rather anecdotal fashion, with particular attention given to the circumstances surrounding key episodes and the characters involved. The writer vividly evokes the speeches, actions and the most memorable sayings of his protagonists. Moreover, Matthew Paris did not restrict himself to politics, but extended his interests to artistic production, cultural affairs and economics. Furthermore, the manuscript is furnished with illustrations, crests, charts and maps – images that both illustrate and supplement the text. That the author was free from political control is clear from his seemingly impartial critique of the authoritarian and centralizing tendencies of the English kings.

Subsequently, from the mid-thirteenth century, the production of histories by Benedictine monks and others in the established monastic orders was slowly eclipsed by the efforts of historians in the mendicant orders. The mendicant orders emerged around the beginning of the thirteenth century. In the hands of mendicant writers, the conception of history and its motives were to be radically altered. History was included on university syllabuses of basic studies in the fields of theology, literature and jurisprudence. In this context, history increasingly became the reserve of the Dominicans or the Friars Preachers, an order dedicated to teaching.

Universal chronicles produced by Dominican writers are characterized by their encyclopaedic form. As teaching resources, such textbooks were arranged logically and didactically, the contents selected and rendered in such ways as to underline their exemplary moral significance. Dominican historians gave considerably less scope to recent history than their counterparts in other contexts, while their treatment of it is inevitably moralizing in purpose. In parallel, the concept of history, and the very term itself, was frequently replaced by multiple 'histories'; in place of a singular conception of the organic unity of the experience of humankind, the Domenicans emphasized the multiplicity of human endeavours or fates, each of which has its own exemplary significance. This trend lies behind the writing of texts with titles such as *Flores temporum* and *Flores historiarum*.

Perhaps the most representative example of this movement, and one of the monuments of the scholastic culture of the thirteenth century, is the *Speculum historiale*, by the Dominican historian, Vincent of Beauvais (*c*.1190-1264). The *Speculum historiale* was to form part of a vast encyclopaedia – the *Speculum maius* – which was also to include the *Speculum naturale* (on the natural sciences), the *Speculum doctrinale* (on theological science), and the *Speculum morale*. The *Speculum historiale* was conceived as a universal history from the Creation to around 1250. It includes histories of various peoples from antiquity to the thirteenth century, for which it draws on ancient and recent sources. The text is interspersed with legends and accounts of the passions of Christian martyrs, and passages from classical authors and the fables of Aesop, apparently chosen for their moral message. Moreover, the author includes a discussion of the teachings of ancient philosophers, as well as extracts from the Koran and descriptions of Muslim customs.

Each chapter of the *Speculum historiale* is dedicated to a given subject. Vincent listed his sources at the head of each chapter. Throughout the text, the author interrupts the narrative in order to refer to the sources of his information, and to suggest interpretations of the subject under discussion. The contents of the text are clearly set out in the form of indexes. Summaries of individual chapters are given, and the entire text is subject to a rigorously systematic presentation, all of which was intended to make this monumental work easily accessible to readers and students.

Another example of this tendency to the practical and systematic exposition of historical knowledge is represented by the *Chronicon pontificum et imperatorum* by the Dominican historian Martin of Troppau (b. before 1230; d. 1278), also known also as Martinus Polonus. Martin was a professor of theology and papal confessor and chaplain. Shortly before his death he became bishop of Gniezno, in Poland. His history is made up of parallel lists of all the popes after Christ, who in this context was considered to be the first pope, and the emperors from Augustus to 1277. When the book was opened, the list of popes occupied the page to the left, the emperors the page to the right, enabling the reader to see their chronological relationship at a glance. Short historical sketches were added alongside the names of the emperors and popes. The commentary takes on much greater breadth and coherency when dealing with recent circumstances or events, for which the author offers much first-hand observation and original comment. The work was intended for the use of scholars and jurists, as a chronological companion for the study of historical and juridical texts.

Like the encyclopaedia of Vincent of Beauvais, the chronology of Martin of Troppau enjoyed enormous success. Together, the two texts were the sources of countless numbers of historical compendia belonging to a distinct genre of historiographical writing that appears from the end of the thirteenth century and in the early 1300s. This genre is represented by frequently anonymous texts generally referred to as *martini*, or Martinian chronicles, and *vincenzi*.

From the end of the thirteenth century, the writing of history among the mendicant orders was characterized by extensive compilations of mostly secondhand material from historical and hagiographical sources. The *Flores temporum* or *Flores chronicorum* are examples of compendia of this kind, which were intended as repertories of material for use in preaching.

Among the characteristic forms of historical writing developed by the mendicant orders, one was to be particularly original. This is the writing of the history of the orders themselves, and their development and diffusion throughout the Christian world. Among the most prominent examples of the genre is the *Chronica* or *Memorabilia* of Giordano di Giano (b. *c*.1195; d. after 1262), a disciple of St Francis. Giordano was sent by St Francis to Germany, with instructions to establish the Franciscan order there. The text gives a straightforward summary of the origin of the order and its growth, with some important observations on the experience and the ethos of the first generation of Franciscans. Of comparable significance is the *De adventu fratrum minorum in Angliam*, the history of the introduction of the Franciscan order to England, completed around 1258 by the English Franciscan, Thomas of Ecclestone. In these histories, the experiences of the friars are interwoven with observations on events in the wider world, and for this reason the texts are important sources for thirteenth-century history.

Historiography in the kingdoms

During the thirteenth century, the pursuit of ordered and systematic forms of written history, and the existence of a much wider audience for such works, influenced historiographical production in other areas.

Particular significance was achieved at this time by the authors of royal histories in the kingdom of France.

From the time of Abbot Suger, the monastery of Saint-Denis, near Paris, was the equal and later the successor of the abbey Fleury as the principal purveyor of history to the kings of France. Around 1180, an anonymous monk of Saint-Denis composed the biography of King Louis VIII; later, the monk Rigord (d. 1220) prepared an exposition of events in the career of Philip Augustus prior to the year 1208. At that time, the monks of Saint-Denis did not yet enjoy the monopoly on royal history. The royal chaplain, William the Breton (d. after 1226), continued Rigord's history at court until the end of Philip's reign. In addition, William was the author of an epic poem, *Philippis*, written in hexameters to celebrate the king's victory against the English, the traditional enemies of the kingdom, at Bouvines. In the same years and in another Parisian monastery, St Germain-des-Près, the *Gesta Francorum usque ad annum 1214* were composed, telling the history of the people and the kings of France from their mythical Trojan origins. A short time later this version of Frankish history was rewritten by monks of St Germain in the vernacular, clearly for a secular audience with little or no schooling in Latin. During this time, Saint-Denis continued to function as the official depository of royal records, while acting as the sanctuary in which the kings were buried and the royal insignia kept. The work of William the Breton was incorporated into the corpus of histories composed by the monastery's scribes. Around 1250, the historians of Saint-Denis set out to revise the key texts for this history of the kingdom of France, from Aimon's *Historia Francorum* and the Carolingian annals, and including the most recent biographies of Philip Augustus. This project provided the material for a vast compilation initially written in Latin; later, in 1274, Primat, a monk of Saint-Denis, translated the text into French, adding translated extracts from other texts including earlier compilations by monks of St Germain-des-Près. Primat dedicated his great vernacular history to King Philip III. In this way an integrated version of royal French history was brought into being, both in Latin and in the vernacular. These histories were intended for the information and education of a wide and diverse audience, one made up by all the political classes of the kingdom.

The two histories, Latin and vernacular, were periodically updated with the biographies of successive kings. In 1286, the Latin text was expanded with the addition of biographies of Louis VII and Louis VIII by an anonymous author, and subsequently with the lives of Louis IX and Philip III by the monk William of Nangis (d. *c*.1300), who was also responsible for a revised edition of the entire royal chronicle. William's life of Louis IX was translated into French and added to Primat's vernacular history. The elaboration of this great collective work accompanied and assisted the affirmation of the French monarchy. Successive stages in the project were carried out at intervals in the middle of the fourteenth century, when the vulgar version was revised and expanded with the addition of the missing biographies, probably at the initiative of another monk, Richard Lescot (d. after 1344).

The French royal chronicle represents an almost unique instance of a history conceived and continually updated at the very heart of the kingdom. In England by contrast, the life of the realm was recorded by the authors of the monastic chronicles referred to above. In addition to these, for the second half of the century we have the *Historia Anglicana* by Bartholomew Cotton (d. *c.*1298), a text rich with its author's knowledge of archive documents, and enlivened by his attentiveness to local conditions.

In England, as in France, the activity of secular historians is by no means unknown in the thirteenth century, though the evidence is rather sporadic. The appearance of lay writers is another symptom of the transformation of history and history writing. Here one is dealing with private individuals writing from memory or on the basis of particular personal interests. Generally, these writers did not claim to be interpreters of, or apologists or spokespersons for, official institutions of either secular or ecclesiastical kind, as was the case with most of the writers referred to up till now.

The tradition of eyewitness accounts and the written memoirs of veterans of the Crusades provided the inspiration for the *Conquête de Constantinople*, an account of the conquest of Constantinople in 1204 by Geoffrey of Villehardouin (b. *c.*1152; d. after 1212), a vassal to the count of Champagne. Geoffrey took part in the Fourth Crusade and its culmination, the conquest of Constantinople. Breaking with the tradition of crusader histories, Geoffrey wrote in French, as he intended his memoirs to appeal to a lay audience. A few years after Geoffrey's death, a biography of King Louis IX was written in French by another layman, Jean de Joinville (*c.*1224-1317), a seneschal of Champagne, nobleman and acquaintance of the king. The writer had followed the king on the Crusade from which the latter was never to return. As his biography was initially intended to garner support for a campaign to have the dead king recognized as a saint, the author neglected to draw attention to the darker sides of his subject's personality – his anger and wrathfulness and his hatred of his wife. Still more original are the author's autobiographical interventions, the references to his duties as administrator and warrior, and other passages relating to his own private affairs. The text is an expression of aristocratic culture, one that breaks the traditional moulds of the official royal biography by combining biography, personal memoirs and courtly literature.

Probably the most significant historical work to be written by a layperson in England at this time was the *Chronica Maiorum et Vicecomitum Londoniarum*, composed between 1258 and 1272 by Arnold Fitz Thedmar, a citizen of the capital. This text is a vindication of municipal interests and local concerns, even ones opposed to the values of the royal administration.

Historiography in Italy in the thirteenth century

But it was in Italy that secular historians enjoyed their greatest advances in the course of the thirteenth century. Written histories were produced in a number of the political centres of the peninsula, in response to prevailing cultural attitudes and interests. At the same time, the conception of the historical narrative became more complex, and the writing of history more closely tied to its political context, as its literary forms were revitalized and diversified.

In the world of the communes of the thirteenth century, the epic treatment of exceptional events, which had characterized history writing in the previous century, was gradually given up in favour of more systematic treatments. Taking local annals and other civic records as their point of departure, whole narratives were dedicated to the histories of individual cities, from the origins to the present. In writing of this kind, the city is regarded as a subject of moral and political interest. An early experiment in this direction is represented by the work of Giovanni Codagnello, a notary of Piacenza (d. *c.*1235), who kept an annual register of political and military history for the Lombard region of Emilia from sometime in the 1220s to 1235. Later, he made use of this material for an anthology of historical writings covering the period from the origin of the world to his own lifetime, which also incorporated legendary and historical material by other writers, including some rather fantastical information on the origins of Piacenza and Milan, and descriptions of imaginary events in the history of the cities of Lombardy at the time of the barbarian invasions. In this account, the ancient episodes foreshadow events of contemporary history. A rather more systematic approach to communal history and its political development is represented by the *Gesta Florentinorum*, the work of the Florentine historian Sanzanome. This describes the growing authority and dominion of Florence from 1125, when the rival city of Fiesole was destroyed, to 1231. Sanzanome may have been a notary at Florence. The annalistic arrangement of his history did not prevent the author from introducing a strong narrative element, which is enlivened by the discourses attributed to the prominent protagonists, and by the inclusion of the texts of official documents – as well as by Sanzanome's own commentary, which is redolent of his personal views and his enthusiastic civic patriotism. The recent history of Florence is preceded by an introduction describing the origins of the city, following a legendary tradition according to which the foundation of the city was attributed to Julius Caesar. The same tradition provided material for the *Chronica de origine civitatis*, the work of an anonymous Florentine writer active in the first half of the thirteenth century. Here, the origins of the city are associated with the

Trojans. The *Chronica* enjoyed much success – numerous vernacular translations were made, bearing witness to the important role of the city's early history in constructing Florentine civic identity.

The development of unitary, systematic approaches to political history, and the cultivation of novel literary forms for such writing, was not limited to communal narratives. In the Veneto region, between Padua, Treviso and Verona – a region known in the thirteenth century as the Trevisan March – the growing hegemony of the da Romano family, under the brothers, Alberico and Ezzelino, provided a context for narratives of rather different sort. These are the work of writers whose perspective extended beyond the confines of the communes where they lived to take in the varied political life of the region as a whole. One such was Gerardo Maurisio (d. after 1237), a notary of Vicenza, whose account of events in the region is dominated by the activities of the da Romano brothers. A more complex and sophisticated treatment is developed by the *Chronica in factis et circa facta Marchie Trivixiane* by Rolandino (d. 1276), a master of grammar and rhetoric at the university of Padua. Rolandino's *Chronica* reveals its author's great skill in embracing multiple events within a coherent narrative. Writing after 1260, Rolandino has a clear understanding of the structural relations between civic and regional history. He was the son of a notary; he describes how he received historical records from his father which he used for writing his chronicle. Indeed, in Italy in the thirteenth century, the writing of history was most often the business of notaries. Educated professionals, these individuals had convenient access to public records through their offices in the communal administration. The status of their historical writing was probably enhanced for contemporaries by the writers' status as public officials; their narratives were considered to be accurate and reliable, in proportion to the degree of authority and respect in which these writers were held. In the communes, the public demand for reliable historical records was satisfied by the 'publication' – that is, by a sort of official control and validation of the texts through a variety of means. There is evidence, for example, that Rolandino read his *Chronica* aloud in public, and in the presence of the teachers of Padua university, who thus confirmed and authenticated the history. On other occasions, communal magistrates promoted the making and keeping of historical records in the public interest. Following the death of Caffaro di Caschifellone in 1166, at Genoa the communal records were kept up by chancellery scribes and, later, by a committee of chroniclers appointed by the communal administration. Despite this bureaucratic tendency, the resulting records are by no means deprived of literary form or merit. The authors were educated and cultured individuals, and they were concerned to apply the most appropriate form and style to writing of this kind. In some cases, they wrote in a clear and unmannered style, in order for their writings to be accessible to the widest audience; in others, communal writers deployed an elevated style con-

sistent with the importance of their subject and the dignity afforded to
the principal protagonists. These writers were conscious of their role not
only as the compilers and narrators of events, but also as cultural
mediators and arbiters of fame and honour. In the communes, the
writers of narratives acted as interpreters of collective identity for the
citizenship.

Narratives produced in southern Italy during the thirteenth century
display similar characteristics. The world of the communes did not
extend to the south, where the institutional framework continued to be
provided by the Normanno-Swabian kingdom. In this context, history
was perceived through the actions of the king and his government, and
set in relation to the particular place or region in which individual
writers lived. In common with the situation in the north, in the south
the writing of history was dominated above all by notaries engaged in
public administration. Like the communal historians, these writers
began with the straightforward accounts of annals, from which they
developed progressively more studied literary expositions. Riccardo di
San Germano (active 1186; d. after 1242), a notary and functionary in
the financial administration of the kingdom, composed the *Chronica
regni Siciliae*, a history of southern Italy from the death of the last
Norman king, William II, in 1189, to 1242. This is a detailed exposition
of political events and the progress of government, with particular
attention reserved for the reign of Frederick II. The text is animated by
the author's vivid experience of life in the kingdom. Rather than an ideal
patrimony, the kingdom is presented as a political and administrative
structure, the career of which involves the destiny of all subjects.
Riccardo's *Chronica* is modest in its literary ambitions, though certain
salient events are treated with metrical and rhythmic compositions in
which the author gives vent to his own sentiments.

During the reign of Frederick II, the writing of official chronicles was
not promoted in the kingdom, perhaps as the emperor preferred to
deploy other media of spreading information and propaganda. That
said, the kingdom was the context for writing of the *Historia de rebus
gestis Friderici II imperatoris eiusque filiorum Conradi et Manfredi,
Apuliae et Siciliae regum*. The text is attributed to one Nicolò Jamsilla,
a mysterious and otherwise unknown figure sometimes identified by
scholars with Goffredo of Cosenza (d. 1269), a jurist and advisor and
intimate of King Manfred, in whose service Goffredo carried out important duties. The best part of this text concerns events between the years
1250 and 1258, when Manfred came to power and was engaged in
seeking the consent of the popes. The text reads as an official statement
of royal policy, one intended to raise support for Manfred's actions and
his political programme; as such, it may have been conceived in the
context of negotiations with the popes. The image of Manfred that
emerges is that of a feudal sovereign obedient to the papacy, and with
no intention of extending his political influence beyond the limits of the

kingdom. In the same context, Bartolomeo di Neocastro (d. after 1294) composed the *Historia sicula*, an account of life in the kingdom from the death of Frederick II to 1293. Bartolomeo was a royal notary, judge and court functionary. The text does little to disguise its author's contempt for the Angevins, while celebrating the crown of Aragon as the true ruler of Sicily, a dominion established in the wake of the terrible war of the Sicilian Vespers in 1282. Bartolomeo's writing has none of the character of an official document, though it was probably conceived as a source of information for the author's fellow citizens of Messina. But Bartolomeo was by no means indifferent to the literary potential of his work; initially, he wrote in verse; later, he prepared a prose version of the history at the request of his son, who was unable to understand his father's refined verse. The prose history, which survives, is probably an expanded and updated version of its verse predecessor. And it is not without a certain literary distinction and distinctive narrative structure; in particular, the text is coloured by the author's taste for the romance of the events he describes.

As in northern Italy, the writings of southern-Italian historians take the form of monographic treatments dedicated to the great scheme of political history in the kingdom. These are the work of writers who were entirely capable of presenting the course of events in structured and organic ways.

Ecclesiastical history was not unknown in thirteenth-century Italy, where it was closely tied to the world of the communes. Church historians took their models from earlier universal histories and the traditional forms of monastic historiography. The most significant exponent of this genre was the Franciscan, Salimbene de Adam (1221-1288), whose *Chronica*, covering the period between 1168 and 1287, is a singular document, which departs from traditional historiographical schemes. Although it appears to be an annual chronicle of events in northern Italy, it is in fact an assortment of autobiographical records, anecdotes, caricatures and didactic and moralizing exemplars – as well as personal opinions and observations on strange and marvellous things. The commentary concerns both political life and that of the Franciscan order; its treatment is characterized throughout by the author's educative and moralizing purpose. The *Chronica* provides a vivid sense of the mood of the time in which it was conceived, with a strong commitment to the values and the ways of life of communal society. A less original but equally important record of the relations between ecclesiastical and communal history is provided by the *Chronicon Ianuense* by the Dominican, Jacobus de Voragine, archbishop of Genoa from 1292 (d. 1298). This is the history of the city from its mythical foundation by the Trojans to the year 1294 – an account based on Vincent of Beauvais and a variety of local and mostly legendary traditions. Slightly later is the *Historia satyrica* by the Franciscan, Paolino Minorita (*c*.1270-1345). The classical reference in the title of this work announces its thoroughly eclectic nature. In part, this is a reworking of material taken from Vincent of Beauvais, which Paolino extended to cover the period before 1335, while adding fresh material on the history of Venice and the Levant.

From the last decades of the thirteenth century communal narratives in Italy were written in the vernacular in order to be accessible to the widest possible audience. Possibly the earliest text of this kind is the *Estoires de Venise* by Martino da Canal, written between 1267 and 1275. Nothing is known of the author except his name, though it is probably safe to suppose that he was a Venetian. The text belongs to the genre of communal narratives, beginning as it does with the city's ancient origins and continuing into the author's own day, while providing a vehicle for his unabashed civic patriotism. Histories of this kind incorporate historical records, memory and legendary traditions; they were intended to be entertaining as well as informative, a circumstance that explains the more romantic aspects of writing in this oeuvre. In theory, the writers intended their work for a universal audience; in practice, these writings were directed to an audience made up of the authors' fellow citizens and by the large numbers of westerners present in the Mediterranean Levant since the time of the Fourth Crusade and the institution of the French principates of Greece. This may explain why the writer reverted to French, which may have been considered more apt than Italian for a work destined to be widely circulated.

Yet Italian was the language chosen for the *Historia fiorentina*, by the patrician Ricordano Malespini (d. after 1282). Like its predecessors, this is a history of Florence from its mythical origins to the thirteenth century. What is different is the heightened subjectivity of the author, who expresses his nostalgia for the time when Florence was inhabited and ruled by a class of nobles, and when life in the city was characterized by simple and honourable customs. Malespini's history is a polemic aimed against social and cultural change in his time. This is not official writing but an example of private history composed in the spoken Florentine language with immediacy and spontaneity.

The same characteristics appear in the *Cronaca delle cose occorrenti ne' tempi suoi* by the Florentine Dino Compagni (1246/7-1324), a merchant schooled in grammar and rhetoric. Compagni held an important post in the government of Florence until 1302, when his party was banished by the political opposition, and Compagni forced out of office. He wrote the *Chronica* in retirement, in the period between 1302 and 1312. The text is a meditation on the dire implications anticipated by Compagni for the city of Florence following the political upheavals of 1302. Compagni is anxious to identify and denounce those responsible, while predicting grave consequences for the city's internal order. Given his urgent political agenda, Compagni does not bother to explain the ancient origins of the city, in the tradition of Florentine communal history; instead, the account opens at the beginning of the thirteenth century, with a summary description of the origins of the civic factions, before coming to more recent events and the author's theoretical interpretation of their consequences. Despite the text's harsh and polemical tone, it is likely that Compagni's intention was to persuade his fellow townsmen to overcome division and to allow wisdom and moderation to prevail, thus restoring peace and prosperity to Florence. Compagni was writing history in order to have his say in the political life of his city once he had been excluded from civic government.

In Italy at the end of the thirteenth century and during the first decades of the 1300s, the writing of history was enriched in its forms and conception by a revival of interest in classical models. This is apparent from a verse history, the *De gestis in civitate Mediolani*, written by Stefanardo of Vimercate (d. *c*.1297) in hexameters reminiscent of Virgil. Stefanardo was a theologian and Dominican canon at the monastery of Sant'Eustorgio in Milan. His verse history deals with events leading up to the emergence of Archbishop Ottone Visconti as the lord of Milan in the period from 1259 to 1277. Ottone is celebrated as the bringer of peace to a city torn by strife. The poet has written a historical narrative, though his prime purpose is admittedly and unmistakeably eulogistic, hence the choice of a distinctly aulic or courtly literary form with classical references.

In even more significant ways, the classical influence affected the work of two writers active at Padua at the end of the thirteenth century. Evidence of an impressive revival in the study of Latin literature at Padua at this time has provoked some discussion of a Paduan prehumanistic movement. Prominent in this context is the figure of Albertino Mussato (1261-1329), a judge at Padua and the author of two long historical works: the *Historia augusta de gestis Henrici VII*, covering the expedition of Emperor Henry VII to Italy; and the *De gestis Italicorum post Henricum VII caesarem*. Both works describe the situation in central and northern Italy and the drive to re-establish peace and order there in Mussato's lifetime – an undertaking that was to have been carried out by Henry VII. Notwithstanding the failure of that enterprise, as a writer of history Mussato maintained a wide perspective, thanks to his knowledge of the works of classical historians. What is more, Mussato developed the cultivated conception of Italy as a single integrated politico-cultural orbit. However, Mussato was also strongly committed to communal autonomy, and his history expresses Paduan hostility for the Scaligeri of Verona and their imperial protectors. This rivalry provided the context for the *Ecerinis*, a historical tragedy written in the style of Seneca, in which Mussato gloomily recalled the tyranny of Ezzelino da Romano, seemingly as a warning to Paduans to ward against the return of tyranny.

Curiosity for rediscovered models of classical historiography, and a fresh interest in ancient Roman history, was provoked in other parts of Italy by the short-lived revival of the empire under Henry VII. This is witnessed by the writing of Riccobaldo of Ferrara (b. 1245; d. after 1316), a notary and active participant in the political and administrative life of the city of Ferrara under the powerful Este family. Riccobaldo encountered the thriving cultural life of Padua during his many periods of exile there. In his numerous historical works (*Pomarium ecclesiae Ravennatis*, 1297-8; *Historiae*, 1305-8; *Compilatio chronologica*, 1313; *Compendium Romanae historiae*, *c.*1316), the encyclopaedic treatment of universal history, based on the model of Vincent of Beauvais, progressively gives way to a specialized interest in Roman history. For Riccobaldo – and thanks to his reading of Livy – Roman history is regarded as the source of general values and meanings. In certain works, particularly the *Compendium*, the exposition of Roman history continues with a collection of the names and deeds of the medieval emperors, from Charlemagne to the author's own day. This was intended to suggest the continuity of the imperial institution and the resilience of its function. Riccobaldo was also the author of the *Chronica parva Ferrariensis*, a history of Ferrara. His account of contemporary political history, particularly that of his own region, sets out the framework in which imperial authority was expected to be exercised in Italy.

Other aspects of thirteenth-century historiography

In the course of the thirteenth century, the decline of imperial authority put paid to the production of universal histories in Germany. Apart from some Martinian chronicles, the most significant achievements in this area are represented by the *Sachsenspiegel*, a chronicle attributed to the jurist, Eike von Repgow (b. *c.*1180; d. after 1233), in continuation of the work of Ekkehard of Aura; and a verse chronicle composed around 1280 by the Viennese writer, Jans Enikel. The most striking aspect of these two texts is not the peculiarity of the historiographical or political positions taken by the authors, but the condition of the authors themselves – both writers were middle-class laymen, and both wrote in German.

The new territorial and dynastic states did much to foster development in the writing of history. This is clear from the rather different approaches taken by Magnus of Reichersberg (d. 1195), a Bavarian chronicler whose writing relates the history of that region to the wider picture in the empire, and Conrad of Luppburg (d. *c.*1245), author of the *Chronicon Schirense*, and abbot of the family monastery of Wittelsback at Scheyern, in whose writing dynastic and territorial interests are most apparent.

In northern Germany, the priest and warrior missionary Henry of Lettonia (b. *c.*1188; d. after 1259) wrote his *Chronicon Livoniae* around 1225 or 1227. This text represents an important record of the political and religious history of the Baltic peoples before the thirteenth century.

Other original developments in thirteenth-century historiography followed from the Christian conversion of the Scandinavian regions. Saxo Grammaticus (d. after 1218) was the author of a history of the Danes, written about 1200 – the *Gesta Danorum*, a composition comprising Viking-age traditions and legends concerning the mythical origins of the Danes and the heroic exploits of their legendary early kings. Such material was transmitted through oral discourse and in the form of sagas and heroic plays. Saxo was proud of the rich heritage of national Danish history and its originality and importance, to which he gave much attention. However, this pride is tempered by the prominence given to the progress of Christianity, and by the author's knowledge of the refined forms of Latin literary culture, which he took from the schools of France. The influence of this learning is apparent from the narrative's elaborate structure and Saxo's debt to such ancient writers as Justinus, Valerius Maximus and Orosius.

An analogous work undertaken at almost the same time was by the Icelandic author Snorri Sturlusson (1179-1241), a military leader and poet who played a key role in political relations between Iceland and Norway, and who was later assassinated in a vendetta. Between 1223 and 1235 he composed the *Heimskringla*, a history of the kings of Norway from their mythical origins involving the god Odin, to the reign of King Magnus Erlingsson and the year 1184. Again, this is based on epic oral traditions in which Snorri was well versed, having been educated by a pagan priest; traditionally, the priests were the custodians of social memory in the form of poems and lays. Although he was a Christian, Snorri was less concerned than Saxo to isolate or untangle the traditions of ancient (and pagan) origin. Moreover, he wrote in the national language, Norse, making much play of the expressive potential of Nordic poetry. Thus, Snorri's work may be regarded as a literary and poetic history as much as a national or political one.

Historiography in the fourteenth century

The recognizable characteristics of fourteenth-century history are the outcome of developments made already in the thirteenth century. In the 1300s, the writers of history were most commonly laypeople or members of the mendicant orders. The traditional models were disregarded or roundly transformed, and novel forms engendered to suit writers' particular intentions and the context or purpose of their work. The language of fourteenth-century histories, especially that of lay writers, is the spoken vernacular.

In addition to these characteristics of historiographical production in the period, one should mention the growing confidence with which writers dealt with unprecedented quantities of material. At this time, writers of history had access to a greater and more diverse range of sources than their predecessors at any time in the Middle Ages, thanks to ever more expansive networks of political, ecclesiastical and commercial relations, in a world where travel between distant countries was becoming increasingly frequent. Another characteristic is the authors' penetrating ability to analyze actions and events in empirical and rational ways, though this concern did not always exclude a moral preoccupation with the values of human action, as on this subject history was summoned to provide essential teachings.

These characteristics are most apparent in the narratives of secular writers, and are exemplified by the *Chronica* of the Florentine merchant Giovanni Villani (1280-1348). At sometime in the 1320s, while engaged in the government of Florence and with his own affairs as a merchant in that city, Villani began to make records of contemporary events. His purpose was to write a new history of Florence, which he composed between 1333 and his death in 1348. The *Chronica* places the history of Florence in the context of universal history, for which Villani made much use of the work of earlier mendicant historians. That said, roughly half of the material presented in Villani's twelve-volume history is related to events that took place in his own lifetime. Villani's vision of communal history is considerably wider than that of earlier Florentine chroniclers. In this account, the life of Florence is set in relation to events in Italy as a whole, and in some cases the narrator's attention extends even to the European panorama, for which he provides no shortage of detailed and reliable information. Villani's perspective is that of the successful international merchant and financier, a man well placed to receive information and opinion from informants in all parts of Europe – and a man given to pragmatism in his handling and interpretation of such material, whether it refer to economic or political affairs. Of course, this is not to deny Villani his primary purpose, which was to give testimony to the honour and the authority of his city and to educate his fellow Florentines in civic virtues.

Although Villani's history may be considered an exceptional instance of secular writing in the fourteenth century, especially in terms of its literary accomplishment, the achievement of Italian historians at this time is witnessed by a number of important texts.

In Venice, for instance, the doge Andrea Dandolo (1306-1354) ordered the composition of the great *Chronica per extensum descripta*, for which he sought the assistance of the staff of the state chancellery. This was to be a full, official version of the history of Venice and its political dominion in the Mediterranean, from the city's origins with the alleged arrival of St Mark at Aquileia in AD 48 to the mid-fourteenth century. Conceived in the image of the old universal histories, the text retains the traditional annalistic arrangement. Its authors made systematic use of earlier chronicles and records, as Villani did for his history of Florence. As the history was being compiled, the doge was busy revising the statutes of the city's administration and law. This was the context for the writing of transcriptions or summaries of a large number of official documents, the texts of which were copied into the chronicle, providing a documentary history of the Republic's political and commercial relations. Dandolo's intention was to provide a definitive and irrefutable statement of Venetian authority, thereby legitimizing the Republic's claims to political rights at a time when these were being challenged on a number of fronts.

The tendency towards exhaustive and systematic treatment of historical records can also be seen in the work of the Milanese historian Galvano Fiamma (b. 1283; d. after 1344), a Dominican from a merchant family, who was educated in theology and medicine. Fiamma's writing is animated by his civic pride, which he expressed in a number of works dedicated to the history of Milan, such as the so-called *Chronica galvagnana*, *Chronicon extravagans de antiquitatibus Mediolani*, *Chronicon maius* and the *Manipulus florum*. These have little in common with Milanese communal narratives of the previous centuries, as now the lordship of the Visconti family was established in the city. Fiamma supported and collaborated with the Visconti. The works no longer display the communal spirit; now, the emphasis is on the city and its people, its historical traditions, ancient monuments and institutions. The city becomes the subject of historical and moral interest independent of political regimes. Fiamma also turned to earlier historical literature for his description of the city and made use of it as well as contemporary traditions.

Not all communal narratives produced in the fourteenth century were motivated by the same systematic and exhaustive tendency. A *Chronica* composed by an anonymous author at Rome shortly after the middle of the century presents an impassioned and colourful account of contemporary events in the city. In particular, the work is characterized by its author's attachment to the more dramatic and violent episodes in contemporary experience, circumstances that precluded any proud exaltation of the city itself. However, some sense of civic pride is apparent in the writer's nostalgia for Rome's past grandeur, a nostalgia rendered all the more poignant by Cola di Rienzo's doomed attempt to reorganize the city's government in 1347. The use of Roman dialect, and the narrative's subjective tone, marks this out as a work of private history by a lay author.

Private memoirs occur in other forms at this time, as in the *libri di famiglia* (family books) or *libri di ricordanze* (books of remembrance), the use of which became common in the fourteenth century, especially at Florence. These books contain running lists of important events in the life of a family. Records of this kind were often kept by merchants along with books of accounts, and handed down from father to son. As well as biographical information regarding family members, and references to the affairs of the family business and the management of its estate, these sources provide insight to the family's involvement in public life. Moreover, the books shed some light on the conduct of the family and its management, and they thus provide evidence of primary importance for the social life of the period.

It would be difficult to summarize the historiographical production of fourteenth-century Europe even in the most general terms. The period witnessed a proliferation of historical writing in a variety of forms. At this time, writers had access to an unprecedented quantity of material, which they subjected to progressively more systematic and analytical treatments. The impetus for most fourteenth-century writing was provided by local or regional affairs, although the same circumstances provided for such a variety of forms of writing that it is impossible (and unhelpful) to group the texts according to type. The practice of history among an ever-wider section of society is witnessed, among other things, by the appearance in Germany of civic chronicles written in the local vernacular by members of the patrician class and bourgeoisie. Likewise, in France and Belgium members of the urban middle classes prepared histories of their cities, most often in the form of memoirs or private journals.

But it is in the courts of nobles that we find the foremost writer of history in fourteenth-century France – Jean Froissart (1337-1404). Froissart was the author of the *Chroniques*, a vivid and detailed account in French of events during the Hundred Years' War, as seen from an aristocratic point of view. This history is one of honour and gallantry, governed by the complex rituals of chivalric society.

Ecclesiastical history at this time is restricted to the traditional forms developed by the mendicant orders. Martinian chronicles continued to be produced, along with anthologies of universal history, such as the *Mare historiarum* by Giovanni Colonna (d. after 1343), and the *Cronica* of the Franciscan Francesco Pipino, writing in the first half of the fourteenth century. In Germany, the Franciscan John of Winterthur (b. c.1300; d. after 1348) composed a chronicle that combines the characteristics of the universal history with the most distinctive forms of mendicant histories. The text of this chronicle for the years between 1198 and 1348 survives; it contains information of every kind, including accounts of occurrences and phenomena of marvellous and demonic sort, and as such represents a vivid record of the ways of life and thought of common people.

Significant changes in the traditional plan of universal chronicles were introduced in some works by ecclesiastical authors under the influence of the politico-theological doctrines put out by the papacy during its sojourn in Avignon. The Dominican Tolomeo of Lucca wrote his history, the *Historia ecclesiastica*, at Avignon some time between 1313 and 1317. For the most part this is a history of the popes from the time of Christ, now deemed to be the first pope. The basic form of the Martinian chronicles, which were based on parallel lists of popes and emperors, is abandoned. In Tolomeo's history of the Church, the emperors are given no role in the progress of history, which is dominated by the popes. A similar view lies at the heart of the *Flores chronicorum* by the Dominican Bernard Gui (1261/2-1331), a theologian and inquisitor who saw history as the collected lives and deeds of the popes.

Another representative product of fourteenth-century historiography is the *Polychronicon* of the English Benedictine, Ranulph Higden (d. *c.*1363-4), a text modelled on Vincent of Beauvais, and with the usual assortment of exemplary and wondrous anecdotes. Significantly, the author added a variety of material on geographical, scientific and historical themes, making the *Polychronicon* one of the richest and most interesting works of the period. It was translated into English in 1385, a clear sign of the widening use of texts of this kind.

Even this summary profile of medieval historiography will be enough to invalidate the statements frequently made by those who claim that history had little or no place in medieval culture, either as a vehicle for knowledge about the past or as a medium for interpreting the present. Moreover, this account of the medieval production of history reveals the limits of methodological approaches that assume that medieval histories can be read as straightforward receptacles of historical information. As we have seen, records of this kind are better considered as products of one of the main concerns of medieval culture – the interpretation of the progress of humankind and the significance of political actions. There are no convenient or ready-made methodologies for the use of material of this kind. Certainly, medieval narratives impart information or inferences regarding the events and personalities and institutions under consideration, but in the first instance they reflect back on their authors, and on the condition and context and culture of those individuals. The special meaning of any historical source is situated in its production. In order to get at this meaning we must endeavour to understand the writers' conditions and motives. The historian must read the sources in their entirety before selecting from their contents, as the formulation of any text is contingent on the context and the motives of writers.

6

Documentary sources

Alongside the sources that preserve a record of events in the form of historical narrative, another important category of medieval records is concerned with the juridical rights enjoyed by institutions and persons – rights resulting from the dispensation of a public authority, or from agreement between interested parties. These rights may be of the most varied nature, including the property of possessions, and the exercise of jurisdiction, as well as exemptions and privileges, and guarantees of economic kind, ranging from agreements to cultivate land to commercial contracts. As today, in the Middle Ages whenever legally defined and protected rights were brought into being or modified, it was customary for a formal record of the process to be made, in order to protect the exercise of such rights and to defend them in case of disputation.

Developed societies have made use of diverse expedients to communicate and sanction the rights of their members. At the beginning of the Middle Ages, among the Germanic peoples who invaded the Roman empire the peaceful enjoyment of rights was rooted in a system whereby rights were established and acquired before an assembly of freemen, which enacted and maintained such rights through the delegation of the people.

In the Roman world, on the other hand, and at least from the late Republic, the recording of rights was entrusted to written documentation – a more precise, durable and convenient witness than oral and collective memory. Once they had settled within the imperial territories, the Germanic peoples also adopted this use of written documentation, which they combined with their traditional procedures.

In the Romano-barbarian kingdoms, use of juridical documents was made most frequently by public authorities and the Church. The practice was more or less uncommon among the rest of society, depending on local traditions and ethnic and social background. Progressively, though, recourse to written documentation increased, and in the latter part of the Middle Ages, particularly from the thirteenth century onwards, it was the custom in all the territories of Europe and among all social ranks, on account of having become the most appreciable witness in the judicial process. Following the barbarian hiatus, therefore, and in the course of the Middle Ages, the use of the written act as the fundamental form of juridical documentation was re-established. Without further interruption, this practice has continued down to our own day.

The critical study of juridical documents came into being towards the end of the seventeenth century. It should be remembered that the rights acquired during the course of the Middle Ages by ecclesiastical institutions, territorial lordships and aristocratic families, continued to be considered valid, at least in principle, right up to the French Revolution, among the society of the 'Ancien Régime'. Thus, written acts (*acta*) pertaining to such rights were routinely preserved in the archives of institutions and families. In the seventeenth century and even in the eighteenth, claims to property, rights and jurisdiction were often based on precedents of medieval origin. This circumstance produced the so-called *bella diplomatica*, or 'war by documents', in which the interested parties took up as arms diplomata (acts given by constituted authorities, kings and popes above all) which their holders now presented as witnesses to rights in question. Under such circumstances, there was pressing need for a method of critical analysis of medieval juridical documents, in order to evaluate their validity independently of the force of advocatory pleading and the authority of the conflicting parties. Above all, there was a requirement to distinguish genuine documents from forgeries. The history of this problem was already a long one. The juridical document, on account of its very function as the foundation and proof of rights, has always been exposed to the risk of alteration and falsification. Notwithstanding the measures taken in the production of acts to guarantee their authenticity and to make falsification difficult, already in the medieval period itself false documents were frequently made, often by the very persons and offices deputized to redact authentic documents. The practice of altering and forging documents continued well after the end of the Middle Ages, out of practical interest and as a form of erudite entertainment. Though the need to scrutinize juridical documents for authenticity was felt already in medieval times, documentary criticism came into its own only after the birth of humanistic textual philology. There is the famous case of the so-called Donation of Constantine, a document which had been of great importance in the history of the medieval papacy, and which, around the year 1440, the humanist Lorenzo Valla showed to be false, basing his case above all on linguistic considerations.

However, it was not until the second half of the seventeenth century that a critical method was established for the scrutiny of old juridical instruments. A major cornerstone in this enterprise was provided by the treatise *De re diplomatica*, by the Benedictine scholar Jean Mabillon, published in 1681. Mabillon established a system of criteria and objective rules for the critical analysis of documents or diplomata (hence the treatise's title), on the basis of their formal characteristics, both in terms of the exterior aspect (such as the material on which the document was written, the kinds of handwriting used, and the various signs used in validating documents of this kind, including signatures, symbols and seals), and from the form and formulae of the text. Mabillon's work signals the birth of a specialized discipline – Diplomatics. Subsequently, in the course of the nineteenth and twentieth centuries, the resources and objectives of Diplomatics have been greatly expanded. As well as the formal analysis of documents, diplomatists undertake historical research on the offices, the persons, and the occasions that determined the writing of documents; and they are concerned with the scribal, literary and juridical culture of scribes, with the value of documents in juridical practice, and the jurisdictional and political activity of authorities – even with the function of documents as symbolic expressions of political power. Hence, juridical *acta* may be evaluated for at least three types of information: one relating to the act itself, its nature and characteristics; a second relating to the event, the juridical action or negotiation, to which the document refers; and a third level regarding the organization, culture, institutions and practices of the society in which the act was produced. Studies of juridical documents, therefore, have witnessed an immense broadening of perspective, comparable to that which has characterized the study of medieval historiography. As we saw in the previous chapter, there has been a shift away from the earlier tendency to regard historical narratives simply as repositories of facts and information, towards an understanding of their value as evidence of the political ideas, literary culture and theological and historiographical doctrines particular to their authors and the context in which they lived. In the same way, juridical documents are now regarded as historical witnesses not just to single negotiations and their registration, but also to the entire network of institutional and cultural factors which imposes on the production of every written act.

The kind of document of concern to students of Diplomatics may be defined as 'a written witness which is drawn up in a certain predetermined form and serves as proof of some action or fact of a juridical nature'. This definition applies equally to *acta* made, following established forms, by an institutional authority in granting a person or other entity rights of various kinds (typical among documents of this kind are royal 'diplomas'), as it does to acts recording the will of private persons (the most common form of which is the notarial act). In juridical terms, acts in the former category are classified as *public acts*, because the acting authority, which is the source of rights conferred by such acts, is a public authority exercising state powers. The others – in which the rights in question do not arise from the provision of public authorities, but are those of the private sphere – are defined as *private acts*, even in cases where a public authority figures in transactions. This distinction is reflected in the process of document production, with the result that public acts are different from private ones, not only on account of the juridical origin of the rights in question, but also in terms of the documents' external appearance and the form and formulae of the text.

Hence, in the following sections of this chapter, public and private acts are analyzed and described separately, in order to highlight the distinctive characteristics of each category.

There are other types of juridical documents which fit more or less exactly with the definition given above – the deliberations (or *placita*) of the courts of justice, for instance, and the acts of administrative offices, to take just two examples. These types of documents may also be subject to analysis and study by diplomatists, given that they respond to canonical typologies, and present recurrent external and internal characteristics. However, in the pages that follow, public and private acts only are considered, as previously defined. Traditionally, public and private acts are most commonly the object of the science of Diplomatics; and, what is more, between them they make up by far the greatest proportion, quantitatively speaking, of the medieval juridical records extant.

Public acts

The public documents studied in Diplomatics are not acts of government in the true sense; that is, we are not concerned here with the promulgation of laws or the communication of political deliberations. Instead, what concern us are those manifestations of power which, from a juridical point of view, may be defined as 'acts of gracious or benevolent jurisdiction'. These may involve the granting or recognition of rights of various kinds by those in authority to the advantage of a beneficiary.

The concept of authority requires some clarification in the medieval context. By definition, the only real holders of public authority in the period were emperors and kings, who exercised sovereignty through the institutional structures of which they were the heads (i.e. kingdoms and the empire). Therefore, in the strict sense, only the acts of emperors and kings may be considered 'public acts'. That said, the category is usually made to include documents enacted by other authorities whose appearance is less clearly definable in terms of the analogy with modern public jurisdiction. By way of example, papal documents have the appearance of public acts, though they relate not to temporal but spiritual and ecclesiastical jurisdiction. Rather more complicated is the case of those authorities that exercised political and jurisdictional powers of wide-ranging and autonomous kind, but not real sovereignty – the lords of feudal *principates*, say, or, on the ecclesiastical side, bishops and archbishops.

Even the acts of these authorities may be regarded as public in quality, however, as in the Middle Ages the formal jurisdiction exercised by those in authority tended to assimilate to the exercise of public powers, whatever their origin and their relation to royal or imperial sovereignty. Therefore, a necessarily broad and indefinite conception of authority is taken here, in order to admit the authors of public documents made in the exercise of institutional powers in the medieval period.

A public act had to respond to various requirements. It had at once to define the right or privilege being instituted, and to provide unarguable testimony to that right, being clearly valid and unimpugnable. The document's juridical validity derived from the authority that brought it into being (and which is technically considered to be the 'author'). This notwithstanding, the act had to display certain formal and material characteristics in order to be recognized as authentic. In other words, as an object and a tangible expression of authority, the public document had to have a prestigious external aspect.

In order to meet these essential requirements, all authorities in the business of producing written acts availed themselves of the services of professional clerks or scribes, persons able not only to write up such documents, but also to confer upon them the required characteristics. Hence, close by all seats of government and power in the Middle Ages there were usually to be found one or more specialists engaged in the writing of acts. These scribes were organized into more or less complex and autonomous offices, which operated in close connection with the authority from which they depended. This was the case already in the Romano-barbarian kingdoms, which inherited the tradition and often the organization of the offices of the provincial governors of the Roman empire. This bureaucratic system was not a very complex one – one or more *referendarii* (who owed their office and title to the Roman system) took up the petitions and pleadings of interested parties, referring them to the king (hence the title), and subsequently ensuring that acts were written out in correspondence with the king's decisions. The writing was done by *notarii* and *cancellarii*. The *referendarius* then checked the finished text, had it signed by the king, and completed it by signing it himself.

This procedure is well documented in the Merovingian kingdom, whence a considerable number of original documents enables us even to distinguish the various phases in the writing of acts. The system was more or less the same in the Lombard and Visigothic kingdoms. What characterizes this production is the participation of the king, and the condition of the *referendarii* and notaries who, as laymen, may be considered the last heirs of the public functionaries of the ancient world.

As the Carolingians came to power, this organization declined. From the time of Pippin III (reigned from 751), the new kings engaged only churchmen to write their acts, entrusting one of them with the responsibility for the entire production. This development was probably caused by declining levels of secular learning, particularly in the northern regions of the Frankish kingdom whence the Carolingian dynasty hailed; it is also symptomatic of the Church's close involvement with the new regime. It will be remembered that the first Carolingian kings were illiterate, and therefore in need of a trustworthy deputy to control the work of scribes and notaries on their behalf. The new system was rapidly brought to perfection. Though as yet no distinct and autonomous office was formed, as those involved in the production of diplomata were members of the court clergy with functions in the royal chapel, the technical expertise of clerical notaries rapidly increased. Juridical formularies were renewed, and improvements made to the language and the external aspect of acts, through the increasingly correct use of classical Latin and the development of good scripts. From 820, under Louis the Pious, the cleric with overall responsibility for the production of imperial acts became an influential presence at court, often chosen by the emperor from his closest political aides. At first, he took the title *archinotarius* (archnotary) or *summus cancellarius* (supreme chancellor); by the middle of the ninth century, the title most frequently used was that of archchancellor, an office maintained under the administration of the German empire – which in many aspects was the heir to the Carolingian empire – and in the kingdoms connected to it, Italy and Burgundy.

The office of chancellor derives from the bureaucracy of the Roman empire. In its original context, it referred to the keeper of the gates that separated the judge from the people in Roman courts, and, by extension, to the secretary charged with drafting minutes of hearings and proceedings. The term had the same meaning under the Merovingian and Carolingian kingdoms of Francia. At court it also referred to the writer of royal acts, perhaps suggesting an air of superiority with regard to the office of notary. This circumstance would explain the use of the title *cancellarius* to designate the head of the whole service. The title gives the modern English terms 'chancellor' and 'chancellery' or 'chancery' (and the French 'chancelerie'), from *cancellaria* in late Latin. Since the twelfth century the word 'chancery' has referred to the office engaged in the production of royal or official acts. The term is often used as a convenient anachronism in referring to periods and contexts in history when distinct, organized writing offices did not exist in the courts.

The archchancellor did not participate directly in the writing up of acts, being the political rather than the technical head of the service. Technical supervision was provided by a notary charged with overseeing the activity of other notaries, who often doubled for the archchancellor at that very stage in the production of acts which, at least in theory, remained the latter's particular prerogative – namely, the *recognitio*, the final verification of documents in completed form. Reference to this was always made in the last line of royal diplomas as the responsibility of the archchancellor, though it was often carried out by the head notary instead. From the end of the Carolingian era, the head notary assumed the title of chancellor with ever-greater frequency. Thus, in the reorganization of the service at the time of the renewal of the empire in Germany, under the Ottonians, the hierarchy of chancery functionaries was as follows: archchancellor, chancellor and notary.

The archchancellor was normally an archbishop, in most cases from the see of Mainz, a political figure of the highest rank, and a close ally of the king. Increasingly, the archchancellor became distanced from the business of the chancery, at least until the age of Frederick Barbarossa, when for some time, the archchancellors of the empire regained control of their chanceries.

Directly beneath and responsible to the archchancellor was the chancellor, the effective head of the chancery. Like the archchancellor, this figure was usually a churchman promoted from within the court, and he was well rewarded for his trouble, perhaps with an appointment to a prosperous bishopric. He would live at court, though, receiving his orders directly from the throne as well as from his superior. In addition, he was charged with keeping the seal used for authenticating official documents.

Beneath the chancellor were the notaries, whose principal concern it was to prepare the text of documents according to the most appropriate literary and juridical forms. Notaries did not always write up texts themselves, however; instead, they might pass their drafts to scribes to be formally written out (*engrossment – in grossum* or *in mundum*). The functions of the chancery became still more complex in the twelfth century, with the appearance of specialized offices such as that of *registrator*, responsible for registering acts, and the *sigillator*, charged with applying the seal.

Another sovereign institution with a particularly well-developed chancery was the papacy. Like many of the successor kingdoms of early-medieval Europe, at first the forms and practices of the papal bureaucracy followed those of the administrative offices of the Roman empire. The very name initially given to the papal office, the *scrinium*, corresponds with that of the imperial offices. The *scrinium* was made up of a group of notaries or *scriniarii*, who formed a professional association, or *schola*, under the guidance of a *primicerius notariorum*, or head notary. From the end of the eighth century, the acts of *scriniarii* were authenticated by high officials of the papal curia, the palatine magistrates or *datarii* – so-called as it was their task to add the date to the end of the document, using the formula '*datum per manus*' ('given by the hand of') before the name and title of the presiding magistrate. This formula had the same function as the *recognitio* of official documents in the imperial context.

The palatine officials represented the civic nobility in the papal administration. For this reason, in the course of the ninth century, the popes looked to install a chancery official who would be directly dependent on the Apostolic see and active only in its interests. This was the papal librarian, whose official tasks also included those of archivist or keeper of documents. This office, which was usually held by a cardinal bishop, gradually assumed considerable significance, though rarely did its holders threaten the influence wielded by palatine magistrates before the middle of the tenth century. By 983, though, St Peter's librarian had become the sole *datarius* of papal acts.

In the course of the eleventh century, the organization of the papal chancery was progressively transformed. In imitation of the imperial chancery, the office of chancellor was introduced to exercise the librarian's role as the effective head of the service. The chancellor, too, was a cardinal, deacon or priest, and was at times substituted by a representative. Moreover, the organization and role of notaries was modified. Alongside the traditional professional figures who continued to carry the title of notaries and *scriniarii*, and who retained their links with the civic organization, another group of notaries was appointed to follow the pope on his journeys outside Rome; these notaries were exclusively tied to papal authority. Later, the German popes imposed by Emperor Henry III brought with them notaries and chancellors from north of the Alps, who modified the traditional aspect of papal documents in imitation of imperial diplomata.

The process of change continued into the twelfth century, as notaries in papal service broke away from the traditional order of notaries and *scriniarii*; the latter, in turn, lost their role in the papal chancery, becoming civic scribes. The chancellor was confirmed as the head of the chancery. Then, around the mid-twelfth century, the chancellor was joined and frequently substituted by a vicechancellor, the former office having become an honorary one, as it was in the empire. As yet, though, there was no strict division of function among the various employees of the chancery; this came with the reform of the papal chancery instigated by Pope Innocent III (1198-1216), in response to growing demand for privileges, grants, and judgements in all parts of the Christian world. Now a rigorous bureaucratic structure was imposed, the office of chancellor was withdrawn, and sole responsibility given to the vicechancellor, who was now more likely to be a specialist in law rather than an élite churchman, and who thus was required to swear an oath of allegiance to the pope. He was served by a group of six or seven *notarii domini papae* (papal notaries) who were assisted in turn by the *auditor litterarum contradictarum* (auditor of contested documents) and the *corrector*. These officials were charged with receiving petitions presented to the papal see, evaluating them and taking them before the pope – and, subsequently, setting down the provisions emerging from the deliberations of the papal court. They were assisted by abbreviators, who drafted the minutes of documents which the distributors then assigned to the scribes. The latter belonged to a college, and were bound under oath to the vicechancellor; they were responsible for formally writing out (or *engrossing*) acts in definitive form. Subsequently, the completed document was passed for inspection to the *corrector*, who could order it to be re-written at the scribe's expense were errors to be found. Finally, the document was passed to another office, the *Bullaria*, for application of the bull. During the process, petitioners were assisted by official procurators accredited to the curia. Prior to the application of the bull, the procurators were able to contest documents the provisions of which did not meet the approval or expectations of petitioners. Such cases were addressed to the official detailed to deal with disputed acts, the *auditor litterarum contradictarum*. The acts (or rather the minutes of acts) were transcribed into registers kept in the papal archive, which formed a record of outgoing documents and the respective provisions and dispensations. This was not a new practice, but one that became systematic and obligatory only with the reforms of Innocent III. All the apparatus of the chancery depended directly from the pope.

Further modifications to this bureaucratic organization were undertaken by the Avignon papacy. Hence, the roles of the various chancery officials were distinguished according to the nature of the acts with which each was engaged, separating the completion of formalities for grants from those for justice. Even the business of registering acts was differentiated according to material. By the end of the thirteenth century, the papal chancery had become by far the most complex and developed bureaucracy in medieval Europe.

The chanceries of kings and princes were considerably less complex by comparison. In fact, prior to the thirteenth century, they might be served by just one or two ecclesiastical scribes under a chancellor, who doubled as keeper of the seal. From the thirteenth century and above all during the fourteenth century, the offices of the royal chanceries of England and France were diversified, and a greater number of functionaries employed, including an increasing number of lay experts in the field of law.

Following this brief account of the offices engaged in the production of public acts, let us now consider the material aspect, the composition and the essential parts of the medieval public document, with particular reference, once again, to imperial and royal documents. We may begin with the document's exterior form or physical aspect; that is, with what are known to diplomatists as 'extrinsic characteristics'. In the first place, we are concerned here with the very material on which acts were written out. In antiquity it was normal to use papyrus sheets; even the acts of Merovingian kings were written on papyrus, which had to be imported from regions where it was produced, principally Egypt. As trade links became difficult, and the supply of papyrus ever more expensive and unreliable, the use of parchment became widespread. Parchment had been used for writing from as early as the second century BC if not before. It takes its name from the Asiatic city of Pergamum, where King Eumenes II (197-159 BC) used it for the books in his great library. Parchment is formed from the skins of animals, particularly those of young calves, goats and sheep. The skin is removed from the slaughtered beast, dried and put through a variety of processes in order to smooth and whiten its surface. Unlike papyrus, parchment can be produced wherever cattle are raised. That said, it was expensive and its production laborious, though it was found to be much more durable than papyrus. Parchment thus became the medieval material of choice for forms of writing which were intended to last, and for single documents as well as entire books. Papyrus, by contrast, continued to be used only in a few regions of Italy, where it could be obtained from Sicily; at Rome, for instance, papal documents were written on papyrus until the first half of the eleventh century.

Parchment also successfully withstood the spread of paper, which was introduced to the West from the eleventh century. At times, paper was employed as writing material for documents, as it was in Sicily in the twelfth century, but it was long considered too perishable for the purposes of documentation.

Script is another characteristic element of public *acta*. Few will need reminding that documents, like every other kind of written text, were executed by hand in the Middle Ages, and that the appearance of handwriting may differ according to the occasion and the kind of document in question. The same situation obtained well into the twentieth century, prior to the widespread use of the typewriter and, later, the word-processor. The scripts used for medieval public documents were not only executed with particular care and elegance, and carefully arranged within an armature of ruled lines and margins – often they took on forms different to those of scripts in everyday use, with the intention of conferring upon such documents a studied, solemn appearance.

The public act was usually completed with the addition of graphic symbols in the form of signs and seals. These were intended to validate and authenticate the document, and to underscore its authority and dignity. Among the most common marks of this kind is the monogram, a symbol formed from the letters that make up the name of the issuing authority, which are interwoven (or elided) in the form of a cipher. In late antiquity, the monogram was used by private persons to identify precious objects and personal possessions; subsequently, it was adopted by the Merovingian kings for authenticating royal acts, and it remained in use throughout the Middle Ages. Another symbol of this kind is the *rota*, which appears in papal documents from the year 1049. The *rota* consists of two concentric circles enclosing a cross, the arms of which divide four fields in which the names of St Peter and St Paul and the present pope were written. Chancellors and archchancellors often completed their own signatures with complex graphic devices, which also had value in authenticating documents. Essential in completing the acts of public authorities was the seal. Medieval seals might be made from wax or from metal, usually lead – and, in some rare cases, gold. Seals were applied either directly to the surface of the parchment, or as attachments hanging from cords of hemp or silk. The choice of each of these variable characteristics was determined by the standing of the issuing authority and the nature of the document. Medieval seals present an enormous variety of images. They usually depict the issuing authority in official guise, and with its proper insignia. Hence, when they appear on seals, images of figures were carefully contrived and stylized, and every detail given some symbolic significance, in order to convey the quality, the rank and the claims to power of the authority depicted.

These are the principal external or extrinsic characteristics of the medieval public document. Similarly, the document's very text was drafted and formally written out according to norms aimed at conferring authenticity and solemnity upon an act. Therefore, let us now consider the principal 'intrinsic' or internal characteristics of the public document's form. Once again, the focus here is on the most typical imperial and royal diplomata.

Invocatio

Public acts open by invoking the name of God, in which the deliberations and the document itself were made. Normally the invocation is composed of two parts: symbolic invocation, in the form of a cross or the more elaborate *chrismon*, a symbol produced by combining the Greek letters *chi* (X) and *rho* (P), the first two letters of the name of Christ (or *chi-rho*); followed by a verbal invocation of Christ or the Trinity, a formula introduced in royal diplomas under Charlemagne.

Intitulatio

The public act continues with an identification of name and titles of the authority responsible for the document. These formulae are important not just as means of identifying the author of a given document, but also as sources for the history of medieval juridical and political ideas. The *intitulatio* may be regarded as a sort of verbal self-portrait – an official statement of the author's self-image, standing and traditions. Much careful consideration was taken over titles in the Middle Ages, from the barbarian epoch onwards. In the Carolingian era, the devotional formula 'by the grace of God' or 'by the will of God' was added to the royal title; this practice remained in use to the end of the Middle Ages. This not only expresses the king's devotion, but above all it attributes divine origin to his power; hence it was often used as a claim to autonomy. Subordinate authorities could not pretend to have received their powers from God, as such powers depended from the king or a high-ranking prince. For one to claim power by the grace of God, as often happened in the period's more fluid political situations, was to claim autonomy from the constituted authorities.

Inscriptio

There follows an identification of the *destinatarius*, or addressee, be that a person or some other entity, and the addressee's name, titles and official qualifications. This part of the document may be of the same level of interest as the *intitulatio*, offering as it does a view of the juridical and ideological quality of the addressee and that party's relationship with the document's author. In this last respect, much use was made of kinship terms when defining the relations between authorities; for instance, it is common to find authorities referring to others of the same status as 'brothers', and to lesser ones as 'sons'. This stylization occurs with particular frequency in ecclesiastical documents, but was also used by the Byzantine emperors, in imitation of whom it was adopted by western emperors. In certain cases, the addressee might be impersonal or collective in nature (as in 'to all the faithful in Christ' for instance, or 'to all the dukes and counts' of the empire), when the act contained dispositions of general bearing.

Salutatio

An expression of greeting, benevolence or respect completes the opening part of the document, often concluding with such formulae as '*in perpetuum*' (perpetually), '*feliciter*' (happily), or, simply, '*amen*'.

The combination of clauses described above constitutes the *protocol* of a public document, or the opening section in which the principal parties involved in an act are presented. The invocation and *intitulatio*, which normally occupy the opening line of a document, were often written using taller and more stylized letter forms than those used for the remainder of the text, in order to confer visual solemnity upon the document as a proclamation of authority.

Following the *protocol*, the second part of the public document is the *corpus* or *contextus*, in which the juridical substance of the act is set out. The *corpus*, too, was divided into distinct parts, which together made up an ordered treatment of circumstances in question.

The *corpus* opens with an *arenga*, or preamble, consisting of a statement of religious, moral or juridical nature, emphasizing the opportuneness, the significance, and the characteristic merits of the act. Though invariably made up from a limited stock of established formulae, the preamble is nevertheless of considerable interest for what it reveals of the theory of sovereignty, and the functions and quality of power. The *arenga* normally refers to the sovereign's beneficent sentiments and virtues, often with allusions to classical or Biblical precedent.

This is followed by a *promulgatio* or *notificatio*, a statement of notification (along the lines of the expression 'let it be known'), which introduces the *narratio*. The *narratio* gives the background and circumstances that caused the author to make an act of juridical nature. Typically, reference is made to requests previously submitted by the *destinatarius*, the intervention of influential persons on that party's behalf, and the properties and rights at issue. Hence the *narratio* gives the substance of an act, and is essential in understanding the interests of the *destinatarii*, and their relationships with the authors of documents and those persons surrounding them. Thereafter, the juridical decision is revealed in the following part of the act, the *dispositio*, which, in many cases, opens with a deliberative statement (such as 'we order', 'we bestow', 'we concede' etc) setting out the nature of the act, and often repeating the description of properties and rights made in the *narratio*. The *dispositio* is followed then by a series of *clausulae* specifying the juridical conditions attached to the enjoyment of rights or properties under the act.

The *corpus* concludes with a *sanctio*, a formula sanctioning and reinforcing the dispensation, and threatening transgressors or violators with divine or worldly retribution. (Royal diplomas often stipulate the value [in coin or precious metal] of fines to be paid to the royal treasury and the injured party.) This is followed by a *corroboratio* which consists of various means adopted to guarantee the authenticity of the act, usually involving a seal and the validation of the king or other authority. Hence, the public document closes with a series of formulae and signs, confirming its authenticity, and the date. This final part of the document is called *eschatocol* or final protocol. It consists of the signature of the issuing authority, sometimes given in full but more often in the form of a monogram, in which the author inserted a line in his own hand confirming the act. In practice, as chanceries became ever more complex organizations, the *subscriptio* was added by an official charged with this particular responsibility. Finally, the document is verified by a senior chancery official or his representative, and certified free of irregularity through the *recognitio*.

Public acts were usually dated with reference to the year of the reign of the pre-eminent authority (as in the first, second or third year of the reign), taken from the first day of the ruler's accession to power (by coronation, consecration, or, in rare cases, by election). Other indications might be given in the interests of precision. It is important to remember that the custom of referring to the years of the Christian era was by no means widespread, and therefore a certain expertise is required in converting the dates of medieval documents to modern chronologies. Computing dates from medieval documents is a specialist discipline within the orbit of the science of Diplomatics, one known as *chronology*.

Only rarely were public acts signed by witnesses. The virtue of public authority was its own guarantee; thus, public authorities had no need of the testimony of private persons in imparting credibility to their acts.

All the same, the presence and signatures of witnesses might be brought to bear on the writing of acts by major authorities, in order to confer particular solemnity on their documents – as when cardinals were summoned to sign papal *bullae*, for instance. Of a rather different order are the signatures sometimes found in documents produced for subordinate authorities or persons whose institutional condition was not totally clear; and, moreover, in situations of particular weakness or mutability of political power, as in the case of the kings of France, who, in the tenth and eleventh centuries, had their acts underwritten by vassals.

Public documents are essential sources for the history of power and the powerful in the medieval period. It could be said that, through these sources, one witnesses the daily exercise of government and the mundane business underlying the plot of political events which comes to us from the narrative sources. In particular, public acts reveal the relations of kings and lords with the institutions of the Church and other powerful persons under their dominion, as such subordinates were most commonly the addressees of acts of this kind. The same sources offer much insight into the organization and make-up of the court – not only the chancery – through references to the high-ranking figures who often interceded on behalf of petitioners. Details of governing institutions may be gleaned from the titles of rank and function attributed to persons mentioned in acts of this kind. Further information is provided by the dating formulae, which normally also give the place where a document was redacted; thus, details emerge regarding the locations of royal palaces and the movements of sovereigns, from which it may be possible to verify and enlarge the information available from narrative sources. And from this evidence, too, a picture emerges of the organization of the royal dominions, the existence of public palaces, and the routes followed by the court and its retinue in their displacements – and even the preferred resting places.

Both in their exterior and interior forms, public acts are witnesses to the medieval conception of power in both institutional and juridical terms, to say nothing of its ideological aspects. Chanceries were not simply administrative offices – they were also cultural centres of high profile, where theories of sovereignty were elaborated and subsequently given official sanction. Archchancellors and chancellors were often outstanding personalities in their day, not only in the juridical field of their speciality, but also in the sphere of literature. Such was Pier delle Vigne, protonotary and archchancellor to Frederick II in the kingdom of Sicily. Delle Vigne was the king's principal propaganda architect, an active player in the cultural life of the court, and the author of vernacular poetry. Hence, the study of the medieval chancery is not concerned exclusively with bureaucratic organization: it extends to the intellectual and political lives and personalities of chancery functionaries; and thus represents a key element of the history of medieval culture generally.

The private act

It has already been said that the private act is the written registration of the will of one or more actors engaged in exercising rights or establishing agreements relating to issues in the sphere of private law. In order to understand precisely what type of rights are implied here, let us consider the ownership of land, say, or a farm – property that may be sold, acquired, donated, ceded or inherited under a variety of conditions, and passed on as inheritance. All such transactions occasion the production and use of documents, in the past as in the present. From a juridical perspective, a fundamental problem arises when dealing with private acts, in determining the function of private documents in relation to the transactions they describe. It is important to distinguish whether the act was a simple record of a negotiation, or was considered to exert the power of proof, as the basis and witness in itself of the rights to which it refers.

In the latter instance, the private act assumes public validity; that is, it requires that members of a society recognize the rights stated by the document and that the constituted authority defend them. It could be said that the history of private documentation in the Middle Ages is characterized precisely by the development of the social function and the juridical nature of the written act.

The practice of keeping written records of juridical negotiations between private persons was established already in the age of imperial Rome. Under the empire, documents of this kind were acquired from private notaries (*notarii*) or scribes in public service (*tabelliones*) in return for payment. Documents originating in this way had no legal value in case of dispute. Instead, proof that a negotiation had taken place was guaranteed by witnesses present at the contract, and only their word had judiciary merit.

Under Constantine, in the fourth century, documentary practice was reformed, and procedures were adopted to guarantee the authenticity of private records, and to confer upon them the value of proof. The central, provincial and municipal organs (the *curie*) of public administration were instructed to receive acts stipulated between private persons, in order to preserve them and, if necessary, produce authentic copies that were held to be publicly valid. The depositing of private acts in public offices in this way was called *insinuatio*; it was a costly procedure, and was not always strictly followed, but it had certain advantages and was mentioned in the acts themselves as these were drafted.

Insinuatio was abandoned with the crisis of Roman institutions in the wake of the barbarian invasions; we have seen that the barbarians had their own systems for making individual rights known through local assemblies and social memory. Yet even under barbarian dominion Roman society held on to its documentary practices as much as possible.

Use of the written act thus continued, albeit with far less frequency than in the past. Scribes, *notarii* and *tabelliones* continued to operate in the Roman territories dominated by the barbarians; and the barbarians for their part progressively adopted the practice of written documentation, even in the orbit of private jurisdiction. So the new political formations had to face the problem of the validity of private acts.

The attempts that were made to tackle and resolve the problem may be described in relation to the situation in Italy, which is not only particularly clear and well-documented, but which also presents a development that was to give rise to solutions later adopted in many other European countries.

During the sixth century, the Italian peninsula was effectively divided into two broad cultural spheres by the effects of the Lombard invasion. In coastal centres in the south and east, Roman systems were maintained by the imperial Byzantine administration. Elsewhere, and particularly in the north and down through the peninsula's mountainous interior, by contrast, the invasions resulted in the formation of a mixed Italo-Lombard society with its own organizational and institutional forms.

In the Byzantine territories centred on the cities of Ravenna, Rome and Naples, the public scribe continued to practise, even retaining the office's old Roman title – *tabellionatus*. The *tabelliones* were organized into professional associations or colleges, which provided technical training while seeking to guarantee the validity of acts drawn up by their members. Thus, the procedure of *insinuatio* was kept up, or at least some memory of it survived, at Ravenna into the tenth century; while at Naples the college of public scribes, known locally as the *curiales*, maintained an archive containing the minutes of their acts from which copies could be taken. At Rome and Naples, the scribes used a particular form of script in the writing of acts, one different from scripts in everyday use. In time, this script became increasingly elaborate and affected, almost as if it were a guarantee of authenticity in itself. Similarly, in the tenth and eleventh centuries, the Neapolitan script known as *curialesca* became practically incomprehensible for anyone outside the ranks of the *curiales*.

In the territories conquered by the Lombards, the professional colleges followed the municipal courts (*curiae*) into decline. Private records continued to be produced, however, by scribes working independently, unsupported and uncontrolled by any professional organization. Access to the profession was through individual apprenticeship, with no fixed curriculum. These scribes no longer went by recognizable professional titles. Lombard writers are mostly referred to by the terms *scriptor*, *scriba* and even *notarius*; the latter term referred simply to the writer of documents, though it was also employed to indicate writers in the service of the king (*notarius domini regis*, *notarius regiae potestatis*) or other public authorities such as dukes.

In early-medieval Italy, the production of private documents (known as *chartae* or *chartulae*) was a simple business. The scribe registered the will of the interested parties directly, in the form of oral discourse ('I, so-and-so, give/lend/sell etc.'). The text was worked up from notes or minutes using traditional formulae possibly taken from manuals. Once the text had been written out, it was delivered to the interested parties, and no copy kept by the scribe. Obviously, under these circumstances, the written record was vulnerable to loss, theft, damage and forgery. And of course the scribes themselves might easily produce false or unlawful documents. The Lombard kings went to some lengths to restrict such abuses, setting strict punishments for forgers.

On occasion, attempts were made to overcome the limitations inherent in this kind of documentary practice. From the ninth century, the contracting parties to a private transaction applied to a judicial court where a simulated dispute was conducted, the outcome of which always corresponded with the agreement previously made between the two parties. The written record of the debate was signed by a judge, and was thus considered to be a much stronger guarantee than the notarial act. This toilsome procedure was later done away with in favour of another whereby simple declarations were made by both parties before a judge and registered in a written act of the court. Among the Lombards of the Duchy of Benevento in the ninth century, the judge intervened directly in signing and thereby authorizing records of private transactions.

In Lombard Italy, the principle underlying these practices reveals that private acts were not publicly valid, even when written in the presence of witnesses. Public validity was conferred only by recognition before a judicial authority. This principle was consolidated and perfected by the Carolingian rulers of Italy, under whom scribes were subject to greater control on the part of public authority, which saw to professional training and subjected scribal activity to appointment by counts or kings. The title of notary, often accompanied by specifications that referred to the public context of the office (such as 'notary to the sacred palace', or 'king's notary') thus became more frequent. At the same time, it was established that notaries were not to engage in the *rogatio* of acts (*rogatio* being a technical term which refers to the redaction of a written document) outside the administrative district, usually the county, in which they resided. The counts had their own notaries, to write up acts of administration, and particularly the proceedings of courts (or *placita*). Notwithstanding these checks, however – and despite the considerable improvement in the juridical status of such documents – private deeds still required formal validation if they were to assume validity as public documents.

The Church saw to its own needs where documents were concerned, whether it was in Roman or Lombard territory. The archiepiscopal *curiae* of Rome and Ravenna were staffed with ecclesiastical scribes who took the title of *notarii* (and at Rome, *scriniarii*), and were organized in offices under the leadership of a *primicerius*. Elsewhere, in Lombard and Carolingian Italy, the episcopal churches maintained their own notaries, men most commonly drawn from the ranks of the clergy. Episcopal notaries were occasionally called upon to provide documents to private persons.

Ecclesiastical notaries had no need of royal nomination, even in the Carolingian era. Their documents were not by themselves of any greater authority than those of lay notaries; where necessary they had to be ratified by the king or by a judge. For the sake of convenience, kings ratified long lists of acts put forward by church officials. However, the religious statute and the moral and social prestige of the Church gave particular credit to acts stipulated by ecclesiastical notaries.

Hence, a number of rather different solutions to the problem of the public validity of private acts was developed in the diverse cultural and institutional contexts of early-medieval Italy, based on the authority of the professional college and the Church, and alternatively on the confirmation of the authority of state.

Out of this complex and frequently confusing situation, a number of new criteria for authenticating and validating private acts were established under particular conditions in the tenth and eleventh centuries. The most important developments took place in the cities of the Lombard-Carolingian kingdom, where public institutions continued to function effectively, despite the crisis of royal authority witnessed at the end of the ninth century. In this context, notaries made powerful claims to competence as experts in law, regularly taking the title of royal notaries, a title that referred to the public origin of their functions. They also frequently took on the functions of judges, the office traditionally recognized as having the capacity to confer public validity on private acts. As a judge, the Italian notary found himself in the position of being able to validate acts he had written up himself.

The notarial act took another step towards becoming indubitably probative as notaries began to keep copies of their acts. The earliest-known instance of this practice is the register or *protocollo* of the Genoese notary Giovanni Scriba, dated 1154. Presumably the practice had been established already a decade or two before the date of Giovanni's register. Once notaries began to transcribe their acts into registers, it became possible to compare documents held by private persons with copies preserved by the notary which counted as proof. As a consequence, the private act took on the force of proof without the need for complex juridical procedures. Alongside these practical innovations, theoretical reflection on the nature of the authenticity of juridical acts served to strengthen the tendency to regard notarial acts as publicly valid – a development driven by the rediscovery of Roman law in the twelfth century. Consequently, in the course of the twelfth century, the notary who had been properly trained and authorized by public powers – and who produced acts to established forms, maintaining a register of these in his studio – finally came to possess a quality meriting *fides publica*. In other words, he had the capacity to create authentic, valid acts as legal proof – acts on a par with those issuing from the chanceries of public and ecclesiastical authorities. Thus, the notarial act assumed the quality of *instrumentum publicum*.

This transformation provided the basis of the functions that notaries continue to perform in drafting records of negotiations between private persons to this day. It was undoubtedly influenced by developments in economic and social relations, which set a premium on the rapid and effective registration of business and property transactions, which were becoming increasingly complex and frequent in comparison with the preceding period, when the entire economy had revolved around the possession of land.

Having taken up his new jurisdiction, the notary replaced all other figures previously engaged with private documentation. With their archaic procedures, the corporations of the *tabelliones* lost profile and prestige. Gradually even the Church gave up its own notaries. There was change, too, in the practice of notarial documentation. Now the essential pieces of information relating to a transaction (the place, date, identity of the parties and the terms of the transaction) were written directly into the notarial registers. No longer were the parties' statements written out as they had been in the early Middle Ages; instead, the notary set down the terms of the transaction in an objective manner, according to the terms of law. The act written in such synthetic form is known as *imbreviatura*. Subsequently, and at the request of the interested parties, more extensive and detailed redactions could be written out from information given in the *imbreviatura*, in more or less complete form, according to need and available funds. A first level of such elaboration is represented by the document written out *in grossum* (or *instrumentum ingrossatum*), in which the fundamentals of a case are given in the most straightforward terms, without fixed and repetitive *clausulae*, which are given in abbreviated form or as *etceteratae*. The complete redaction of the text is called redaction *in mundum*. A document of the latter kind acquired the quality of *publica forma*, a quality recognizable from the solemnity of the document's formal presentation, the use of parchment, clear and ordered scripts, and the notary's signature complete with particular signs of authentication. However, the proof of such an act was always guaranteed by the *imbreviatura*, which was kept in the notary's studio and handed down to his successors.

Nonetheless, the system did not do away with every occasion for fraud. There was nothing to stop a dishonest notary from altering the *imbreviatura* or from interpreting the content of these records in misleading ways. In order to restrict such abuses, the urban communes of Italy instituted official public registers during the thirteenth and fourteenth centuries, known as *libri memoriales*. They were filled with transcripts of contracts already registered in notarial protocols. In addition, notarial archives were established to preserve the registers of *imbreviaturae* of retiring notaries for future use.

With this extension in the functions of Italian notaries came further developments in their professional organization. Associations of notaries were influential corporations in the communal cities. At Bologna, where the notarial profession was most advanced, there is evidence for an association of notaries from as early as the beginning of the thirteenth century. One of the main purposes of the corporations was to see to the training of future generations of notaries. This they did by offering a course of professional instruction followed by practical apprenticeship in the studio of an established notary, himself a member of the association. Students were schooled in grammar and rhetoric, following the *artes* or *summae dictaminis*, books of *dictamen* which had been composed ever since the twelfth century; and they were given juridical instruction based on the principles of Roman law. The manuals of formulae used for styling acts were furnished with juridical commentaries. The first treatise of this kind, the *Formularium tabellionum*, appeared in Bologna some time between 1200 and 1205.

With the development of the *ars notariae*, the notary's office was distinguished from other juridical professions, by laying claim to a theoretical basis, and boasting an autonomous professional identity equal to that of the other professions. In this context, the *Ars notariae* (1226-33) by Ranieri of Perugia was the first treatise to attempt to tackle and resolve the problems experienced in professional practice. Slightly later, in the middle of the thirteenth century, Salatiele and Rolandino de' Passaggeri, two prominent members of the corporation of notaries of Bologna, produced theories that were to establish the *ars notariae* as a sector of civil law. Rolandino's treatise, *Summa totius artis notariae*, was known throughout Europe, becoming the key text for the notarial profession.

Outside Italy, the notarial profession emerged with rather different patterns and timing in different countries. In southern France, where juridical traditions and social developments were similar to those of northern Italy, the notary had emerged already in the course of the twelfth century, in a similar way to his Italian counterpart, able to produce authentic acts. In Spain, the influence of Roman law saw to the emergence of notaries public and acts of legal value in the thirteenth century. Elsewhere, progress was somewhat slower. In Germany, the notary public was established in the first half of the thirteenth century, but for a long time to come his documents were not attributed legal value. In medieval Germany, the notary merited *fides publica* only with the granting of a licence from the emperor or the pope.

In northern France a variety of methods were used to safeguard the accuracy and authenticity of private *acta*, such as the declaration of interested parties before a court; on other occasions, documents were deposited in safe places, or submitted for approval to communal, seigneurial or ecclesiastical authorities; or given over into the hands of the king's bailiffs to receive the seal. The dominant principle dictated that notarial acts had to be authenticated with the seal of a jurisdictional authority in order to have public validity. Only at the end of the medieval period, under the influence of Roman law, and with increasing monarchical centralization, were these old methods replaced by notaries in royal appointment with powers to produce valid acts.

This transformation in the production of private *acta* determined an equally significant change in the nature and composition of the documentation available to modern scholars.

Of the kind of private document made in single copy and kept only by private individuals, only comparatively rare examples survive in cases where private archives have survived. In this instance, in almost all cases we are dealing with ecclesiastical institutions, which were unique in having enjoyed the kind of longevity and stability necessary for the preservation of archives from periods as remote as the early Middle Ages.

By contrast, early-medieval secular archives are practically unknown, though we know that they once existed. Lay documents seldom enjoyed the same security as those preserved in Church archives, and in many cases were lost or dispersed, unless they found their way into church archives. The appearance of private secular archives in Italy coincides with the origins of the great noble families in the thirteenth century. Many of these collections continued to be maintained by successive generations into the modern era.

The circumstances behind the preservation and transmission of documents have important implications for the student of early-medieval history. In particular, all the evidence presented by private acts is glimpsed from the point of view of ecclesiastical institutions. Moreover, the fact that the greater part of the surviving documentation relates to land-ownership can be accounted for by the predominantly agrarian nature of early-medieval economics.

With the appearance of notarial registers, the nature of the documentary evidence changes in a significant way. Although notaries continued to compose extensive and formal acts on parchment (a practice that continued, increasingly sporadically, into the seventeenth century), the notarial register was to become by far the most rich and engaging source, presenting as it does a much wider and multifarious view of the economic and social life of the period than it is possible to glean from individual archives. Almost all classes of late-medieval Italian society had recourse to notaries; all kinds of people went to notaries for records of negotiations and transactions of all kinds. As well as for the sale or exchange of property, records were made of commercial agreements, loans of money, leases of houses and workshops, and as declarations of marriage agreements and the wills of the dead. Documents were made registering the emancipation of male heirs, and in recognition of undertakings of the most diverse kinds. In one case, a written statement was made confirming the purchase of a sack of chestnuts! Each day, the notaries opened their doors and their registers to all comers. Notarial registers thus supply extraordinary details of medieval social life in all its aspects.

The formal characteristics of medieval private *acta* are, in general, those of the public acts, if in rather simplified form and with some variations. There follows a brief description of the most complete and elaborate form that private acts may take.

In terms of external or extrinsic form, it will be remembered that the private act was normally written on a sheet of parchment; the use of papyrus was abandoned after the seventh century, due to problems of supply. Only at Ravenna and at certain other centres in Byzantine Italy did the use of papyrus continue into the ninth century. Paper was not used for notarial documents prior to the modern era; even the registers of *imbreviaturae* were made up of parchment folios. Notaries used a clear and legible script for texts written out *in mundum*, in order to lend the document prestige and credibility. Finally, medieval notaries executed their own distinctive and intricate graphic devices or signs alongside their signatures; these signs served to underline the authenticity of the document. Only on rare occasions were seals used for private documents.

As for the text, this was arranged in much the same way as that of public acts, though in rather simplified form. The opening *protocol* of a private document most commonly begins with devotional or invocatory formulae preceded by the *chrismon* or the sign of the cross. The date is sometimes given at the opening of the text, otherwise it is kept to the end. Only on rare occasions is the author's name given at the beginning of a document, as it is in the *intitulatio* of public acts; more often, it is given in the *corpus* part of the text, in the *narratio*. The *corpus* itself may begin with a preamble, which, in a more simplified form of the *arenga* of public documents, sets out the moral or religious motivation which caused the author to make a juridical act (this is particularly commonplace in documents granting dispensations to religious institutions). This is followed by a formula of notification ('let it be known'), which introduces the *narratio*, the narrative exposition of circumstances causing the juridical act (such as a request from one of the interested parties, reciprocal agreement, or the deliberation of the author), with a description of the act itself and the property or rights in question. This is followed in turn by the *dispositio*, which opens with a dispositive statement in which the will of the author is described (for example, 'I sell', 'I give', or 'I concede'), followed by a further description of the properties or possessions subject to the transaction, with the terms of the transaction, and *clausulae* imposing the limits and conditions on its enjoyment. These formulae may be followed by others imposing sanctions for violators of the act, be they the contractors themselves or third parties; as in the case of public acts, punishments of spiritual or material kind are set. The text concludes with a variety of forms intended to guarantee the authenticity of the manuscript, or *corroboratio*, and consisting above all in the presence and signatures of witnesses, and in an instruction to the notary to write up the act (*rogatio*).

The *eschatocol* includes the signatures of witnesses and, on certain occasions, those of the parties themselves; the date, in cases where this is not included in the *protocol*; and the signature of the notary, which validates the completed document.

Notarial documents are a source of information regarding scribal practices and the cultural context in which such documents were made. Moreover, they offer a vast quantity of precious information on a wide range of aspects and phenomena relating to medieval society. First of all, this information concerns juridical negotiations, laws in contemporary use, legal regulations and their application. But it also relates to more general aspects, such as:

- the origin, make-up, range and use of land holdings by individuals and institutions;
- the exploitation of the land, agrarian cultures and tenancy agreements;
- the characteristics of habitat and settlement structures, which are frequently described in their various parts, their nomenclature and distinctive elements, often even with dimensions;
- place names or toponyms, which can reveal aspects of the stratifications of settlement and the nature and use of land, as well as of the culture of local society (including religious cults, for example);
- the institutional organization of territories – acts frequently refer to the political or ecclesiastical districts in which persons or places referred to in the text were to be found;
- the make-up of the population – private documents often refer to the professional role, the origin and nationality, and the juridical status of individuals involved in negotiations;
- proper names: the names of people, with all their cultural significance; nicknames, which were usually determined by a person's personal demeanour or socio-economic condition; and surnames;
- family structures: genealogy, inheritance, and the political strategies of inter-marriage; and the economic and juridical relations between husband and wife and between parents and children;
- biographical information regarding the life, the inheritance, the place of residence and the social context of individual persons when they occur in the documents;
- means of payment and monetary systems – these are often mentioned in private acts, as a measure of the value of goods or properties, or in recording payments received or due in connection with a particular transaction;

- and, finally, this type of source can be used to reveal the relative levels of literacy among the parties engaged in negotiations; literacy can be assessed on the basis of the individuals' ability to underwrite the document in their own hand.

Private documents may also be read for what they reveal of political history. For a long time it was customary to date private acts according to the years of the reign of lords in whose dominion the act was produced. From these indications we can reveal the political orientation of different regions and localities. Information of this kind is of particular interest to historians when dealing with marginal and frontier communities, or recently conquered or disputed territories.

Even in such a summary account as this, the potential of private documents as sources for historical research should become clear. In concluding this discussion, it is important to bear in mind that the kinds of information referred to here take on consistency and significance only when they are found in a considerable number of documents. In other words, a single reference should not be read as evidence of a general situation. When working with archive documents, the historian will look for quantitatively verifiable bodies or stocks of information, which can be used to verify the frequency, the incidence and the variation in time and space of the phenomena witnessed by the juridical documentation.

Coins

Coins as historical evidence

Of the many types of material evidence available to students of the Middle Ages, one of the most fascinating is provided by coins. This is due both to the rarity and preciousness of these objects, and the images and inscriptions emblazoned upon them. Enthusiasm for coins is not a recent development. In the West, collectors have sought after coins at least since the Renaissance; earlier still, Petrarch is known to have had a coin collection. At first, collectors were predominantly attracted by Greek and Roman coins, which, with their images, portraits and other symbols, represented an authentic illustration of ancient history, and thus appealed to the exponents of the classical culture dominant in courtly and scholarly circles in Europe from the fifteenth century. From the end of the seventeenth century, the revival in antiquarian and philological culture prompted a systematic approach to the study of ancient coins. Experts sought to identify, classify and compare pieces from collections, and to disseminate this knowledge through the publication of catalogues and learned papers. In this way, scholars developed the ability to verify the authenticity of pieces, since the art of counterfeiting grew steadily in pace with the passion for collecting. During the eighteenth and nineteenth centuries the study of coins became a specialized discipline – *numismatics* – while the interest of numismatists extended to medieval and modern coinage. All the same, antiquarian interests remained dominant, and for some time to come the numismatist's principal motive was to compile ever more accurate and complete catalogues of the major private and public collections, systematically piecing together the coinages of the various ancient and modern states.

Just as coins are a fundamental tool of economic life, so numismatists progressively recognized the possibility of using their material as a means to investigating and better understanding the economic aspects of life in the past. Particularly during the twentieth century, significant advances were made in establishing links between numismatics and economic history; and while the discipline's antiquarian heritage has proved tenaciously resilient to change, the most interesting contemporary research is in the area of monetary history, which is considered an element of economic history. From this perspective, the usefulness of numismatic evidence for historians should be obvious. As far as medieval history is concerned, numismatics and monetary history can make a significant contribution to our understanding of the period's complex and unusual economic culture. It is the aim of this chapter to present a brief summary of the contemporary state of our knowledge of medieval monetary history, in order to illustrate the potential of this area of study.

Firstly, however, it is important to establish a number of key principles regarding the nature of this category of evidence, and the methods used in interpreting its historical significance. The first thing to bear in mind is that this type of source requires specialized analysis, which is not limited to the straightforward identification and classification of individual coins, indispensable though these operations may be. Rather, the numismatist's work extends to the analysis of complex sets of coin data, while taking into account written records and archaeological research.

In the first place, the historical value of coins resides in their material characteristics. Coins are metal objects of predetermined weight and shape. As means of exchange, they have legally determined value, which is guaranteed by the official markings they carry. Therefore, each coin is characterized by the images and text impressed on its two sides (obverse and reverse); by its weight; and by the type of metal from which it is made. From analysis of these characteristics, it is usually possible to place a given coin within a chronological and/or political context, and to determine its value as a means of exchange. In the western tradition, from the first appearance of objects of this kind – probably in the Greek cities of Asia Minor, and in the kingdom of Lydia with its mythical king, Croesus, in the seventh century BC – the production of coinage has always been associated with sovereignty or the exercise of politico-institutional power. Public authorities had their names and titles impressed upon the surfaces of coins, thereby imparting legal value to the objects. Coins thus supply the names and often even the portraits of emperors and kings, as well as such emblems of power as the crown, the official insignia and standards, and other symbols referring to the governing regime or to the official religion.

On the basis of these data it is usually possible to relate individual coins to political or institutional contexts, and to give them more or less precise dates. It is rare that ancient or medieval coins will be found bearing the date of issue, unlike modern coins.

As well as acting as a guarantee of value, the image of the issuing authority was intended to make known the identity and the physiognomy of the sovereign to his subjects and others who might encounter his coinage. To some degree, coins were vehicles for propaganda in periods when media of mass communication were unfamiliar. As such, they could be used to display and disseminate particular aspects of official political culture.

The other principal diagnostic characteristics of coin are its metallic composition and weight, both of which determine a coin's value as a means for exchange. It goes without saying that metal coinage, unlike paper money, has an intrinsic value determined by the quantity and the type of metal involved. In the case of coins struck from precious metals (gold and silver), this value may be fairly high. What is more, state authorities have the power to issue coins that are more valuable than the quantity of metal in them; this they do by fixing rates of exchange against other coins and pure metal. However, in most ancient and medieval economies, metal and weight were the essential elements that determined the exchange value of coin in respect of goods or coins of other kind; consequently, metal and weight together determined the market value of coin and its capacity to operate as an adequate means of exchange. Therefore, the metal and weight of coin are the principal concerns of modern scholars in attributing intrinsic value to single coins and distinguishing the denominational values of coin types such as the denier, gross or florin. Thus, it is possible to define the relationship between the denominations, and to interpret the monetary polices of past regimes, which are frequently reflected in the rise and fall of the metal value of coins.

In antiquity and the Middle Ages, the metals most commonly used for coinage were gold, silver and bronze (or copper). It was rare for precious metals to be used in their pure state; rather, they were alloyed with variable quantities of less valuable metals, both in order to give durability to coins and for reasons of economy. In this way, not only bronze (copper and tin) coins but those of gold and silver are, in effect, alloys of one sort or another (gold and copper, gold and silver, silver and copper). The quantity of precious metal used was normally fixed by law, as, in theory, each and every coin of a given denomination was to contain exactly the same weight of precious metal. In practice, the weight of precious metal might vary for any number of more or less acceptable (and legal) reasons. Therefore, in order to identify the intrinsic value of a coin, it is necessary to analyze the composition of the metal alloy from which it was made.

Medieval people were probably able to satisfy themselves of the quality of their coin from their experience of handling and seeing sound coin. Modern collectors and coin specialists once engaged similar empirical methods, before sensitive scales and other instruments replaced the experienced eye and feeling hand. It is possible to calculate the quantity of precious metal in a coin by comparing its weight with that of the same volume of pure metal. Far more reliable results can be achieved by chemical analysis. The techniques of laboratory analysis are now sufficiently sensitive to reveal the presence of substances in the tiniest quantities, and so to provide information concerning the provenance of metals and the techniques employed in their working. Despite its enormous potential, this kind of analysis comes at a cost, for it causes irreversible (if limited) damage to sample coins. This being so, archaeological scientists now prefer to use less destructive techniques, which involve provoking the emission of X- or gamma-rays from coins by bombarding them with emissions from subatomic particles (neutrons and protons). As different metals give off different rays, scientists are able to extrapolate the composition of metal alloys from the spectrum of radiation produced. The results of this work are more or less precise, depending on the techniques used.

The weight of coins was also fixed in law by issuing authorities. A given quantity (or weight) of metal would be expected to produce a given number of coins of equal weight and value. In the Roman empire and the early Middle Ages, the unit of weight for the metal was the *libra* (pound), which was equivalent to 327.45g in the Roman period, or approximately 409g following the Carolingian reform. From the eleventh century, the *mark* was more commonly used; the Troyes mark, one of the most widely used in the Middle Ages, weighed 244.75g. Given that coins were made by hand, however, in practice there were frequent discrepancies between the weight of precious metal required by the authorities for each coin and that achieved by the moneyers. Following one of the most widespread techniques, coins were made by cutting discs from thin sheets of metal, and placing them between paired metal dies made from iron or steel; previously, the striking surfaces of dies had been cast or incised with the negative impression of the design to be impressed upon both sides (obverse and reverse) of the coin. One by one the metal rounds were placed between the dies and the upper die hammered down – and the coin struck. As a result of this process, each coin is slightly different from the next in appearance and weight, though such small variations had to be tolerated as an unavoidable condition of the moneyer's craft.

Variation in the weight of coin could be caused by a number of other factors. The moneyers themselves (false moneyers) could make short weight coins, illicitly removing the surplus as profit. Still further alteration in the weight of coins might occur as a result of their handling and use. Once in circulation, coins are subject to wear, as a result of which their weight is reduced. Coins struck from precious metals might be subjected to illegal clipping, 'shearing' or 'sweating', through which processes small quantities of metal may be extracted from coins without altering their face value. Periodically, public authorities were concerned to standardize the value of coin in currency. To this end, coins were recalled to the mints, melted down, and recast into reformed coinage of legally determined value. On many occasions, the fineness of coin was altered by the mints under instructions from the issuing authorities, and in line with monetary policy. Official intervention was determined by the very fact that the production of coined money depends on the limited availability of metal, particularly precious metal. This is true of any period in history, not least the Middle Ages, when reliable supplies of metal were difficult to come by – a circumstance that affected both the quality and quantity of medieval coin.

Therefore, alloy and weight are both indicators of the intrinsic value of coins, and the conditions of their production and use. Nonetheless, these data are insufficient when it comes to considering the extent of monetary circulation as a whole in any given period. To this end, it is necessary to chart the composition and volume of currency; in other words, what is needed is information on the quantity of coin present in a particular institutional or economic context, the relationship between the various means of exchange in use, and the capacity of the various denominations adequately to penetrate the markets.

Naturally, the greater the complexity of the problems we face, the greater are the technical and methodological difficulties involved in research. For instance, it is very difficult to calculate how many coins of a given denomination were struck with each issue, though clearly this kind of information is vital if we are to comprehend the economic function of a given coin (which is going to differ according to whether the coin was struck in a few thousand or several millions), and the relative liquidity of a particular monetary system.

It is calculated that a single medieval moneyer could produce up to three thousand coins in a day. However, as we do not have access to information concerning the number of moneyers engaged in a single issue or the number of days worked, we are no closer to understanding the volume of this production. Equally unhelpful is the criterion some-times employed by observers who claim that the coin types that survive in the largest numbers were those minted in the greatest quantities. Our perception of the surviving evidence is influenced by a number of factors, not least the arbitrariness inherent in patterns of ancient coin loss and modern recovery. What is more, in antiquity and the Middle Ages, currency was frequently recoined; that is, coins were withdrawn in order to be melted down and reformed – a process that presumably involved considerable quantities of coin at a time. This circumstance presents an enormous impediment to any attempt to calculate the volume of coin in circulation at any one time. For these reasons, numis-matists and others now look to more effective methods of calculating the volume of coins struck in a given period. And to this end, particular consideration is now being given to methods of calculating the output from minting dies.

When the number of coins to be struck is high, it is obvious that more than one set of dies will be required. Even during a single issue, dies may have to be replaced, as they are damaged and worn out by regular use, thus ceasing to make a sharp impression. Each die in a pair operates (and wears out) in different ways. Naturally, the die receiving the hammer blow, which usually carries the impression of the reverse of the coin, will wear out more quickly than the other (the obverse). It has been calculated that in the thirteenth century, an obverse die was good for between 30,000 and 35,000 strikes, the reverse for about half that number. Obverse and reverse dies can be identified from small variations in the images with which they were cast or engraved. In some cases, dies themselves were differentiated by the stamp of the issuing authority. From the number of dies and the incidence of obverse and reverse parts, one can calculate the overall number of coins produced. This method seems to offer considerable potential, though its workings continue to be refined and its criteria reviewed.

Another important aspect of these studies is concerned with the quality and quantity of the coin types in currency in a particular politico-economic context – or the 'monetary system'. It is rare to come across situations in which only a single denomination was used; when we do, the circumstance should imply that we are dealing with rather simple economic systems and limited trade. In most cases, two or more denominations were issued, and their relative values fixed. In a developed economy there are certain advantages to be had from using multiple denominations suited to a variety of economic transactions and a wide range of monetary values, such as those implied by international commerce and local trade, say, or the property market and the market in foodstuffs.

When dealing with antiquity and the Middle Ages, monetary systems are commonly characterized according to the number of metals used for coinage. Hence, it is said that the late-Roman monetary system was a trimetallic one, based on the use of gold, silver and bronze coinage concurrently in an integrated currency system. In the same way, the Carolingian monetary system was monometallic, based as it was on silver coinage alone. Beginning in the thirteenth century, a multi-metallic system of gold and silver coinage was introduced in most parts of western Europe. A different bimetallic system, based on gold and bronze coinage, operated for some time in Byzantium and Byzantine Apulia in the tenth and eleventh centuries. From the fifteenth century onwards, the general tendency in Europe was towards the trimetallic system. Each system has particular implications for the organization of economic activity, as we shall see in the second section of this chapter. However, one ought to bear in mind that number of metals alone is an inadequate indication of monetary circulation in a given system, as different denominations were often struck from the same kind of metal. Moreover, it is by no means rare to find imported or imitative coin in use alongside the official currency, so much so that the circulation of money is frequently a far more complex business than we would be led to believe from the study of the legal currency alone.

Clearly, in order to reconstruct these aspects of monetary history, we must take account of a wide range of evidence relating to a particular context or time period. First of all, the specifically numismatic data must be integrated with information derived from relevant written records. For instance, extant documents contain the administrative acts (or ordinances) with which the kings of France stabilized circulation at the end of the Middle Ages; others provide treasury records and rates of exchange of metals and coin types. Moreover, references to coins occur in charters, in relation to the price or value of goods transacted. Similarly, in the late Middle Ages, references to coins and their values were made in trading manuals, among information and instructions for merchants. These and other documents are indispensable to the exact and thorough treatment of the workings of medieval monetary systems.

Additionally, important information on the history of coinage may be supplied by archaeological research. When systematically recorded, the spatial distribution of coin finds presents a picture of the diffusion of different coin types, one that may enable us to understand whether particular coins were used for local, regional or international trade, and whether they served an economy of limited sort or one of expansive and wide-ranging scope. Other information can be deduced from the position or context of coin finds in the archaeological record. Coins are usually found in deposits resulting from human activity or occupation, in layers of soil and refuse which constantly build up in the course of everyday life. Otherwise, coins may be found where they were intentionally hidden and subsequently – inexplicably – abandoned. Coins lost during everyday business were most often the smallest denominations in common use. As today, in the past one did not routinely go about with quantities of cash in large denominations without being careful not to lose it. On the other hand, coin hoards were purposefully stashed away or hidden as treasure. Collectively, the coins in a hoard might amount to a considerable sum, and even individual coins often may have been of high value. Hoards are particularly revealing of the make up of monetary wealth, as on many occasions hoards will be found to contain diverse coin types from different periods. Therefore, comparison of the archaeological context of coin finds can shed instructive light on the functions and uses of different issues in currency.

Thanks to these complex and diverse methods of research, the study of coins becomes the study of monetary practices in past economies.

The monetary history of medieval Europe

As in previous chapters, it would seem appropriate to begin an account of the monetary history of medieval Europe with a description of the situation in late antiquity.

In the wake of the reform of the emperor Constantine, the late-Roman empire operated a trimetallic monetary system based on the circulation of different denominations of gold, silver and bronze coinage, the relative values of which were determined by fixed rates of exchange. The foundation of this system was the gold *solidus*, the weight of which was fixed at 4.55g; the solidus was struck 72 to the Roman pound (327g), or 6 to the ounce. The principal silver coin was the *miliarensis*, which may have been so-called as in theory it was valued at 1/1000 to the pound of gold. In practice at least two different types of miliarensis were produced, one rather heavier than the other; depending on the type these were the equivalent to 1/15 or 1/18 of the solidus. The content of precious metal in these gold and silver coins was close to 100%, as guaranteed by the state, which had the monopoly on minting.

Bronze coinage was minted in at least four denominations, of which the *nummus* was by far the most common. In theory, the value of the nummus was fixed at 1/7200 of the gold solidus, though this rate varied considerably during the fifth and sixth centuries. Other large denominations were used, such as the half solidus or *semissis*, and the third of a solidus, known as the *tremissis* or *triens* – and the silver *siliqua*, which weighed 2.65g, and its fractions. Multiples of the bronze nummus were issued, such as the *follis*, which was produced in Italy from AD 480-90 to the value of 40 nummi. In addition, very small bronze coin existed, which was completely devoid of intrinsic value.

Such a complex system met the varied requirements of a developed economy in which coinage was used for transactions of every kind, from the everyday purchase of goods in urban markets, for which purpose bronze coin was the most suitable, to the payment of state taxes and property revenues in gold. However, in the fifth and sixth centuries, the system was simplified. Certain denominations were suspended, though the basic trimetallic system remained in place. The barbarian kingdoms inherited this simplified system, which they endeavoured to maintain by continuing to issue the most commonplace denominations. Moreover, the barbarian kings took steps to reaffirm the public nature of coinage by having their names stamped on coins, at first alongside the title of the emperor, and later in its place. Notwithstanding these efforts, however, the system went into further decline. In the course of the sixth century, bronze coinage ceased to be issued, perhaps because it was not worthwhile for the mints or because it had become worthless in economic terms. In the same way, silver coinage disappeared from circulation in the second half of the sixth century, due to the scarcity of metal. After the sixth century, the barbarian kingdoms produced gold coins almost exclusively; as well as being inherently valuable, these barbarian coinages provided the kings with a conspicuous symbol of power and prestige. The only references in the documentation are to the Roman type of gold coin, which was the unit of prices and fines stipulated in barbarian law codes. In practice, the production of moneyers was limited to tremisses (three to a solidus), which were lower in gold content and purchasing power than the solidus. The quality of this coin was promptly debased. In Merovingian Gaul and Visigothic Spain, from the end of the sixth century the percentage of precious metal present in coins diminished as supplies of gold became scarce. The causes of this scarcity are many and complex. On one hand, precious metals went to pay for expensive luxury commodities in thriving eastern markets;

otherwise, gold and silver coins were hoarded or used in non-monetary ways. Given that gold and silver were no longer mined in the West, they would have had to be imported in large quantities (and at great expense) from the East in order to sustain new emissions of valuable coin. In any case, the supply of eastern gold and silver was in decline at the time of the barbarian invasions, falling still further during the first half of the seventh century.

Given these circumstances, it is perhaps remarkable that coinage did not cease to be minted altogether. Surprisingly, some 500 coin production centres are known in Merovingian Gaul in the sixth century. In this context, coins were made by private moneyers, possibly under licence from the kings; in any case, we know that monarchs guaranteed these media by having their names inscribed upon the coins. Likewise, we know of numbers of mints active in Visigothic Spain at this time. In regions where imperial Roman mints had not existed, as in England and Frisia (a region roughly comprising the area between the river Weser and the Rhine), gold coins of imitation Roman type were minted for a short time in the seventh century, in the shape of Anglo-Saxon *thrymsas* and the Frisian *trientes*.

How this coinage was intended to function is currently unclear, as we lack detailed information regarding the quantity of coin produced, the careers of individual mints, and the areas covered by single emissions. The proliferation of production centres in Gaul and Spain may indicate that coin was destined for local markets, thus implying that the kings were no longer in a position to issue currency to the kingdom as a whole. The ancient monetary system had fully collapsed by the second half of the seventh century, by which time production of a new denomination began in Merovingian Gaul. The Merovingian *denarius* (or denier) resembled the golden triens in form and weight (approximately 1.3g), though it was silver and otherwise unrelated to Roman silver coinage. Also at this time, new forms of silver coinage began production in England and Frisia. These are the so-called *sceattas*, or pennies, coins similar to the Merovingian denarius, and minted by the million.

Following the failure to introduce gold coinage to the region, the birth of Anglo-Frisian silver coinage is symptomatic of the growing vitality of trade around the North Sea, which was to reach its greatest intensity in the period between the seventh and the ninth centuries. In accounting for this development, we face the problem of identifying the source of the silver that made the new money possible. It is likely that the Franks intensified their exploitation of silver deposits at Melle in Poitou at this time. Silver was extracted there in Roman times and with even greater intensity in the Carolingian period. It may be that Frankish silver reached Frisia in exchange for luxury commodities such as animal skins brought by Frisian merchants from markets in Scandinavia. However, it is less clear if it was Frankish silver that supplied the production of Anglo-Saxon sceattas. Certainly, it seems that the northern regions of

Merovingian Francia, such as Austrasia and Neustria, gravitated towards North Sea trade, bringing their silver coinage with them. The move was given political sanction by the military conquest of Frisia by Charles Martell in 719.

In the Mediterranean, gold coinage of Roman origin survived rather longer, thanks to links with Byzantium; gold coin was still to be found in Spain and Provence at the beginning of the eighth century, and in Italy after 750. On the other hand, and in contrast to the situation in the North, production of silver coin was sporadic in the Mediterranean in early-medieval times.

As time went on, the Mediterranean regions also faced shortages in the supply of gold. Scarcity of gold led to continual depreciation of the currency in Lombard Italy, while in Spain production of gold coin ceased altogether in the first half of the eighth century. At the end of the seventh century, the political and economic configuration of the Mediterranean was redrawn by Arab expansion in the Middle East and in North Africa. This circumstance drove the Byzantine empire into recession, as the Byzantines saw their provincial revenues drastically cut; traditionally, these revenues had been paid in gold. The growing scarcity of gold in the East made the Byzantines even less inclined to lose their gold to the West. The vast Islamic dominion had its own monetary system, set up by the caliph Abd al Malik in the years between 696 and 699. This was based on the *dinar* and the *dirham*. The dinar (weight 4.25g) – or *mancus* as it was to be known in the West – was a gold coin of slightly lesser value than the Romano-Byzantine solidus; the dirham (weight 2.97g) was a silver coin modelled on the Persian drachma. This Arabic coinage was made possible by the opening of silver mines in Armenia and gold mines in Egypt and the Sudan, territories now subject to Islamic control. In the eighth century, Arab coin reached the southern fringes of western Europe. Production of the silver dirham began in Spain following the Arab conquest, while dinars changed hands in the coastal towns of Italy, presumably in exchange for goods.

In north-western Europe, in contrast, the eighth century witnessed the triumph of Frankish silver coinage, which became the common currency over a vast territory, in the service of the new political and economic order inculcated by the Carolingians. As soon as he was crowned king of the Franks, Pippin the Short concerned himself with the kingdom's currency; he took the production of coin out of the hands of private moneyers, concentrating the activity in mints subject to the direct control of the crown. At the same time, Pippin adopted a new type of coin that was to be thinner and larger than the Merovingian denier, and inscribed with the name or monogram of the king. Under the reform it was stipulated that 264 coins were to be struck from one pound of silver; previously, 288 coins were struck from the same quantity of metal. Pippin's reform brought the weight of the Carolingian denier to approximately 1.3g. In 794, Charlemagne raised this weight to approximately 1.7g, by stipulating that a pound of silver was to yield 240 deniers, and at the same time increasing the value of the pound as a unit of weight.

By this time the use of gold for coinage had been completely abandoned. The solidus survived as a unit of account equal to the value of 12 denarii (1/20 of a pound). This value was purely theoretical, as in practice there were no such gold coins to be exchanged. Thus, a monometallic monetary system was established, one that was to survive in Europe until the mid-thirteenth century. Even with the reintroduction of gold coinage, this system of calculating monetary values remained in practice in European countries right up to the introduction of the decimal system – and in the United Kingdom until the monetary reform of 1971. The new system and its coins were accepted in all regions subject to Frankish rule – in Saxony and Bavaria, and in the Spanish March and the Lombard kingdom of Italy. In Italy, use of the surviving gold coin was outlawed, thereby resolving problems provoked by the scarcity of precious metal. The denier of Carolingian type was introduced to regions of central Italy under the papacy, while in England, Offa, the king of Mercia, reformed the Anglo-Saxon currency by raising the weight of the penny in line with Charlemagne's denier.

The Carolingian supply of silver was provided by the mines of Melle and by other deposits opened at the beginning of the ninth century. It is difficult to ascertain precisely how the kings intended the coinage to be used. To a considerable degree, the economy of Carolingian Europe was based on self-sufficiency and small-scale barter, and in most cases the exchange of goods took place in the absence of coin. However, coins seem to have been widely circulated – at least in some regions of the empire. The overall interpretation of the Carolingian economy is still a matter of debate.

The area comprised by the Carolingian monetary system was not closed and self-sufficient; on the contrary, it absorbed silver and gold from the Mediterranean and above all from Muslim Spain, in return for an expensive and much sought-after commodity – slaves captured and shipped from central Europe, from the frontiers of the Christian world. Morevoer, silver was exported to Scandinavia in exchange for skins and other goods, though some of these losses were recouped thanks to the activity of the Frisian merchants trading Frankish produce in northern markets. Subsequently, in the second half of the ninth century, the Carolingian system ran into crisis on two fronts. Firstly, the ransoms and tribute demanded by Vikings did much to drain the supply of precious metal available for coin; it has been estimated that the Frankish kings lost a total of eighteen tons of silver in this way. Secondly, and at precisely the same time, the Carolingian silver mines were becoming exhausted, while export trade went into decline as a result of a paucity of tradable goods and the perils facing traders on the road and at sea.

The fate of Dorestad exemplifies this crisis – it was a major Frisian port before its destruction by Vikings shortly after 875.

In response to the crisis of royal authority brought about by the breakdown of the Carolingian empire, the great secular and ecclesiastical lords took over control of the mints in territories under their jurisdiction. Although these individuals did not question the royal prerogative implicit in the issue of coinage, they nonetheless set about minting coins themselves. In doing so, they often maintained the image and sometimes even the name of a king on their coins, though typically neither one nor the other was related to the king reigning at the time of issue. The practice was therefore but an acknowledgement of the ideal royal associations implied by the issue of coin, associations that did little to abash the ambitions of local lords. In the course of the tenth century, the most powerful and ambitious feudal lords went so far as to add their own names alongside that of the king, and in some cases reference to the king was omitted altogether. Moreover, the lords altered the type and weight of coin in currency at their own discretion.

Thus, with the disintegration of the Carolingian empire, the production and circulation of coin were reorganized within a regional context. By the twelfth century we know of around 90 feudal mints active in France. In the same period, the currency depreciated due to the general dearth of available silver, as local lords had neither the power nor the means to command sufficient supplies of precious metal.

Only along the northern and southern margins of Europe did precious metals continue to be traded. Already in the course of the ninth century the emporium of Birka, in lake Mälaren in Sweden, was where Frisians traded for natural products from Finland and northern Russia. Towards the end of the ninth century, the Swedes seized territory in northern Russia, thereby coming into contact with the Bulgar population living around the basin of the middle Volga. Bulgar traders were engaged in trade with Turkistan and the Abassid caliphate in Baghdad – as well as with Byzantium. By selling animal skins, slaves and other commodities in southern markets, Swedish traders amassed enormous quantities of Arabic silver coin, which had become especially plentiful and widespread due to the exploitation of mines in central Asia, an initiative begun earlier in the ninth century by Islamic Turks. Approximately 200,000 dirham have been recovered from archaeological deposits in Scandinavia, giving a clear idea of the scale of this exchange.

It is perhaps remarkable that trade on this scale did not lead to the issue of autonomous currency by Scandinavian peoples. In fact there was to be no Scandinavian currency before the eleventh century. Until then, Scandinavian traders continued to measure silver by weight, using both whole and fragmentary coins as well as ingots for the purpose. The final destination of this extraordinary wealth is unclear, though it may be that traded silver was used to substitute the silver previously acquired as loot and ransom from the Frankish kings, the supply of which had dried up along with the kings' wealth and the cessation of the Vikings' raiding activity. The silver must have been hoarded, though to what end we are unable to say. In any case, at least part of the Scandinavian silver went in trade with the Baltic and North Sea – and thence to England, where silver coinage continued to circulate. The Viking settlements of the Danelaw, along the northeast coast of England, around York, and others in Ireland, minted pennies and halfpennies in abundance. In 930, once the Saxon King Aethelstan had succeeded in expelling the Vikings, restoring his authority in the region, a law was passed prohibiting the circulation of foreign coin within the kingdom. The outlawed coin was to be melted down and recoined as national currency under royal control. This measure may have been dictated by fiscal interests, since the royal mint was to keep back a quantity of the newly minted coin; subsequently, one coin in every four was retained. This production implies the continued availability of foreign coin, which must have come in part through Scandinavia, perhaps in exchange for wool, the basis of the commercial economy of England throughout the Middle Ages and beyond.

Supplies of Islamic coinage nourished commercial activity on the southern periphery of Europe and in the Mediterranean in a rather more direct way. In this context, one is dealing with gold coin of African origin. The countries of North Africa had access to large quantities of gold brought across the Sahara from the gold producers of Niger and Senegal. African gold was transported in the form of dust; it was used to produce dinars and the smaller denomination *tarì* (weighing approximately 1.05g); four tarì are equivalent to one dinar. When the Saracens conquered Sicily in the ninth century, they introduced the tarì. From Sicily, the coin spread along trading and raiding routes to Campania in central Italy. By the end of the ninth century and the beginning of the tenth, tarì were turning up in the coastal towns of Campania, such as Amalfi, where they were used in local and regional exchange. However, it seems that gold coinage did not penetrate the mountainous interior of the Italian peninsula; in fact, the distribution of tarì is limited outside Campania. At Venice, where a certain amount of gold was available in the form of Arab and Byzantine coin, new issues were already being made for use in exchange with western merchants at the time of Louis the Pious. This was silver coinage of a Carolingian type, production of which continued in the first half of the tenth century, despite the dwindling supply of silver.

The use of gold coinage as an alternative to silver was thus not generally adopted even in southern Europe. Instead, in certain parts in the tenth century, it would seem that non-monetary objects were offered in exchange, as they were in areas of central Italy.

The waves of commercial and monetary exchange which lapped Europe's northern and southern coasts could only gather in force and spill over to inland parts when a political system suited to long-distance trade emerged in the European mainland. In particular, new sources of precious metal were needed to supply the mints. In Germany, the conditions for a revival of long-distance trade were met during the second half of the tenth century, thanks to the discovery of new silver mines in the Harz mountains near Goslar in Saxony; and thanks, too, to the ascendance of the dukes of that region – the Ottonians. At this time, the Ottonians seized the royal and imperial thrones, imposing German hegemony over the neighbouring territories.

It is certain that the Ottonians exploited the silver of Saxony in order to sustain their political programme; simultaneously they encouraged the widespread use of silver coinage in trade. Numerous mints were opened, some under royal control, others controlled under royal licence by ecclesiastical institutions, monasteries and bishoprics, and by powerful lay lords. The mints were situated alongside the most important trade routes, such as the road between Cologne and Magdeburg, on the border with the Slavic countries; others were located close by the sites of markets.

The coinage produced by the Ottonians' moneyers – the *pfennig* – is related to the Carolingian monetary system, in that it was in effect a new version of the silver denier. However, as it was not centralized coinage, the weight of the pfennig varied from mint to mint. Thanks to its silver, Germay under the Ottonians was able to import foreign goods such as furs from the Baltic and Slavic countries, and exotic and precious commodities from Venice – as well as wool and craft products from the Low Countries and England. In exchange, it sent silver.

In Scandinavia, supplies of Arab dirham were broken off after political events of 970 put paid to commercial links with central Asia. The shortfall was made up by enormous quantities of German pfennigs, as Rhinish merchants returned to the Baltic, followed closely by the Frisians.

Silver from Saxony supplied the royal mints of England, whether as coin or bullion carried by Anglo-Saxon traders returning from the Baltic. In Poland, Bohemia and Hungary, local princes set about forging new state systems under the hegemony of the German empire. Under the influence of German practices, these states began production of coinage of German type.

Likewise, German silver came to Italy as a consequence of trade after Otto I annexed the kingdom of Italy in 951. The diffusion of silver coinage in Italy may also have been encouraged by imperial support for the royal mints of Milan, Verona and Lucca, and above all Pavia, the capital of the Italian kingdom. Deniers minted in Italy at this time are named after the heads of the German empire; hence the *denari ottolini*, named after Otto III, and the *denari enriciani*, after Henry II.

This coinage circulated widely in central and northern Italy and at Rome. At Gaeta, on the threshold of the markets of Campania, it replaced Islamic coin. Venice, too, had commercial relations with the

German empire, particularly at the time of Otto III. These connections ensured a steady flow of silver to Venice, where consequently we see an upturn in production of silver deniers by the local mint. Moreover, German silver facilitated the first experiments with national currencies in Norway and Denmark at the beginning of the eleventh century, though it failed to penetrate France, where both royal and feudal issues continued to be produced in tiny quantities of miserable quality. By 1040, the mines of the Harz were worked out, leading to a new wave of monetary crisis in Europe. Though less severe than the crisis of the preceding period, the shortage was sufficient to interrupt production of the newly established Scandinavian coinages and those of the Slavic countries. The crisis led to serious difficulties for northern Italy, too, where, in order to satisfy the demand for coin, the royal mints turned out deniers containing progressively smaller quantities of silver. These heavily alloyed coins are known as *brunetti*, for such was the colour of their lustreless metal, with its minuscule silver content. In Italy, the crisis gave way to the circulation of coin of diverse and unreliable value, a circumstance that fostered distrust in the market and inflation in prices.

However, the growing scarcity of silver in Mediterranean countries after the middle of the eleventh century was to be compensated by abundant supplies of African gold. From around 970, gold coinage was struck at Granada, Seville and Almeria in Muslim Spain. Intensification in commerce caused this production to spread to Cataluña, where imitation coins were struck during the first half of the eleventh century. By the end of the century, sufficient quantities of gold were available in northern Spain to enable the production of a Spanish currency. This was the *maravedi*, which circulated along northern Mediterranean seaways to the ports of Provence and Liguria, and to Genoa, where such coins were known as *marabotins*. Likewise, in southern Italy, gold became available in considerable quantities in the eleventh century, thanks to the intensification of trade links with Sicily and Africa. Tarì of Sicilian type were minted in Amalfi and Salerno around the middle of the eleventh century. In the north, the coastal cities of Genoa, Pisa, and Venice continued to enjoy a supply of European silver in exchange for imported luxury goods from Constantinople, the Holy Land and Egypt. This traffic with Eastern merchants was underpinned by precious metals of every kind, making good the trade deficit and ultimately allowing for the production of silver currencies at Genoa and Pisa in the period *c.*1138-*c.*1150.

In the second half of the twelfth century, silver was once again in plentiful supply in most parts of continental Europe, thanks to the discovery of massive deposits at Freiberg near Meissen (Saxony). Around 1200 further mines were opened in the Harz mountains in Germany, and others in Tuscany. Subsequently, between 1220 and 1230, silver deposits were identified in Jihlava in Bohemia and at

Iglesias in Sardinia. Moreover, by the end of the thirteenth century, silver was being mined at Kutna Hora in Bohemia.

Among the first signals of this new wealth was a proliferation in the number of mints, and a number of attempts at currency reform. At the end of the twelfth century, the number of mints active in northern Italy rose from three to twenty-six, while in Tuscany the number increased from one to five. The numbers continued to rise in the first half of the thirteenth century. In France, by contrast, the fragmentation of the feudal age was brought to an end by the activity of a small number of very powerful mints turning out coin for use in regional markets. Thus the Melgueils denier came to prominence in Languedoc, and Tours deniers (or *deniers tournois*) in western France, while the *deniers provins* were pre-eminent in Champagne, where they fuelled the region's famous fairs. In this context, the kings of France took steps to reform the currency. Beginning around the middle of the twelfth century, this initiative produced the *parisis*, weighing slightly more than 1g and with a silver content of about fifty per cent. After the battle of Bouvines and the subjection of the western provinces to royal control in 1214, the denier tournois became the royal currency. Later, in 1226, King Louis VIII laid the basis for the monetary reunification of the kingdom, by decreeing that only the royal currency be permitted to circulate within the kingdom, while feudal coin was to be allowed only in the dominion within which it had been issued.

In England, mintage rights were completely controlled by the monarch and counterfeiters were heavily punished. Maintenance of the coherence and stability of coinage was a factor of considerable importance to royal prestige. Silver had always been relatively abundant in England, allowing the mints to produce enormous numbers of pennies of the highest quality during the thirteenth century. It has been calculated that the two principal mints of the realm, London and Canterbury, between them put out around four million pennies each year at the beginning of the thirteenth century. By mid-century, and by the same reckoning, there were one hundred million pennies in circulation in England.

Silver from Saxony and Bohemia spread to all parts of Europe in exchange for goods or coin. It reached England and the Baltic via Cologne, and by way of the trade fairs of Champagne and the Low Countries. In central parts of Europe, as in Poland and Hungary, silver was imported in quantities sufficient to maintain consistent production of coinages of German type. The same silver spread in still greater quantities to the great trading centres of coastal Italy. The Mediterranean remained the centre of gravity of international trade throughout the thirteenth century and for much of the first half of the fourteenth century. The Mediterranean was the source of luxury and exotic goods as it had been in previous centuries; in addition, it now provided a market for raw materials such as cotton, and agricultural produce such as grain, oil and sugar, and objects of domestic consumption including ceramics and glassware. Italian merchants continued to export silver to Africa and the East, to markets in which silver was rare and where it enjoyed considerable purchasing power.

The quantities of European silver reaching North Africa and the Near East were sufficiently large to revitalize the monetary economies of Egypt, Syria and Iraq. In the region between the Black Sea and the Sea of Azov, Mongul governors issued a local silver coinage; in Italy, where they were imported by Genoese and Venetian traders, these coins came to be known as *aspri*. Very considerable quantities of continental silver circulated in Italy at this time, too; in fact, for a while the deniers provins of Champagne were the local currency at Rome, where they provided the model for the city's own currency, production of which began in 1184.

The explosion of international trade posed rulers and moneyers with the problem of how to create forms of money of sufficient worth to clear the enormous values involved in contemporary commerce. As a result of its progressive transformation, the traditional silver denier was insufficiently valuable to be convenient in clearing medium- and large-scale payments. In transacting expensive sums, coins were reckoned by weight and not by number, such was the quantity of old silver deniers involved. Thus, international traders carried silver in bullion form, as bars or ingots rather than as coin. Certain mints turned out currency bars stamped, like coin, with symbols of authorization and ready for use in trade. In the towns and regions where the monetary economy was most advanced, even local trade suffered from the weakness of the currency. This created the preconditions for an overhaul of the Carolingian monetary system and the creation of a new system, one based on the co-existence of different denominations of silver coinage and the reintroduction of gold.

This transformation took place during the thirteenth century. It began in Italy, where the commercial economy was prosperous and well established, and where precious metals were far more plentiful than they were elsewhere. Subsequently, and by degrees, the movement spread to other European countries, in response to the needs of regional economies.

In order to meet demand for coin of very high unitary value, Italian mints raised the silver content of the denier, thereby creating the so-called *denaro grosso*, or *grosso* ('big penny'), which in English became the groat. The first issues of this pioneering coinage were made in Venice in 1202. The Venetian grosso (also known as the *matapan*) is a large coin of almost pure silver (weighing 2.18g). Similarly, around 1220, Genoese mints went into production of heavy deniers (1.4-1.5g), and in this they were followed by other Italian cities. The *grossi* – or *gros* – were the first coins to be developed which were without precedent in terms of the old Carolingian system. As the production of thin fabric deniers continued – these were now called *piccoli* to distinguish them from *grossi* – coinage in many cities consisted of two types of silver coin, one for use in transactions involving expensive goods, the other for small-scale, everyday use. The grossi were also used in international trade, though their value was insufficient to clear high-value transactions, and ingots and currency bars therefore remained the money of choice for long-distance commerce for some time to come. To some degree, this explains the reintroduction of gold coinage, not in the form of imitation Islamic coin, but in an original form tailored to the needs of international trade. It is no coincidence that this gold coinage began life in the Italian cities that led the vanguard of European trade. Only the Italian cities could rely on regular supplies of gold by way of their trade with Africa, and, in the case of Venice, contact with Hungary, where gold was mined in Transylvania.

Gold coinage was familiar to the inhabitants of Italian cities on account of their trade links with Byzantium and the Islamic world. Already in 1231, Fredrick II, the emperor and king of Sicily, was issuing gold coin of 5.2-5.3g in weight, though mostly in the interests of prestige to judge from the fact that these coins were known as the *augustale* – a reference to the issuer's imperial dignity. A few years later, the Christian states of Spain (Castille, Leon and Aragon) ceased production of imitation Islamic gold coin. Instead they issued the *doblas*, which was worth two dinars and was thus tied to the African monetary system. However, Spanish coin seldom crossed the borders of the regions in which it was made, as these regions were unconnected to wider trade networks. Much more successful was the gold coinage issued by the great Italian trading cities. Particular prominence was achieved by Florence and Genoa – Florence even took over from Pisa in terms of the volume of its international traffic at this time. Almost simultaneously, in 1252, the Florentine and Genovese mints coined the gold *fiorino* (3.54g) and the gold *genovino* (3.53g) respectively, each from 24-carat gold. Compared to silver, gold has a lower weight by volume, and greater value by weight. In the late Middle Ages, the value of gold oscillated from eight or nine times to around thirteen or fifteen times the value of silver. On this basis, gold was suited to the production of coin in very large denominations. When first issued, a single fiorino (florin) or genovino was equivalent to a pound of Tuscan silver deniers, or to 2/5 of a pound of the broadest Genoese deniers. These figures reveal how Italian gold coinage could be used to effect payments of large sums easily and quickly, while making bookkeeping easier. Moreover, golden coins were more flexible than ingots. With their supplies of gold from Transylvania and southern Italy, the Venetians continued to make use of minted bars long after 1252. Only later, from 1285, did the Venetians join other Italian cities in issuing their own currency in the form of gold *ducats* similar, in alloy as in weight, to the florin and genovino.

The development of gold coinage signals the climax in the development of monetary systems in the most developed commercial cities. Gold coinage was hereafter to be the medium of choice for international trade. It was particularly powerful in both eastern and western markets, where it enjoyed advantageous rates of exchange against silver.

Outside Italy, the demand for strong currency was soon felt in those countries where the volume of trade was becoming more intense and its organization more developed. In France in 1266, King Louis IX issued reformed silver coinage, the *gros tournois*, weighing 4.2g or the equivalent of twelve deniers tournois (one sou). That the gros tournois came into wide circulation is proof that it satisfied real demand. In the following years the *gros d'argent* came into use in the Low Countries, in the form of the *baldachin* (approximately 2.3g) and, from *c*.1300, the *grooten* (*groot*), which was similar to the French gros tournois. The picture is rather different in England, where the silver currency was already strong – so strong in fact that it came to be recognized as the benchmark of silver currencies among England's continental neighbours.

In Germany, in contrast, in the Rhineland and among the Hanseatic cities, the silver gros was a rather less familiar sight. Once so vigorous in the early-medieval centuries, the Baltic markets played a more modest role in the late-medieval European economy, which was characterized by the trade in manufactured goods and natural raw materials. The gros was a late arrival, too, in parts of eastern Europe. Only after the mines of Kutna Hora were opened did the kings of Bohemia issue coins equivalent to and actually heavier than the gros tournois, above all for the purposes of international trade.

In terms of gold coinage, once again it was France that was first to follow the lead set by the Italian mercantile cities. In 1266 Louis IX issued a gold coin, the *écu*, which at 4.2g was heavier than the florin and equivalent to ten solidi or gros tournois. However, the écu was to enjoy only limited circulation. In 1290 Philip the Fair revived the French experiment with gold coin by issuing the *royal*, which was equal to the florin in fineness and weight (3.5g). At the same time, the French crown prohibited the circulation of florins in the kingdom. This strategy was intended not only to establish the fiscal authority of the king, but also to force merchants and money-changers to hand over their gold coin to the mints, so feeding the royal mints and raising revenue. In fact, gold was brought to France principally in the purses of Italian merchants. However, like the écu, the royal was not greatly successful, due to the fact that it continued to be equivalent in value to ten gros tournois; thus, while the royal weighed less than the écu of Louis IX, it was more valuable in terms of silver. The first successful French gold coin was the *agneau*, issued between 1311 and 1326.

Other countries were even slower to introduce gold currency. In England and the Low Countries, the first gold coins were issued in the 1330s – and even then the motive seems to have been political rather than economic. Edward III of England issued two new gold coins, the *leopard* (equivalent to the florin) and the *noble* (equivalent to two écus), which he used above all to buy the allegiance of Flemish and German princes in preparation for the war with France. Indirectly, English gold coinage stimulated the production of gold coin in the Low Countries (such as the *gulden*, modelled after the florin and the écu) and, later, in the Rhineland. Subsequently, gold currency was issued in Hungary in a form resembling the florin. No gold currency was developed by the Scandinavian states, as these did not participate in the handling of precious metals. Among the cities of the Hanseatic League, only Lübeck had its own gold coin, albeit in very limited quantities.

The slowness in the spread of gold currency might suggest that silver, either in coin or bullion form, continued to provide an adequate means of exchange. In other words, in most parts of continental Europe, gold was regarded as a supplement to silver, and not as indispensable in itself. All the same, in the course of the fourteenth century, all countries with well-developed economies came to adopt the bimetallic system of gold and silver coinage.

Currency continued to be the source of problems for European governments into the late Middle Ages. National economies and international trade depended on the supply of coin for their survival. Traders had to be assured of adequate quantities of coin in the appropriate denominations. Furthermore, both buyers and sellers needed to know that the relative value of different coins (and the value of coin to precious metal) was stable and constant. Various factors combined to prevent these conditions from being met, making the fourteenth century a period of considerable economic instability.

Under the bimetallic system, the availability and the value of precious metals depended not only on their exchange for goods, but also on the relative values of gold and silver. As the value of gold and silver varied in different parts of Europe according to local circumstances, the markets fell prey to speculation – a development that was to affect the supply of precious metal by prejudicing the patterns of distribution in favour of certain markets and not others. Another factor behind the crisis in the supply of precious metals was the introduction of the bill of exchange, which was used by international merchants in order to avoid the risks involved in moving large quantities of valuable coin over long distances. As a result the exchange of goods in the late Middle Ages does not always imply the inverse exchange of precious metals. Nevertheless, perhaps the most significant development was the forceful intervention of the states in the management of their currencies. As they developed their administrations and expanded their territories, the kings found themselves facing growing financial pressures; often their response was to manipulate the currency. By far the most obvious measure was to reduce the content of precious metal circulating as coin while retaining the value of individual denominations; thus, the mints issued more coins per weight of metal bullion, and the surplus was held back by the crown, along with the income from the mints. However, once undervalued, it is almost inevitable that a currency will lose its exchange value. What is more, in countries where mineral resources were scarce, the kings were forced to pay above the market price for precious metals in order to supply the mints; otherwise, they had to order their subjects to renew all coin in circulation, while robbing the people of the share normally paid to the mints in return for this service.

The consequences of the crisis took a dramatic turn in France, where the organization of royal administration was highly developed, but where there were no mines. Moreover, in the fourteenth century, the French kings were engaged in a long series of wars abroad. Philip the Fair in particular needed vast quantities of coin in order to finance military operations in Gascony and Flanders; and so it was that he became the first French king openly to undervalue the currency. His actions encouraged inflation, bringing ruin on those who lived from private means, as sound coin disappeared and the price of gold soared. After Philip's death, the value of the currency was restored with the revival of the gros, though this stability was to be short-lived. The Hundred Years War brought with it a fresh set of financial needs. King Philip VI had to issue enormous quantities of gold coin in order to pay his allies, and to this end he resorted to undervaluing the silver coinage, not only to feed the royal reserves, but also because metal sometimes became so scarce that some French mints were forced to close temporarily.

In 1336, prior to the outbreak of hostilities, the tournois was valued at 1/12 of the *argent-le roy*, which was 96% silver. By 1353, its value had fallen to 1/64 the value of the argent-le roy; for a brief spell in 1359 the tournois was reckoned 500 to the argent-le roy. By this time, the tournois contained almost no silver (approximately 0.093g). An associated problem of concern to all governments, not only the kings of France, was the supply of small coin suited to everyday business and the needs of the poorer classes. The mints were reluctant to make this coin because they derived practically no profit from it; the metal being almost devoid of silver, such coinage became known as 'black money'. In some cases the kings ordered the mints to dedicate one day in the week to the production of low-grade coin, but this measure had little effect. However, at times when the supply of good coin failed, even 'black money' was sought after and hoarded. Periodic attempts to reintroduce sound coin were even more brief and sporadic than they had been before the war; in fact, this intervention complicated rather than improved matters, as it did not begin by withdrawing bad coin from circulation. Although it was less subject to manipulation, gold coinage itself created problems and confusion, as it was issued in types and values that varied frequently; the rates of exchange with silver coin fluctuated capriciously, according to the price of metals and the quality of the issue. The official rates were ignored and alternative rates of exchange imposed, calculated on the basis of the intrinsic value of each type of coin. In this way, money-changers became vital agents in the effective circulation of currency within individual states.

In France the situation stabilized after 1360, during the long truce in the Hundred Years' War and thanks to the shrewd leadership of Charles V. The silver currency returned to stability, though the value of the gros had been halved during the war. The kings held back from interfering with it until 1417, but in the last decades of the fourteenth century – and for reasons beyond their control – the French kings had to deal with further shortages of silver. Beginning in 1385, the paucity of available silver caused even the production of black money to cease, while 'white' as well as gold coin was depreciated.

Other countries faced similar difficulties in the course of the four-teenth century. War led to damaging devaluation of the currencies of the Low Countries and Castille. Even the Venetians struggled to maintain their bimetallic system under stable control. By the middle of the century Venice had ceased production of the silver gros, not because of war but due to the scarcity of metal. Only England was immune to the crisis set in motion by the monetary policies of continental kings, as the English monarchy derived its revenues from taxation rather than cur-rency control. But even in England there were occasional problems with liquidity. At the end of the fourteenth century and into the fifteenth, all of Europe went through a process of monetary stabilization, the effect of which was to consolidate the bimetallic system. Gold was coined by various states in types generally related to the standard provided by the florin, which, together with the Venetian ducat, maintained its role as the international currency par excellence, and as such was often imi-tated. For the most part, the national gold currencies circulated within their country of origin or in the context of political or diplomatic rela-tions between states. Little use was made of gold currency for international trade.

Silver coinage was stabilized at average values lower than the values pinned to the gros during the thirteenth century. In France, following a further period of acute instability during the last phase of the Hundred Years' War (1417-1435), the *blanc* was struck. This weighed 3g and contained 50 per cent of pure silver, though in practice it was only 1/3 the value of the gros tournois of one hundred years earlier. Coins of a standard comparable to the French blanc were issued in the Low Countries, in the Rhineland, and in the duchy of Milan. At Venice, where production of the silver gros was resumed in 1379, and in Eng-land, where the closest comparable coin was worth twice the value of the blanc, the local system was made compatible with the continental one by adjusting the weight of coin or by issuing smaller denominations.

None of this was to make the circulation of coined money regular or free flowing. In fact, one characteristic of this period is the wholesale reduction of stocks of precious metals, particularly silver. Already in the fourteenth century, the scarcity of metal had led to problems; subsequently, the shortage was to be a recurring aspect of European monetary history. Europe continued to export gold and silver to the Levant by way of Italian markets, though these losses were no longer made good by Europe's natural reserves, as had been the case in previous centuries. The mines of Bohemia began to expire after the mid-fourteenth century; and while metal continued to be supplied from mines in Serbia and Bosnia, they scaled down their production in the fifteenth century, before ceasing to supply the West altogether following the Turkish conquest. Although gold continued to reach Italy from Africa by way of Seville, the supply diminished, leading to a reduction in the weight and quality of gold coin in currency. This affected the English noble, the French écu and the German florin, all of which depreciated in the years after 1420.

Therefore, the stabilization of European currencies occurred in the face of a dearth of metal and with the reduction of coin in circulation. Moreover, the process did nothing to stop a slow but continuous drop in the value of coin. Such devaluation was brought about by the habit of recoining, a strategy intended to remove worn and corrupted coins from circulation. As the mints were unable to keep up the amount of silver in currency, governments were forced to lower the content of precious metal circulating as coin or to issue lighter coin. The shortage of precious metals forced a reduction in currency at all levels, leading to a shortage of credit, the deceleration of trade and a general downturn in the economy.

A new cycle was to begin with the discovery of new silver mines in Germany at the end of the fifteenth century, and with the arrival in Europe of silver from the Americas.

It would be impossible to do justice to all the aspects and problems presented by the monetary history of medieval Europe in so small a space. Even where the most important systems are concerned, much work remains to be done. Moreover, there is plentiful scope for original research in local and regional spheres, in plotting micro-economic systems and their relation the bigger picture. The study of coinage thus remains an area of extraordinary potential for our understanding of the workings of medieval society.

The material record

Material culture and society

Every society – every organized and permanent group of individuals –
produces and makes use of a diversity of objects, implements, buildings
and other structures, which are essential for the exercise of economic
and social practices. Part of this apparatus, and the techniques associated with its use, satisfies the essential needs in the life of individuals,
such as food, shelter and clothing, while a considerable part plays an
indispensable role in the life of society as a whole, as in the production
and exchange of commodities, for instance, or in government and religion, defence and military activity, and in the relationships of individuals
and groups.

Naturally, artefacts, buildings and landscapes occur with diverse
functions and forms, and in differing combinations, among different
societies and at different times in the past. Their characteristics and
functions depend on technological knowledge and ability, the lifestyles
of individuals and groups, and exchanges with other societies. Alongside
norms of behaviour, collective mental attitudes and social memory,
objects – artefacts – constitute the 'culture' of a society.

The concept of 'culture' intended here was first developed around the
middle of the nineteenth century by those engaged in anthropological
and ethnographical research on primitive societies that were encountered by Europeans and Americans through geographical exploration or
colonial expansion. These societies were observed, described and interpreted on the basis of their standardized forms of behaviour and oral
traditions – as well as the implements and techniques employed in
everyday activities. The purpose was to identify both the ideal and the
utilitarian principles that governed the actions and organization of
societies apparently so different to those of the western world – principles which were understood to constitute the very 'culture' of these
societies. More recently, the study of artefacts, buildings and tools has
been applied to descriptions and analyses of developed societies, including our own highly developed post-industrial society. Generally
speaking, objects and implements are the tools with which a society
controls and exploits its habitat. They make up an artificial, artefactual
world, which influences the activity and the very psychology of individu-

als. When seen in this way, the personal computer is no more remarkable than the prehistoric flint axe.

Consequently historians became concerned with the material aspects of social organization, which they recognized as a means to a fuller understanding of societies in the past which had deployed artefacts and structures so very different to our own. As far as medieval history is concerned, major advances in the analysis of the period's material remains were made from around the end of the nineteenth century and during the first decades of the twentieth. The key figure here is Karl Lamprecht, whose place in the development of the modern practice of medieval history was described in Chapter 1. In his studies of settlement and economic activity in medieval Germany, Lamprecht directed his attention to the physical conditions of life, such as climate and landscape, and forms of settlement and land use. Lamprecht used the expression 'material culture' to refer to concrete, tangible aspects of social organization. The term 'material culture' reveals the influence of Marxist thought; subsequently, the term was used to refer to an important branch of historical and archaeological studies within the Soviet Academy of Sciences, founded under Lenin, and spreading to the science academies set up in the capitals of eastern-bloc countries after the end of the Second World War. Hence the concept of material culture came to have a strong ideological charge, derived from the theory that the study of material culture should enable the objective representation of the modes of production and class structure in ancient societies, thereby correcting the distortions implicit in the literary and juridical sources, which by their nature express only the perspective of the dominant class.

Nowadays, few would accept material culture and only material culture as the pre-eminent platform for the analysis of socio-economic structures in societies past or present; neither is it considered the vital expression of the culture of subordinate classes. Material culture is but one aspect of the complex configuration of society, to be studied and interpreted in its relation to the other aspects, even those of very different kind, such as institutions and religion. It was this that Lamprecht himself set out to do. But precisely because it relates to a vast spectrum of activities and social practices, material culture constitutes a body of evidence which in many ways completes the historical perception of past societies.

The importance of technology, settlement forms and agrarian landscapes for the overall interpretation of medieval society, was recognized by Marc Bloch, this time without ideological connotations. In his famous studies on the spread of the water mill and the use of draught animals, and their impact on the landscapes of France and England, Bloch illuminated the connections between technology and the organization of society, showing the two to be strictly and reciprocally interlinked.

Once the interest and importance of these aspects of history had been established, questions arose regarding the most suitable ways of documenting them. Both Lamprecht and Bloch were concerned above all with the evidence of written sources, which they combined with geographical and, in Bloch's case, antiquarian material. It was perhaps inevitable, however, that scholars were to become dissatisfied with mere references to artefacts and structures, before setting out track down and study past material cultures at first hand. Hence the lure of archaeology – the essential means of accessing the material record of the past.

Medieval archaeology

The practice of medieval archaeology is not an innovation of recent times, and it was not a novelty even in Bloch's day. In fact, the roots of medieval archaeology can be traced to the eighteenth century. At first, the subject's links with history proper were weak or nonexistent; this situation continued until fairly recent times. Traditionally medieval archaeology has followed two principal paths. The first, which may be defined as the archaeology of monuments, developed out of the fashionable taste for abandoned and ruinous monuments prevalent in England during the second half of the eighteenth century. Particular stock was set by the ruins of medieval abbeys and castles, which were made the subjects of picturesque views in paintings and prints, later becoming the objects of critical studies of their structure, function and architectural style.

With the Restoration and Romanticism, the medievalizing taste spread to France, where it paved the way for schemes for the listing and protection of historic monuments under state control.

Prior to the mid-nineteenth century, however, approaches to medieval archaeology seem rather rudimentary when compared with the standards of today. Analysis of buildings was carried out on the basis of structural and stylistic features visible in elevation. Only seldom were analyses of this kind accompanied by excavation, and frequently those involved were unable even to reconstruct the original form or plan of a building and its historical development. Similarly, building restorations, which were frequently carried out in England and France, were conducted according to criteria that are now mostly obsolete. Commonly, restorers were little concerned with recovering or preserving the original structural characteristics of a building; instead, their aim was to impose an idealized medieval appearance, one more in tune with contemporary tastes and expectations than with the original forms of the monuments themselves. In fact, large numbers of buildings were distorted in order to appear in ways that would have been entirely unfamiliar to their medieval builders.

Nevertheless, archaeological interest soon quickened beyond prestige monumental buildings such as abbeys, cathedrals and castles, to include other, more common forms of medieval architecture, such as the ver-

nacular architecture of dwellings and agricultural and utilitarian buildings. And scholars turned to written sources in order to provide a
historical context for the construction and use of medieval buildings.
Particular consideration was given to reconstructing the fixtures and
furniture of medieval domestic, ecclesiastical and military buildings,
using mostly antiquarian objects, more or less appropriately, as well as
iconographic evidence. A comprehensive synthesis of the state of nineteenth-century knowledge of medieval architecture was composed by
Eugène Emmanuel Viollet Le Duc (1814-1879), inspector in the office
for national monuments in France under the second empire (1852-70) of
Napoleon III. Viollet Le Duc directed the restoration of a number of
important medieval buildings, employing the dubious criteria of his day.
He had a considerable knowledge of medieval texts, monuments and
antiquities, on which basis he prepared two great archaeological ency-
clopaedias: the *Dictionnaire raisonné de l'architecture française du XIe
au XVIe siècles* (10 vols, Paris, 1854-68); and the *Dictionnaire raisonné
du mobilier français de l'epoque carolingienne à la Renaissance* (6 vols,
Paris, 1858-74).

From the late nineteenth century and on into the first decades of the
twentieth century, the study of medieval monuments was to embrace
the very aspect in which it had previously been most lacking – namely,
the understanding of structural sequence. Rarely were medieval buildings the result of a single building operation. Through minutely
scrupulous examination of the materials and construction methods of
particular buildings, the aim was to reconstruct the organization of
building campaigns and the structural sequence or history; to identify
the various trades involved and the extent of their roles; and to explore
the functions as well as the symbolic significance of buildings and their
constituent parts. In this way, medieval archaeology was reconceived in
ways that continue to enjoy credit to this day. It was on this basis that
the discipline defined itself as an alternative or complement to the
formal and stylistic interpretations proper to art history.

In parallel with this development, and in the course of the nineteenth
century, a second major development in medieval archaeology was
made, this time in Scandinavia. The monuments of medieval Scandinavia – monuments dating to the Viking age if not before – are rarely
buildings but megalithic structures and earthen mounds or tumuli, not
dissimilar in kind to those built in prehistoric times. In Scandinavia, the
medieval period followed on directly from the Iron Age, with no intervening classical epoch. Upon investigation, the tumuli were found to
contain princely or high-status burials, normally accompanied by grave
goods in the form of weapons, jewellery, coins, and in some cases entire
ships, which were buried to display status and to accompany the deceased on the journey to the afterlife. Sealed beneath the soil as they
were, such extraordinary evidence needed to be excavated. Excavations
had been carried out from as early as the eighteenth century and

probably long before. During the nineteenth century, the interest in ancient funerary archaeology spread to Germany, where numbers of migration-period cemeteries were investigated archaeologically, and found to contain graves within which weapons and personal items had been placed alongside the bodies of the dead. During the nineteenth century, archaeological material of this kind was subjected to analytical methods derived from ethnography, which was coming into its own as a discipline. The aim was to reconstruct the artefact cultures, the distinctive forms of dress, personal adornment and weaponry – as well as the burial rites and belief systems peculiar to the Germanic peoples. The broader aim was to underline the cultural identity of early Germanic peoples, by using archaeological material to give substance to particular national traditions. Particular attention was paid to the patterns of ornament applied to prestige objects, especially jewellery and weapons. The complex abstract and figurative designs of these objects were considered to be characteristic expressions of an original conception of artistic form unique to Germanic culture. Important work in analyzing and codifying this material was undertaken by the Swedish archaeologist Bernhard Salin, and published in 1904. As a direction in medieval archaeology, the study of material of this kind was progressively advanced during the twentieth century, and it remains an important and dynamic field of research. On this basis, archaeologists are now better able to give more precise dates to burials containing grave goods of identifiable kind, and to trace with ever greater precision the development of decorative styles, therefore reconstructing the dynamics of Germanic culture. Moreover, during the twentieth century, the development of physical anthropology has enabled archaeologists to reconstruct the physical, anthropological characteristics of individuals, as well as the make-up of population groups.

Despite the interest provoked by archaeological research in the two areas outlined above, up until the middle of the twentieth century there was no established basis for collaboration between archaeology and historical studies. The reason for this was the predominant belief that archaeology is concerned with phenomena of a particular kind, different to those with which the historian is concerned; a belief that has yet to be entirely overcome. For this reason, nineteenth-century archaeologists sometimes considered their discipline's relationship to art history to be more pertinent, while historians regarded archaeology as a substitute source of information for periods in which written evidence is lacking, particularly the age of migrations and the early Middle Ages in general. In the presence of abundant written sources, conversely, it has often seemed to historians that they might do without with archaeology altogether.

Significant progress towards the convergence of archaeology and history finally came about following the end of the Second World War. The agent of this change was the emergence of interest in landscape and settlement archaeology. Some archaeological investigations of medieval towns and villages had already been carried out. In Denmark, for example, the major Viking-age town of Hedeby had been brought to light by important excavations conducted there in the 1930s by the German archaeologist Herbert Jankuhn. But the excavation of Hedeby had been motivated by the lack of written sources available to historians of the period. Greater originality was shown by the methodology developed for the study of deserted medieval villages by the two English historians, W.G. Hoskins and M.W. Beresford. Through their studies of economic history, Hoskins and Beresford came to the conclusion that the depopulation of a considerable number of English villages had occurred not in the fourteenth century and due to the Black Death, as had previously been believed, but a century later, and as a consequence of land reforms and the reversion of cultivated land to pasture. Hoskins and Beresford set out to prove their hypotheses through archaeological investigations, with which they intended to establish when a certain number of villages had been abandoned. Such limited objectives were soon widened, and the investigation of the economic and material life of medieval villages became an end in itself. In the space of a few decades, a wealth of new information became available on subjects that had previously been considered worthless if they were considered at all – subjects such as the forms and construction of houses, domestic implements, village planning, artisanal production and social stratification. At the same time, it became clear that increased collaboration between archaeologists and historians offered great potential, as both the foundation and abandonment of the villages occurred during the central and later Middle Ages, periods for which abundant written records survive. In England, this circumstance provided the basis for detailed reconstructions of the socio-economic structure and the material form of villages. Moreover, the same circumstance provided an opportunity to assess the parity or disparity of conclusions drawn on the same subject by the two research techniques, historical and archaeological. Lively debate ensued, and many historians denied that any significant breakthrough had been made. Nevertheless, archaeology had established its capacity to reveal aspects of the life of past societies which were unknown from the written records, particularly as regards the distribution, form and quantity of the material products of social life. The problem was (and remains) how best to make use of this body of evidence.

Research into abandoned villages was profoundly to alter the traditional perspectives of medieval archaeology. As the buildings and structures of medieval villages were frequently of poor construction, the privilege previously shown to monumental buildings was revoked. Consequently, the medieval village in all its aspects – including those formerly considered to be of less significance, such as boundaries and land divisions, and the very shape of fields – became the object of archaeological investigation. At the same time, new importance was attached to a category of archaeological material which hitherto had been largely overlooked – the detritus of everyday life. Attention shifted away from prestige artefacts (which in any case are rarely encountered on village sites, having been carried off by the fleeing village population), to the fragments of vessels and receptacles, food remains, including bones, and the by-products and waste generated by craft activity. Research into abandoned villages thus had the effect of focusing medieval archaeology on similar subjects to those tackled by social and economic history.

From the 1960s the archaeology of lost villages spread to France, Italy and Spain, where it has been responsible for the rebirth, so to speak, of medieval archaeology and the potential for collaboration with historical studies. From their experience of working on abandoned sites, archaeologists began to look at occupied settlements, including towns, for which they developed particular strategies in order to carry out archaeological investigations without disruption to the daily lives of inhabitants. Archaeologists learned to take advantage of the opportunities presented, for instance, by the digging-up of roadworks and the laying of foundations for new buildings. Light began to be shed upon the organization of structures and economic activity in many medieval towns, with results that were richer and more complex than those encountered in rural settlements. After the Second World War, comparable results were attained in Poland and other eastern European states, by archaeologists working on the origins and make up of early Slavic society using material culture and settlement patterns as the main evidence.

Thanks to the increasingly precise knowledge of archaeological materials and the growing number of archaeological discoveries and excavations, the attention of researchers has turned from settlements to the landscape, the organization of production, and the circulation of commodities in the medieval world. Nowadays medieval archaeologists are constantly striving to expand the variety of social experience and phenomena which their discipline is able to detect and illustrate, while refining the methods for collecting and interpreting data.

Techniques of archaeological investigation

The construction of archaeological knowledge follows procedures and rules that are determined by the characteristics of the evidence to hand. Even a sketchy understanding of these procedures is worthwhile, if, as historians, we are going to be able to judge and make use of evidence as it is presented by archaeologists, and in order to integrate this evidence with data derived from other sources. To this end, the remainder of the chapter is taken up with a brief synopsis of the key aspects of archaeological method.

Excavation

Excavation is the principal method used to recover archaeological material from the soil. On every site deposits of earth and other materials accumulate continuously, as the result of natural forces and the activity of people; unless these deposits are removed, the ground level will continually rise, burying beneath it the signs of life of successive generations of inhabitants. As this is an ongoing, cumulative process, each deposit is laid over the previous one. Remains accumulate in stratified layers – or *strata*. The make-up or consistency of each deposit of earth is determined by the action or process as a result of which the layer came to be formed. Thus, strata may result from the deposition of humus and alluvial soils, or building work; others may be formed from the debris of collapsed and demolished buildings, the dumping of rubbish and refuse, and the redepositing of earth for agriculture. In the same way, it follows that the formation of strata may have occurred in an instant or over a prolonged period of time.

The importance of stratification in archaeology was first recognized during the second half of the nineteenth century. At that time, geologists were beginning to explain how the earth's crust resulted from processes of sedimentation and was composed of layers of rock. From the variety of fossilized material preserved in these layers, geologists began to postulate chronological sequences for the development of the earth. By analogy, archaeologists realized that, on sites of human activity, deposits of earth are laid down stratigraphically, in chronological sequence. It follows, therefore, that objects found within layers of soil are related to successive stages of human activity or occupation on a site. This breakthrough announced a revolution in the techniques and the very purpose of excavation. Previously, excavation had been intended simply to remove objects or structures from the soil. Once it was understood that the stratification of the soil is related to distinct phases in the life of a site, archaeologists recognized the importance of separating excavated material according to the strata in which it is found, though at first they struggled to find the best ways of putting the principle into practice. One could say that, during the late nineteenth century and for much of the twentieth, advances in archaeological method have been directed above all to the development of increasingly refined methods of stratigraphic excavation and analysis.

Early in the last century, the pioneers of stratigraphic excavation were eager to apply the principles of geology to the archaeological record. However, they soon found that too close a dependency enabled them to identify only the broadest bands of stratigraphy containing any number of individual layers. At first, attempts to recover archaeological (rather than geological) profiles were haphazard. In certain schools of archaeological practice during the first half of the twentieth century, a method was adopted whereby layers of predetermined depth were systematically stripped away. While this allowed excavators to plot the position of excavated material in the vertical dimension, the method led to great confusion, for it was not long before archaeologists recognized that a single arbitrary layer might contain material from any number of archaeological deposits.

Only after the First World War was the technique of stratigraphic excavation properly refined. This was the achievement of the British archaeologist, Mortimer Wheeler. Wheeler made stratigraphic analysis the basis of archaeological excavation and recording methods. Wheeler's legacy was to be of immense importance for his successors. Like others before him, Wheeler recognized that excavation causes the irremediable destruction of the archaeological record. He developed important new strategies for systematic site-recording based on his innovative excavation technique. In order to reveal and record the stratigraphy of a given site, Wheeler first laid out a grid of square trenches (or 'Wheeler boxes' as they came to be known, usually five metres square) on the surface of the site. These were then excavated leaving baulks of earth intact between the squares of the grid. By doing this, Wheeler found that each baulk presents a section of the excavated deposits in vertical profile. These sections can be reproduced in photographs and detailed drawings to provide a record of the stratigraphic sequence across the site.

Wheeler's boxes marked a decisive advance in the methods of stratigraphic excavation, though the widespread application of the technique revealed its inherent limitations. For instance, the earthen baulks left between trenches – usually one metre wide – were found to present walls of invisible archaeology, which obscure as much as they reveal of the totality of a site. Furthermore, it was difficult to trace connections between layers in widely separated areas of a site. The emphasis on the vertical dimension imposed by Wheeler was less well adapted to representing stratigraphic relations on the horizontal plane, nor was it suitable to record actions that leave a negative stratigraphic impression, such as the clearance or removal of archaeological material which occurs, for example, ahead of building work.

During the 1970s archaeologists sought to free their work from such limitations. The result was open-area excavation. Champions of open-area excavation – pre-eminently, Philip Barker, another British archaeologist – argued that it was better to cut vertical sections not according to an arbitrary grid, but at whatever angle and wherever needed to investigate complex stratigraphy. Across the excavated area, both vertical and horizontal relations are recorded by a more accurate system of three-dimensional co-ordinates, based on a combination of grid references and levels. Open-area excavation is concerned with exposing the upper surfaces of deposits as they were laid down, rather than with cutting sections through them as Wheeler had done. This has implications for site recording, as planning, rather than section drawing, becomes the essential method of documentation. The plans of individual areas and features can be joined to provide an overall plan of the site at a particular stage of its development, and plans of successive phases superimposed to show the transformation of the site over time. During open-area excavation, what are known as running sections will be cut in order to investigate particularly complex stratigraphic relations. Smaller trenches may also be opened for this purpose and the sections drawn, following Wheeler's method.

Open-area excavation has profoundly altered archaeologists' perception of the nature of stratigraphy. The method has shown that material of archaeological interest does not only occur in broad strata uniformly covering the surface of a site. In fact, deposits may be irregular in profile, shallow, discontinuous, or limited in extent. This understanding led to demand for an effective system to recognize and record stratigraphic relations, taking into account the spatial and chronological relations of each single event that makes up the stratigraphic profile of a site. It was Edward Harris, the Bermudian archaeologist, who came up with the solution. Harris developed a method for representing the matrix of physical relations between layers or features – or what he called contexts. In the stratigraphic sequence, each context is recognised as previous, contemporary or subsequent to any other context. Harris developed a method for expressing relationships between archaeological deposits in graphic form, as a diagram – the so-called Harris matrix. The matrix is worked out at the end of the excavation, from information provided by the archive of site documentation; it presents a synthesis of the spatial distribution and the chronological succession of excavated contexts. By following these principles, excavation produces a detailed reconstruction of the history of the site, and the succession of actions and events that have left their traces in the soil.

Although excavation methods and recording techniques continue to be developed and refined by field archaeologists, this is now the most advanced stage of development in archaeological technique. The development was made possible, too, by the experience of archaeologists on the ground. Since the Second World War, qualified and experienced archaeologists have replaced labourers on sites in most areas of Europe. This is important, as, in the final analysis, stratigraphic excavation is based on the archaeologist's empirical capacity to distinguish one deposit from another, sometimes on the evidence of minute changes in the colour and consistency of soil. The archaeologist's sensitivity and skills of perception together make up the vital (but nevertheless problematic) point of contact between the material fact of the archaeological deposit and the representation of that fact in graphic or written form in the archaeologist's report. This last is the only documentation available to non-archaeologists. It follows that the archaeologist's skill actively determines, for good or ill, the construction of archaeological and historical knowledge; in other words, the usefulness and reliability of this knowledge both depend on the inherent ability and sensitivity of the archaeologist.

Dating methods

An excavation carried out according to modern methods will result in the reconstruction of a chronological sequence of activities and events that have left some trace in the stratigraphic make-up of a site. Such a sequence follows a relative chronology unique to the particular context or site in question. In order to relate the relative sequences of archaeological material to absolute historical chronology, we need dating evidence. There are a variety of methods for establishing relative and absolute dating, but the evidence routinely used by archaeologists is provided by excavated finds. Particular importance is afforded in this respect to the evidence of coins and pottery.

As we saw in the previous chapter, coins are frequently marked with the name of the issuing authority. This circumstance allows us to attribute finds of coin to a more or less well defined period in history, if with certain limitations.

Coins are encountered only rarely, however, and certainly not in every archaeological deposit. In contrast, pottery is the category of material evidence recovered in the greatest quantities in excavations. The ubiquity of ceramics needs little explanation. Ceramics belong to a category of artefacts widely used in almost all societies, from the Neolithic to the present day, for the basic purposes of food preparation and for storage of foodstuffs such as oil, wine, pickles and cereals. Moreover, pottery is highly resistant to decomposition when buried in soil.

The importance of pottery as dating evidence derives from the fact that, since ancient times, vessels were often decorated with colours and ornament, or covered with a vitreous emulsion that hardens when fired, creating a glaze. Both the shape of vessels and the forms of their decoration have been constantly adapted and modified in the course of time, in response to the availability of materials and the techniques in use, and to changes in function, fashion and aesthetics. This observation applies equally to medieval pottery. The first systematic studies of medieval pottery were made in the nineteenth century, and some basic typologies established using the formal and stylistic features of complete vessels from securely dated contexts. Much progress has since been made, thanks above all to the methods of stratigraphic excavation, such that it is now possible to identify and give dates to pottery types even when these occur in fragmentary form, as sherds.

Yet it should be emphasized that the dating of archaeological deposits from their finds has its limits. It may be the case that a particular context is found to contain no recognizable material. Undecorated ceramics can rarely be dated with precision, and there are periods for which diagnostic ceramic types are simply unknown. Moreover, coins found in excavations are often so badly worn or corroded as to be illegible. The date of a single coin or a single potsherd – even well-known and accurately datable types – cannot necessarily be extended to the deposit in which the object occurs, as such objects may have been displaced from their original positions in the archaeological record by movements of the earth (by burrowing animals, for instance, or the growth of roots and the action of the plough). For this reason, reliable dating depends on the accurate assessment of stratified and homogeneous assemblages of material evidence.

In every case, finds – even well dated ones – cannot (and should not) dictate the date of a given deposit. This is not only because the production of coins and pottery can be attributed only to fairly broad spans of time (such as the duration of a king's reign, say, or a decorative style), but also because it is seldom possible to ascertain precisely how long such objects remained in use before ending up in the archaeological record. Therefore, the dates given to excavated objects provide only a baseline for dating the deposits in which they are found. Strictly speaking, datable finds provide a *terminus post quem* – a date after which the deposit may be said to have been created. In the same way, finds may indicate a *terminus ante quem* for contexts and objects deposited before them in chronological sequence. In any case, the accuracy of dates suggested by excavated material will range between about 25 and 100 years. Given the present state of their methods, it is rare that archaeologists are able to date finds with any greater precision.

In response to the inadequacy of dating methods based on formal and typological analyses of excavated artefacts, archaeological scientists have developed a range of laboratory methods to provide dates for a range of materials occurring in the archaeological record, of which probably the best known is radiocarbon (or carbon-14) dating. Radiocarbon dating measures the residual radioactivity of atoms of carbon-14. Carbon-14 is produced by high-energy neutrons of cosmic radiation reacting with nitrogen atoms in the atmosphere and absorbed by the cells of plants and animals during growth. Upon the death of an organism, the unstable composition of carbon-14 atoms causes their radioactive content to decay at a regular pace. As the rate of decay is known, it is possible from the residual radioactivity to calculate the age of a find to within one or two hundred years. Given its limited accuracy, carbon-14 dating is useless when looking for more precise dating.

Another widely known scientific dating method in archaeology is dendrochronology, or tree-ring dating. Variations in climatic conditions produce differential growth in plants and trees, resulting in the formation of rings of varying width. An extensive database of tree-ring patterns is now established, and master tree-ring sequences are available from prehistory to the present in different parts of the world. As a ring is formed every year, in some cases dendrochronologists can arrive at very precise dates for the felling of trees from which timbers or wooden artefacts have been cut. Like most dating methods, though, dendrochronology has its limitations. Once buried, wood will resist decomposition only in certain soil types, and usually only in the most arid conditions. When preserved timber remains are found, it may be impossible to extract enough of a profile to refer to a master sequence. And as with pottery and coins, although dendrochronology can point accurately to a date for the felling of a tree, it does not yield information regarding the life span of wooden objects. An object may be carved from wood already centuries old, and the same object remain in use for decades more before it enters the archaeological record.

Other laboratory dating methods are available for various materials. Of particular use to historical archaeology are archaeomagnetic and thermoluminescent dating of baked-clay structures such as furnaces and kilns, as well as bricks, tiles and pottery. Given the degree of approximation involved in these techniques, they are secondary in importance to the other methods employed by archaeologists for the Middle Ages. As such, they are used above all to verify chronologies constructed from other evidence. Finally, one should note that it is rare that a precise date can be attributed to a layer or deposit in medieval archaeology. Archaeologists draw on a variety of patterns of internal dating evidence to form relative chronologies within the framework of the 'absolute' chronology of historians. These relative chronologies relate to long-term historical phenomena. The precise timing of an event for which there is archaeological evidence, such as the foundation or destruction of a building, can be fixed only in rare instances when the date is recorded by some form of written documentation.

Finds

Finds are the objects found in archaeological deposits. This definition has been widely stretched by advances in archaeological research: initially, the definition applied mostly to artefacts; subsequently it was extended to cover remains that may not have been the work of man, but which nonetheless provide evidence of his activity and conditions of life, such as human and animal bones and plant residues, such as seeds, charcoal and pollen.

Through analysis of this great range of evidence, archaeologists are able to reconstruct the material culture of a particular settlement, and that of a particular society. There are certain limitations in this kind of work, which result from the objective conditions of archaeological discoveries. When buried beneath the ground, in most conditions non-organic materials (stone, metal and fired clay) survive better than organic ones (such as fur, leather, textiles and timber). Leather and cloth are mostly preserved in waterlogged sites, and desiccated wood and plant finds in arid conditions. The exception to the principle is bone, which survives well in most soil conditions, though not in high acid levels such as those produced by sand.

It is well to remember that reconstituting material culture is not simply a process of cataloguing and quantifying the material evidence recovered by excavation. Because archaeological finds were once the outcome of productive processes, and as they were intended to serve particular purposes, the study of material culture production and usage is central to the archaeologist's work of understanding past societies. Determining the function of a given object is often more difficult that it might seem, particularly when one is seeking to move beyond summary definitions to a detailed understanding of the object in hand and the differences that distinguish it from other analogous objects. Ethnology often throws up parallels and possible interpretations, but at times it is a case of tracking down similar artefacts (or even making them anew), in order to come to a practical understanding of an object's original function.

The mechanical and physico-chemical processes through which arte-facts were made can be interpreted to some degree from the external aspect of an object, from the way in which a pottery vessel was turned and fired, for instance. Still greater detail may be provided by techno-logical analyses, which can identify the productive processes involved, and the nature and provenance of the raw materials, thus revealing the constituents of a metal alloy, for example, or the type of clay used for pottery. The pursuit of this level of information is not an end in itself; rather, it contributes to an understanding of the essential aspects of economic and technological organization, the circulation of raw materi-als to artisans, and the condition of technological practice. For this reason, archaeological science has developed a battery of specialized techniques with which to interpret and present the enormous range of data available from the material record. This analysis extends to human and animal remains and plant residues. In the hands of physical anthro-pologists, the archaeology of human remains can be made to reveal the sex of individuals and their age at death, and, in certain cases, the cause of death. A range of techniques is employed to evaluate physical appear-ance, standards of diet and nutrition, and the incidence of disease or deformity. Similarly, animal remains can be used to recover important aspects of economic organization, such as domestication and hunting, to say nothing of dietary habits, the types of meat predominantly con-sumed, and the butchering and preparation of meat. Botanical residues, pollens and seeds provide data relating to patterns of cultivation and the natural environment. In order for each of these specific sources of data to assume comprehensive or over-arching significance, they must be regarded in terms of their reciprocal interdependency. This requires the specialist skills of the environmental archaeologist.

Another significant range of information may be provided by the distribution of artefacts. Increasingly, archaeologists have become interested in the distribution of finds over wide areas and its significance. Studies of distribution and spatial analysis are concerned with the condition of production and distribution. Restricted distribution of particular commodities may imply that these were in limited demand, though the same circumstance may also imply that there were difficulties in communication and exchange. Conversely, we might assume that categories of archaeological material found across large areas were (or were associated with) sought-after commodities of some value; that production of these objects was organized in an efficient way; and that conditions were favourable to exchange. Once again, pottery is the staple of this branch of archaeological inquiry. Through the patterns of distribution of particular ceramic types, it is possible to reconstruct the direction of exchange networks and shipping lanes. In cases where pottery vessels changed hands in the form of containers for foodstuffs, the remains of such vessels are evidence for the area and volume of distribution of victuals and provisions.

Survey and other forms of archaeological investigation

The stratigraphic sequence and its artefactual and material constituents together make up the record of the formation, development and function of an excavated site. Information derived from analysis of the excavated data is valid only in the context of the particular site. Strictly speaking, it is not legitimate practice to adduce the same data in statements about other sites or situations. How, then, are we to establish to what degree our understanding of activity at one site may be interpreted as symptomatic of wider tendencies or trends? This question is central to the issue of collaboration between archaeological research and historical studies. Historians are capable of distinguishing between situations of local significance and others of more general import, as they are able to make use of documentation concerning the general character of economic, social and institutional systems particular to various eras and different societies, and in relation to which the significance of particular episodes and incidences may be evaluated.

In archaeology, by contrast, the interpretations suggested by discoveries on a given site may not be readily transposed to other sites or even to other areas of the same site. Instead, the relevance of these discoveries may be established only if similar discoveries are made on other sites with such frequency as to suggest that one is dealing with a situation of general significance. It follows, then, that the possibility of attributing general significance to a given discovery depends in large measure on the quantity of excavations carried out. Yet excavations are costly and frequently time-consuming concerns; and in the field of medieval archaeology, large-scale projects are still relatively few and far between.

Attempts have been made to obviate these difficulties through the introduction of surface reconnaissance strategies, aimed at identifying and investigating remains visible on the surface of the soil, without the need for excavation. Traces of buildings and potsherds are regularly brought to the surface by movements of the soil caused by construction work, soil erosion, planting and ploughing.

Evidence of this kind has always been taken into consideration by archaeologists, particularly when planning future excavations. But in the last decades considerable effort has been put into maximizing the potential of this class of evidence. For instance, it is now understood that, in certain conditions, surface finds of pottery are statistically representative of material concealed beneath the soil; hence, strategies have been devised to ensure that the sample picked up is representative, and that the location and extent of the scatter is accurately plotted on plans of the area under survey. Even when conducted over vast areas and whole regions, surface reconnaissance of this kind involves none of the complex logistics and vast cost entailed by widespread excavation, while rapidly providing an overview of settlement in an area or region and a glimpse of its culture. Moreover, the results of a survey of this kind can be combined with those produced by other methods of remote detection, such as aerial photography, and the study of old maps and archive records. It should be clear, however, that the outcomes of this kind of work are limited. Most commonly a survey is concerned only with settlement patterns, diffusion of ceramic types and particular building traditions; it cannot produce the quantity and variety of data afforded by excavation and stratigraphic analysis. What is more, the very productivity of archaeological surveys depends on reliable knowledge of local pottery and building traditions, knowledge best obtained through excavation. Therefore, survey results can only be sustained by the results of excavation in the area in question. This being so, excavation remains the essential means of acquiring and refining archaeological knowledge.

Still more ambitious attempts to overcome the intrinsic limitations on archaeological knowledge have beaten other paths. Those archaeologists most acutely aware of the problem have turned to the social sciences, geography and anthropology, for models and general laws governing the behaviour of human societies, spatial patterns, and the organization of economic relations, with which to interpret the general significance of local situations. This turn in archaeological practice and theory continues to be the subject of enormous debate, as its results are continually verified and its conclusions tested.

As archaeology proceeds in pursuit of wide-ranging explanations of the processes of change and their social and economic causes, the discipline's objectives are moving further and further in the direction of those of historical research, and so the case for greater collaboration between the two disciplines becomes all the more compelling. By comparing the interpretations and explanations independently formulated by the two disciplines using their proper analytical tools, it is possible for practitioners in both disciplines to test the quality and plausibility of each others' findings, both at the level of local situations and more general phenomena. Of course, the benchmarks of this test are not necessarily to be dictated by historians. Archaeology sheds light on aspects of phenomena for which no evidence is to be found in written records, and by doing so it opens the way for fresh readings of the written evidence. Conversely, the general frameworks produced by historical research provide institutional and structural systems with which archaeological interpretation must be compatible. There is a particular case for collaboration when more than one causal explanation may be offered for a single archaeological discovery, as often happens; in this case, historical expertise may be brought in to guide the archaeologist's choice from the interpretations on offer. In other words, the process of testing must always be a reciprocal and bilateral one. It is the aim of the collaborative process to broaden our understanding of life in the past in ever more complex and comprehensive ways.

Further Reading

The following bibliographies were prepared by the translator, with the interests and needs of an English-speaking readership in mind. For this reason, most references are to modern publications in English.

1. The Middle Ages – the history of an idea

General historiography

M. Bentley (ed.), *Companion to Historiography* (Routledge, London & New York, 1977).

M. Brown & S.H. Harrison, *The Medieval World and the Modern Mind* (Four Courts, Dublin, 2000).

P. Burke, *New Perspectives on Historical Writing* (Cambridge University Press, Cambridge, 1991).

H. Damico (ed.), *Medieval Scholarship: Biographical Studies on the Formation of a Discipline*. Vol. 1: *History* (Garland, New York & London, 1995). Vol. 2: *Literature and Philology* (Garland, New York & London, 1998). Vol. 3: *Philosophy and the Arts* (Garland, New York & London, 2000).

H. Elmer Barnes, *A History of Historical Writing* (Norman, Oklahoma, 1936).

V.H. Galbraith, *Historical Research in Medieval England* (Athlone Press, London, 1951).

A. Green & K. Troup (eds), *The Houses of History: A Critical Reader in Twentieth-Century History and Theory* (Manchester University Press, Manchester, 1999).

P. Heather, 'Late antiquity and the early medieval West', in M. Bentley (ed.), *Companion to Historiography* (Routledge, London & New York, 1977), pp. 69-87.

D. Hay, *Annalists and Historians: Western Historiography from the VIIIth to the XVIIIth Century* (London, Methuen, 1977).

M.D. Knowles, *Great Historical Enterprises: Problems in Monastic History* (Nelson, London, 1963).

L.K. Little & B.H. Rosenwein, *Debating the Middle Ages: issues and readings* (Blackwell, Malden [Mass.] & Oxford, 1998).

A. Marwick, *The New Nature of History: Knowledge, Evidence, Language* (Palgrave, Basingstoke, 2001).

D. Metzger (ed.), *Medievalism and the Academy* II. *Studies in Medievalism* X (D.S. Brewer, Woodbridge, 2000).

N.F. Partner, 'Making up lost time: writing on the writing of history', in B. Fay, P. Pomper & R.T. Vann (eds), *History and Theory: Contemporary Readings* (Blackwell, Malden [Mass.] & Oxford, 1998), pp. 69-89.

G. Sergi, *L'idea di medioevo* (Donzelli editore, Rome, 1998).

T. Shippey & M. Arnold, *Appropriating the Middle Ages: Scholarship, Politics and Fraud. Studies in Medievalism* XI (D.S. Brewer, Cambridge, 2001).

F. Stern (ed.), *The Varieties of History: Voltaire to the Present* (World Publishing Company, Cleveland [Ohio], 1956).

J.M.H. Smith, 'Introduction: regarding medievalists: contexts and approaches', in M. Bentley (ed.), *Companion to Historiography* (Routledge, London & New York, 1997) pp. 105-16.

R.E. Sullivan, 'The Carolingian Age: reflections on its place in the history of the Middle Ages', *Journal of Medieval and Renaissance Studies* 18 (1988), pp. 267-306.

T.R. Tholfson, *Historical Thinking: An Introduction* (Harper & Row, New York, 1967).

J.W. Thompson, *A History of Historical Writing.* 2 vols (Macmillan, New York, 1942).

D.R. Woolf, *A Global Encyclopedia of Historical Writing* (Garland, New York & London, 1998).

L.J. Workman, K. Verduin & D.D. Metzger (eds), *Medievalism and the Academy* I. *Studies in Medievalism* IX (D.S. Brewer, Cambridge, 1999).

Historiography of the sixteenth and seventeenth centuries

L. Barkan, *Unearthing the Past: Archaeology and Aesthetics in the Making of Renaissance Culture* (Yale University Press, New Haven & London, 1999; reprinted 2001).

N. Edelmann, *Attitudes of 17th-Century France toward the Middle Ages* (New York, 1946).

M. McKisack, *Medieval History in the Tudor Age* (Clarendon Press, Oxford, 1971).

R. McKitterick, 'The study of Frankish history in France and Germany in the sixteenth and seventeenth centuries', *Francia* 8 (1980), pp. 556-72.

F. Smith Fussner, *The Historical Revolution: English Historical Writing and Thought 1580-1640* (2nd edn. Greenwood Press, Westport [Conn.], 1976; 1962).

J. Voss, *Das Mittelalter im historischen Denken Frankreichs: Untersuchungen zur Geschichte des Mittelalterbegriffes und der Mittelalterbewertung von der zweiten Hälfte des 16. bis zur des 19.Jahrhunderts* (Fink, Munich, 1972).

R.G. Witt, *Italian Humanism and Medieval Rhetoric. Variorum Collected Studies Series* CS737 (Ashgate, Aldershot, 2001).

Historiography of the Enlightenment and Romanticism

E. Baho, 'Scott as a medievalist', in H.J.C. Grierson (ed.), *Sir Walter Scott Today: Some Retrospective Essays and Studies* (Constable, London, 1932).

J.B. Black, *The Art of History: A Study of Four Great Historians of the Eighteenth Century* (2nd edn. Russell, New York, 1965; 1926).

J.H. Brumfitt, *Voltaire: Historian* (Oxford University Press, London, 1958).

L. Gossman, *Medievalism and the Ideologies of Enlightenment: The World and Work of La Curne de Sainte Palaye* (Johns Hopkins University Press, Baltimore, 1968).

J.R. Hale (ed.), *The Evolution of British Historiography: From Bacon to Namier* (World Publishing Company, Cleveland [Ohio], 1964).

J.G.A. Pocock, *Barbarism and Religion.* 2 vols (Cambridge University Press, Cambridge, 1999; reprinted 2000).

A. Schreiber, 'Das Mittelalter universalhistoriches Problem von der Romantik', *Archiv für Kulturgeschichte* 31 (1943), pp. 93-120.

R. Stadelmann, 'Grundformen der Mittelalterauffassung von Herder bis Ranke', *Deutsche Vierteljahrsschrift für Literatur und Geistesgeschichte* 9 (1931), pp. 45-88.

A.H. Thompson, *Gibbon* (King & Staples, London, 1946).

L.J. Workman, *Medievalism in England.* 2 vols (D.S. Brewer, Cambridge, 1992).

Historiography of the nineteenth century

C. Antoni, *From History to Sociology: The Transition in German Historical Thought* (2nd edn. Merlin Press, London, 1962; 1959).

E. Artifoni, *Salvemini e il medioevo. Storici italiani fra Otto e Novecento* (Liguori, Naples, 1990).

G. von Below, *Die deutsche Geschichtsschreibung von der Befreiungskriegen bis zu unsern Tagen* (Oldenburg, Munich & Berlin, 1924).

T.B. Bottomore & M. Rubel (eds), *Karl Marx: Selected Writings in Sociology and Social Philosophy* (2nd edn. Penguin, Harmondsworth, 1961; 1956).

C.O. Carbonell, *Histoire et historiens: un mutation idéologique des historiens français 1865-1885* (Privat, Toulouse, 1976).

D. Doolittle, *The Relations between Literature and Medieval Studies in France from 1820 to 1860* (Bryn Mawr, Pennsylvania, 1933).

G.R. Elton, *F.W. Maitland* (Yale University Press, New Haven & London, 1985).

G. Falco, 'La questione longobarda e la moderna storiografia italiana', *Atti del I congresso internazionale di studi longobardi* (CISAM, Spoleto, 1952), pp. 155-60.

G.P. Gooch, *History and Historians in the Nineteenth Century* (Longman, London & New York, 1949; reprinted 1952).

E. Hobsbawm, 'What do historians owe to Karl Marx?', in *ibid., On History* (Abacus, London, 1998), pp. 186-206.

—— 'Marx and history' in *ibid.*, pp. 207-25.

G.G. Igers, *The German Conception of History: The National Thought from Herder to the Present* (Wesleyan University Press, Middletown, Connecticut, 1968).

H. Stuart Hughes, *Consciousness and Society: The Reorientation of European Social Thought 1880-1930* (2nd edn. MacGibbon & Key, London, 1959; revised Vintage Books, New York, 1977).

Studi medievali e imagine del medioevo fra Ottocento e Novecento (= Bullettino dell'Instituto Storico Italiano per il Medio Evo, 100), Roma 1997.

G. Tabacco, 'La dissoluzione medievale dello stato nella recente storiografia', *Studi medievali* 1 (1960), pp. 397-446.

Historiography of the twentieth century

N. Cantor, *Inventing the Middle Ages: The Lives, Works and Ideas of the Great Medievalists of the Twentieth Century* (Morrow, New York, 1991).

O. Capitani, *Medioevo passato prossimo. Appunti storiografici: tra due guerre e molte crisi* (Il Mulino, Bologna, 1979).

R. Collins, 'The Carolingians and the Ottonians in an Anglophone world', *Journal of Medieval History* 22 (1996), pp. 97-114.

P. Delogu, 'Reading Pirenne again', in R. Hodges & W. Bowden (eds), *The Sixth Century: Production, Distribution and Demand* (Brill, Leiden, Boston & Cologne, 1998), pp. 15-40.

F. Drion du Chapois, *Henri Pirenne* (Brussels, 1964).

J. van Engen (ed.), *The Past and Future of Medieval Studies* (Notre Dame, Illinois, 1994).

E. Hobsbawm, 'Historians and economists I and II', in *ibid.*, *On History* (Abacus, London, 1998), pp. 124-43, 144-63.

H. Kleinschmidt, *Understanding the Middle Ages: The Transformation of Ideas and Attitudes in the Medieval World* (Boydell Press, Woodbridge, 2000).

B. Lyon, *Henri Pirenne: A Biographical and Intellectual Study* (E. Story-Scientia, Ghent, 1974).

L. Patterson, 'On the margin: postmodernism, ironic history and medieval studies', *Speculum* 65 (1990), pp. 87-100.

B. Rosenthal & P.E. Szarmach, *Medievalism in American Culture* (Arizona Center for Medieval and Renaissance Studies, Tempe, Arizona, 1989).

G.M. Spiegel, *The Past as Text: The Theory and Practice of Medieval Historiography* (Johns Hopkins University Press, Baltimore, 1997).

———— 'History, historicism and the social logic of the text in the Middle Ages', in K. Jenkins (ed.), *The Postmodern History Reader* (Routledge, London & New York), pp. 180-203.

S. William Halperin (ed.), *Some 20th-Century Historians: Essays on Eminent Europeans* (University of Chicago Press, Chicago & London, 1961).

There is now an academic journal – *Studies in Medievalism* – dedicated entirely to the study of post-medieval images and perceptions of the Middle Ages.

2. The problem of periodization

L. Besserman (ed.), *The Challenge of Periodisation: Old Paradigms and New Perspectives* (Garland, New York & London, 1996).

A. Briggs & D. Snowman (eds), *Fins de Siècle: How Centuries End 1400-2000* (Yale University Press, London & New Haven, 1996).

C. Brooke, *Europe in the Central Middle Ages 962-1154* (Longman, London, 2000).

P. Delogu (ed.), *Periodi e contenuti del Medio Evo* (Il Ventaglio, Rome, 1988).

D. Gaimster & P. Stamper, *The Age of Transition: The Archaeology of English Culture 1400-1600. Society for Medieval Archaeology Monograph* 15 (Oxbow, Oxford, 1997).

J. Hines, K. Hoilund Nielsen & F. Seigmund, *The Pace of Change: Studies in Early Medieval Chronology* (Oxbow, Oxford, 1998).

N. Howe, *Migration and Mythmaking in Anglo-Saxon England* (Yale University Press, New Haven & London, 1989; revised 2001).

L. Jordanova, *History in Practice*, ch. 5 'Periodisation' (Arnold, London, 2000), pp. 114-40.

G. Kubler, *The Shape of Time: Remarks on the History of Things* (Yale University Press, London & New Haven, 1962).

R. Lodge, *The Close of the Middle Ages 1273-1494* (Allen Lane – Penguin Press, London, 2001).

H. St L.B. Moss, *The Birth of the Middle Ages 395-814* (Oxford University Press, London, 1935).

J. Moorhead, *The Roman Empire Divided 400-700* (Longman, Harlow, 2001).

D. Norman, *The Arabs and Medieval Europe* (Longman, London, 1975).

R. Reece, *The Later Roman Empire* (Tempus, Stroud, 1999).

A. Schiavone, *The End of the Past: Ancient Rome and the Modern West* (Harvard University Press, Cambridge [Mass.], 2000).

C. Wickham, 'The other transition: from the ancient world to feudalism', *Past and Present* 103 (1984), pp. 3-36.

3. Some general themes in medieval history

Invasions, barbarians, Germans

T.S. Burns, *A History of the Ostrogoths* (Bloomington, Indiana, 1984).

F.M. Clover, *The Late Roman West and the Vandals* (Ashgate, Aldershot, 1993).

W. Goffart, 'The Barbarians in late antiquity and how they were accommodated', in L.K. Little & B.H. Rosenwein (eds), *Debating the Middle Ages: Issues and Readings* (Blackwell, Malden [Mass.] & Oxford, 1998), pp. 25-44.

H. Härke (ed.), *Archaeology, Ideology and Society: The German Experience* (Peter Lang, New York, 2000).

P. Heather, *Goths and Romans, 332-489* (Clarendon Press, Oxford, 1991).

—— *The Goths* (Blackwell, Oxford, 1996).

A.H.M. Jones, *The Decline of the Ancient World* (Longman, London, 1975).

M. Kazanski, *Les Slavs: les origines (Ier-VIIe siècles après J-C)* (Editions Errance, Paris, 1999).

J. Lucassen & L. Lucassen (eds), *Migration, Migration History, History: Old Paradigms and New Perspectives* (Peter Lang, New York, 1998).

J. Moorhead, *Theoderic in Italy* (Clarendon Press, Oxford, 1993).

W. Pohl, 'Conceptions of ethnicity in early medieval studies', in L.K. Little & B.H. Rosenwein (eds), *Debating the Middle Ages: Issues and Readings* (Malden [Mass.] & Oxford, 1998), pp. 15-24.

P.S. Wells, *The Barbarians Speak: How the Conquered Peoples Shaped Roman Europe* (Princeton University Press, Princeton [N.J.], 1999).

C. Wickham, 'The fall of Rome will not take place', in L.K. Little & B.H. Rosenwein (eds), *Debating the Middle Ages: Issues and Readings* (Blackwell, Malden [Mass.] & Oxford, 1998), pp. 45-57.

H. Wolfram, *History of the Goths* (University of California Press, Berkeley & London, 1988).

—— (trans. T. Dunlap) *The Roman Empire and its Germanic Peoples* (California University Press, Berkeley & London, 1997).

I. Wood, *The Merovingian Kingdoms 450-751* (Longman, London & New York, 1994).

Christianity and the Church

J. Burton, *Medieval Monasticism* (Caxton Book Co., London, 1996).

J. Burton Russell & D.W. Lumsden, *A History of Medieval Christianity: Prophecy and Order* (Peter Lang, New York, 2000).

H. Daniel-Rops (trans. A. Butler), *The Church in the Dark Ages* 2 vols (2nd edn. Dent, London, 2001; 1959).

H. Fictenau, *Heretics and Scholars in the High Middle Ages 1000-1200* (Pennsylvania State University Press, University Park [PA] 1998).

B. Hamilton, *The Christian World of the Middle Ages* (Sutton, Stroud, 2001).

R. Kay, *Councils and Clerical Culture in the Medieval West* (Variorum, Aldershot, 1997).

P. King, *Western Monasticism: A History of the Monastic Movement in the Latin Church. Cistercian Studies Series* 185 (Kalamazoo [Michigan] & Leicester, 1999).

C.H. Lawrence, *Medieval Monasticism* (3rd edn. Longman, London & New York, 2001; 1984, 1989, 1996).

A. McGrath, *Historical Theology: An Introduction to the History of Christian Thought* (Blackwell, Oxford, 1998).

T. Nyberg, *Monasticism in North-Western Europe 800-1200* (Ashgate, Aldershot, 2000).

R.E. Reynolds, *Clerical Orders in the Early Middle Ages* (Ashgate, Aldershot, 1999).

—— *Clerics in the Early Middle Ages* (Ashgate, Aldershot, 1999).

J. Shinners (ed.), *Medieval Popular Religion 1000-1500: A Reader* (Broadview, Ontario, New York & Cardiff, 1997).

R.N. Swanson, *Religion and Devotion in Europe 1215-1515* (Cambridge University Press, Cambridge, 1995).

J.A.F. Thomson, *The Western Church in the Middle Ages* (Harvard University Press, Cambridge [Mass.], 1998).

Power and the limits of power

E.A.R. Brown, 'The tyranny of a construct: feudalism and historians of medieval Europe', in L.K. Little & B.H. Rosenwein (eds), *Debating the Middle Ages: Issues and Readings* (Blackwell, Malden [Mass.] & Oxford, 1998), pp. 148-69.

W. Brown, *Unjust Seizure: Conflict, Interest and Authority in an Early Medieval Society* (Cornell University Press, 2001).

J. Denton (ed.), *Orders and Hierarchies in Late Medieval and Renaissance Europe* (London & New York, Macmillan, 1999).

A. Gewith, *Marsilius of Padua: The Defender of Peace*. 2 vols. I: *Marsilius of Padua and Medieval Political Philosophy* (Columbia University Press, New York & London, 1951).

W.C. Jordan, *Ideology and Royal Power in Medieval France* (Variorum Collected Studies, Ashgate, Aldershot, 2001).

B. Jussen (ed.), *Ordering Medieval Society* (University of Pennsylvania Press, Philadelphia, 2001).

M.S. Kempshall, *The Common Good in Late Medieval Political Thought* (Oxford University Press, Oxford, 1999).

J. Nelson, 'The Lord's anointed and the people's choice: Carolingian royal ritual', in D. Cannadine & S. Price (eds), *Rituals of Royalty: Power and Ceremonial in Traditional Societies* (Cambridge University Press, Cambridge, 1987), pp. 137-80.

E. Peters, *Limits of Thought and Power in Medieval Europe. Variorum Collected Studies Series* CS721 (Ashgate, Aldershot, 2001).

G. Tabacco (trans. Rosalind Brown Jensen), *The Struggle for Power in Medieval Italy* (Cambridge University Press, Cambridge, 1989).

B. Tierney & P. Linehan, *Authority and Power: Studies on Medieval Law and Government Presented to Walter Ullmann on his Seventieth Birthday* (Cambridge University Press, Cambridge, 1980).

W. Ullmann, *Law and Politics in the Middle Ages: An Introduction to the Sources of Medieval Political Ideas* (Sources of History, London, 1975).

Nations

D.A. Bullough, 'Ethnic history and the Carolingians', in C. Holdsworth & T.P. Wiseman (eds), *The Inheritance of Historiography 350-900* (Exeter University Publications, Exeter, 1986), pp. 85-105.

S. Gasparri, *Prima delle nazioni. Popoli, etnie e regni fra Antichità e Medioevo* (La Nuova Italia Scientifica, Rome, 1997).

D. Harrison, 'Dark Age migrations and subjective ethnicity: the example of the Lombards', *Scandia* 57 (1991), p. 1.

E. Hobsbawm, 'Introduction: inventing traditions', in E. Hobsbawm & T. Ranger (eds), *The Invention of Tradition* (Canto, Cambridge & New York, 1983), pp. 1-14.

E. James, *The Origins of France: From Clovis to the Capetians* (St Martin's Press, New York, 1982).

———— *The Franks* (Basil Blackwell, Oxford, 1988).

R. Jenkins, *Rethinking Ethnicity* (Sage, London, Thousand Oaks [California] & New Delhi, 1997; reprinted 1998).

R. Miles, *Constructing Identities in Late Antiquity* (Routledge, London & New York, 1995).

W. Pohl, 'Tradition, Ethnogenese und literarische Gestaltung: eine Zwischenbilanz', in K. Brunner & B. Merta (eds), *Ethnogenese und Überlieferung: Angewandte Methoden der Frühmittelalterforschung* (Oldenburg, Vienna & Munich, 1994).

W. Pohl & H. Reintz (eds), *Strategies of Distinction: The Construction of Ethnic Communities 300-800. European Science Foundation – Transformation of the Roman World* 2 (Brill, Leiden, Boston, Cologne, 1998).

W. Pohl, 'Memory, identity and power in Lombard Italy', in Y. Hen & M. Innes (eds), *The Uses of the Past in the Early Middle Ages* (Cambridge University Press, Cambridge, 2000), pp. 9-28.

A.P. Smyth (ed.), *Medieval Europeans: Studies in Ethnic Identity and National Perspectives in Medieval Europe* (Macmillan, Basingstoke, 1998).

H. Zmora, *Monarchy, Aristocracy and the State in Europe: 1300-1800* (Routledge, London & New York, 2000).

The demographic cycle

P. Biller, *The Measure of the Multitude: Population in Medieval Thought* (Oxford University Press, Oxford, 2000).

E. Carpentier, 'Autour de la Peste Noire: famines et epidémies dans l'histoire du XIVe siècle', *Annales: Économies, Sociétés, Civilisations* 17 (1962), pp. 1062-92.

R. Horrox (trans. & ed.), *The Black Death* (Manchester University Press, Manchester, 1994).

D. Keys, *Catastrophe: An Investigation into the Origins of the Modern World* (Century, London, 1999).

P.H. Sawyer & R.H. Hinton, 'Technical determinism: the stirrup and the plough', *Past and Present* 24 (1975), pp. 90-100.

M.R. Smith & L. Marx (eds), *Does Technology Drive History? The Dilemma of Technological Determinism* (Massachusetts Institute of Technology, Cambridge [Mass.] & London, 1994).

L. White Jr, *Medieval Technology and Social Change* (Clarendon Press, Oxford, 1962).

P. Ziegler, *The Black Death* (Bramley, Godalming, 1998; 1997; 1970; 1969).

4. The sources of medieval history

Manuals and aids

B. Bischoff (trans. D.Ó Cróinín & D. Ganz), *Latin Palaeography: Antiquity and the Middle Ages* (Cambridge University Press, Cambridge, 1991; reprinted 1995).

L.E. Boyle, *Medieval Latin Palaeography: A Biographical Introduction* (University of Toronto Press – Centre for Medieval Studies, Toronto & London, 1984).

C. Bozzolo & E. Ornato, *Pour une histoire du livre manuscrit au Moyen Age: trois essays de codicologie quantative* (2nd edn. Éditions du Centre National de la Recherche Scientifique, Paris, 1980).

M.P. Brown & P. Lovett, *The Historical Source Book for Scribes* (British Library, London, 1999).

R.C. van Caenegem, *Guide to the Sources of Medieval History* (North-Holland Publishing Company, Amsterdam & Oxford, 1978).

—— *Introduction aux sources de l'histoire médiévale* (Brepols, Turnhout, 1997).

—— *Manuel des études médiévales: typologie des sources* (Brepols, Turnhout, 1997).

C.R. Cheney, *The Records of Medieval England* (Cambridge University Press, Cambridge, 1956).

U. Chevalier, *Répertoire des sources historiques du moyen âge. Topo-bibliographie*. 2 vols (Honoré Champion, Paris, 1894-1903).

M.A.H. Ferguson, *Bibliography of English Translations from Medieval Sources 1943-1967* (Columbia University Press, New York & London, 1974).

E.B. Graves, *A Bibliography of English History to 1485* (Clarendon Press, Oxford, 1975).

N.R. Kerr (ed.), *Medieval Libraries of Great Britain* (Royal Historical Society, London, 1964).

M.B. Parkes & A.G. Watson, *Medieval Scribes, Manuscripts and Libraries: Essays Presented to N.R. Ker* (Scolar Press, London, 1978).

M.B. Parkes, *Scribes, Scripts and Readers: Studies in the Communication, Presentation and Dissemination of Medieval Texts* (Hambledon Press, London, 1991).

C. Platt, *Medieval Archaeology in England: A Guide to the Historical Sources* (Pinhorns, Shalfleet Manor, Isle of Wight, 1969).

B.S. Pullan, *Sources for the History of Medieval Europe: From the Mid-Eighth-Mid-Thirteenth Century* (Blackwell, Oxford, 1966).

P.R. Robinson & R. Zim (eds), *Of the Making of Books: Medieval Manuscripts, their Scribes and Readers: Essays Presented to M.B. Parkes* (Ashgate, Aldershot, 1997).

J.A. Szirmai, *The Archaeology of Medieval Bookbinding* (Ashgate, Aldershot, 1999).

P.J. Willetts, *Catalogue of Manuscripts in the Society of Antiquaries of London* (D.S. Brewer, Woodbridge, 2000).

The language of medieval sources

A. Blaise, *Lexicon latinitatis medii aevi praesertim ad res ecclesiasticas investigandas pertinens* (Brepols, Turnhout, 1975).

F. Blatt & Y. Lefèvre (eds), *Novum glossarium mediae latinitatis ab anno DCCC usque ad annum MCC* (Ejnar Munskgaard, Copenhagen, 1957-).

N. Brooks (ed.), *Latin and the Vernacular Languages in Early Medieval Britain* (Leicester University Press, Leicester, 1982).

J.F. Collins, *A Primer of Ecclesiastical Latin* (Catholic University of America Press, Washington [DC], 1995).

G. Cremaschi, *Guida allo studio del latino medievale* (Liviana, Padua, 1959).

K.H. van Dalem-Oskam, K.A.C. Depuydt, W.J.J. Pijnenburg & T.H. Schoonheim (eds), *Dictionaries of Medieval Germanic Languages: A Survey of Current Lexicographical Projects. International Research Series 2* (Brepols, Turnhout, 1997).

Dictionary of Medieval Latin from British Sources (Oxford, University Press, London, 1975-).

E.A. Gooder, *Latin for Local History. An Introduction* (Longman, London, 1961).

R.E. Latham, *Revised Medieval Latin Word-List from British and Irish Sources* (British Academy – Oxford University Press, London, 1965).

E. Lofstedt, *Late Latin* (Aschenhoug, Oslo, 1959).

Mittellateinisches Wörterbuch bis zum ausgehenden 13. Jahrhundert. 2 vols (Bayerische Akademie der Wissenschaften – Deutsche Akademie der Wissenschaften zu Berlin) (Munich, Beck, 1959-91).

F.A.C. Mantello & A.G. Rigg (eds), *Medieval Latin: An Introduction and Bibliographical Guide* (Catholic University of America Press, Washington [DC], 1996).

C. Mohrmann (ed.), *Études sur le latin des chrétiens.* 4 vols (Edizioni di Storia e Letteratura, Rome, 1958-77).

J.F. Niermeyer & C. van de Kieft (eds), *Mediae latinitatis minus: lexique latin medieval-français-anglais* (2nd edn. Brill, Leiden & New York, 1993; 1976).

K.C. Newton, *Medieval Local Records – A Reading Aid* (Historical Association, London, 1971).

D. Norberg, *Manuel pratique de latin médiéval* (Picard, Paris, 1968).

R. Sharpe, *A Hand-List of the Latin Writers of Great Britain and Ireland before 1540* (Brepols, Turnhout, 1997).

K. Sidwell, *Reading Medieval Latin* (Cambridge University Press, Cambridge, 1995).

———— (trans. P. van de Woestijne) *Introduction à l'étude du latin medieval* (Gand, 1933).

J. Thorley, *Documents in Medieval Latin* (Duckworth, London, 1998).

Select topics

F.H. Bauml, 'Varieties and consequences of medieval literacy and illiteracy', *Speculum* 55 (1980), pp. 237-65.

C. Bertelli, 'The production and distribution of books in late antiquity', in R. Hodges & W. Bowden (eds), *The Sixth Century: Production, Distribution and Demand* (Brill, Leiden, Boston & Cologne, 1998), pp. 41-60.

R. Black, *Humanism and Education in Medieval and Renaissance Italy* (Cambridge University Press, Cambridge, 2001).

L. Bonfante (ed.), *The Origin of the Romance Languages: Stages in the Development of Latin* (Winter, Heidelberg, 1998).

C.F. Briggs, 'Literacy, reading, and writing in the medieval West', *Journal of Medieval History* 26 (2000), pp. 397-420.

H. Gneuss, *Books and Libraries in Early England. Variorum Collected Studies Series* CS558 (Ashgate, Aldershot, 1996).

D.H. Green, *Language and History in the Early Germanic World* (Cambridge University Press, Cambridge, 2000).

N.R. Kerr (ed.), *Medieval Libraries of Great Britain* (Royal Historical Society, London, 1964).

M.B. Parkes & A.G. Watson, *Medieval Scribes, Manuscripts and Libraries: Essays Presented to N.R. Ker* (Scolar Press, London, 1978).

M.B. Parkes, *Scribes, Scripts and Readers: Studies in the Communication, Presentation and Dissemination of Medieval Texts* (Hambledon Press, London, 1991).

P.R. Robinson & R. Zim (eds), *Of the Making of Books: Medieval Manuscripts, their Scribes and Readers: Essays Presented to M.B. Parkes* (Ashgate, Aldershot, 1997).

J.A. Szirmai, *The Archaeology of Medieval Bookbinding* (Ashgate, Aldershot, 1999).

R. Wright, *Late Latin and Early Romance in Spain and Carolingian France* (Cairns, Liverpool, 1982).

——— (ed.), *Latin and the Romance Languages in the Middle Ages* (Pennsylvania State University Press, Philadelphia, 1991; reprinted 1996).

5. The writing of history in the Middle Ages

Collections

J.J. Bagley, *Historical Interpretation* I: *Sources of English Medieval History 1066-1540* (Harmondsworth, Penguin, 1965; reprinted 1972).

J.M. Bak (ed.), *Mittelalterliche Geschichtsquellen in chronologischer Übersicht* (Stuttgart, Steiner, 1987).

J.H. Baxter, C. Johnson & J.F. Willard, *An Index of British and Irish Latin Writers AD 400-1520* (Paris, 1932).

W. Buchwald, A. Hohlweg & O. Prinz (eds), *Tuskulum: Lexicon griechischer und lateinischer Autoren des Altertums und des Mittelalters* (Artemis, Munich, 1982).

M.T. Clanchy, *From Memory to Written Record: England 1066-1307* (Blackwell, Oxford, 1993).

M.C. Diaz y Diaz, *Index scriptorum latinorum medii aevi hispanorum. Acta Salmaticensia. Filosofia y letras* 13. 2 vols (University of Salamanca, Salamanca, 1958-9).

English Historical Documents. 3 vols (Vol. I, ed. D. Whitelock [London, Eyre & Spottiswoode, 1979]; Vol. 2, eds D.C. Douglas & G.W. Greenaway [2nd edn. London, Eyre & Spottiswoode, 1982]; Vol. 3, ed. H. Rothwell [London, Eyre & Spottiswoode,1975]).

A. Gransden, *Historical Writing in England*. 2 vols (London, Routledge & Kegan Paul, 1974, 1982).

G. Hasenhor & M. Zink (eds), *Dictionnaire des lettres françaises: le moyen âge* (Fayard, Paris, 1992).

O. Lorenz, *Deutschlands Geschichtsquellen im Mittelalter seit der Mitte des XIII. Jahrhunderts*. 2 vols (Herz, Berlin, 1886-7).

M. Manitius & P. Lehmann, *Geschichte der lateinischen Literatur des Mittelalters. Handbuch der Altertumswissenschaften* IX. 3 vols (Munich, Beck, 1923-59).

A. Molinier, *Les sources de l'histoire de France: des origines aux guerres d'Italie (1494)*. 6 vols (Picard, Paris, 1901-6).

A. Potthast (ed.), *Bibliotheca Historica Medii Aevi. Wegweiser durch die*

Geschichtswerke des europäischen Mittelalters bis 1500 (Berlin, 1896; re-printed Graz, Akademische Druck, 1957).

Reportorium fontium historiae medii aevi (Unione Internazionale degli Istituti di Archeologia, Storia e Storia dell'Arte – Istituto Storico Italiano per il Medio Evo, Rome, 1953-).

W. Wattenbach, *Deutschlands Geschichtsquellen im Mittelalter bis zum Mitte des XIII. Jahrhunderts.* 2 vols (Berlin, 1983-1994).

Manuals and aids

D. Aers (ed.), *Medieval Literature and Historical Inquiry* (D.S. Brewer, Wood-bridge, 2000).

A. Callander Murray, *After Rome's Fall: Narrators and Sources of Early Medie-val History* (University of Toronto Press, Toronto & London, 1998).

H. Hall, *A Formula Book of English Official Historical Documents* I: *Historical Documents* (Cambridge University Press, Cambridge, 1908).

A. Cook, *History/Writing: The Theory and Practice of History in Antiquity and in Modern Times* (Cambridge University Press, Cambridge, 1988).

L. De Looze, *Pseudo-Autobiography in the Fourteenth Century* (Florida Univer-sity Press, Gainesville, 1998).

P.J. Geary (ed.), *Readings in Medieval History* (Broadview, Ontario, New York & Cardiff, 1989; reprinted 1992).

——— (ed.), *Authors of the Middle Ages.* Vol. 2, Nos 5-6: *Historical and Religious Writers of the Latin West* (Ashgate, Aldershot, 1995).

J.-P. Genet, *L'historiographie médiévale en Europe* (Picard, Paris, 1991).

W. Goffart, *The Narrators of Barbarian History (AD 550-800): Jordanes, Gregory of Tours, Bede and Paul the Deacon* (Princeton University Press, Princeton & Guildford, 1988).

A. Gransden, *Historical Writing in England.* Vol. 1: *550-1307.* Vol. 2: *1307 to the Early Sixteenth Century* (Routledge, London, 1997).

D.R. Woolf, *A Global Encyclopaedia of Historical Writing* (Garland, New York & London, 1998).

N. Wright, *History and Literature in Late Antiquity and the Early Medieval West: Studies in Intertextuality. Variorum Collected Studies Series* CS503 (Ashgate, Aldershot, 1995).

Select topics

W.R. Brandt, *The Shape of Medieval History: Studies in Modes of Perception* (Yale University Press, New Haven & London, 1966).

E. Breisach, *Classical Rhetoric and Medieval Historiography. Studies in Medie-val Culture* XIX (Kalamazoo Medieval Institute Publications, Western Michigan University, 1985).

J. Coleman, *Ancient and Medieval Memories: Studies in the Reconstruction of the Past* (Cambridge University Press, Cambridge, 1992).

P. Damian-Grant, *The New Historians of the Twelfth-Century Renaissance* (Boydell & Brewer, Woodbridge, 1999).

R.H.C. Davis & J.M. Wallace-Hadrill, *The Writing of History in the Middle Ages: Essays Presented to Richard William Southern* (Clarendon Press, Oxford, 1981).

D.H. Green, *Language and History in the Early Germanic World* (Cambridge University Press, Cambridge, 2000).

H. Moisl, 'Kingship and orally transmitted Stammerstradition among the Lombards and Franks', in H. Wolfram & A. Schwarcz (eds), *Die Bayern und Ihre Nachbarn* I (Verlag der Österreichischen Akademie der Wissenschaften, Vienna, 1985), pp. 111-19.

V. Murdoch & G.S. Couse (eds), *Essays on the Reconstruction of Medieval History* (McGill-Queen's University Press, Montreal & London, 1974).

R.C. Pales, *The Intellectual Life of Western Europe in the Middle Ages* (Brill, Leiden, New York & Cologne, 1992).

L. Shopkow, *History and Community: Norman Historical Writing in the Eleventh and Twelfth Centuries* (Catholic University of America Press, Washington [DC], 1997).

G.W. Trompf, *Early Christian Historiography: Narratives of Retributive Justice* (Seabury Press, New York, 1997).

C. Wickham, 'The sense of the past in Italian communal narratives', in *ibid.*, *Land and Power: Studies in Italian and European Social History, 400-1200* (British School at Rome, London, 1994), pp. 295-312.

6. Documentary sources

Collections

Papal documents

W. Holtzmann, 'Kanonistische ergaenzungen zur Itali Pontificia', *Quellen und Forschungen* 37 (1957), pp. 55-102; *ibid.*, 38 (1958), pp. 67-175.

P. Jaffé, *Regesta Pontificum Romanorum ab condita ecclesia ad annum post Christum natum MCXCVIII.* 2 vols (Weit & Co., Leipzig, 1851-88).

A. Potthast, *Regesta Pontificum Romanorum inde ab anno post Cristum natum MCXCVIII ad annum MCCCIV.* 2 vols (De Decker, Berlin, 1974; reprinted Akademische Druck, Graz, 1957).

Regesta Pontificum Romanorum. Italia pontificia (IP). 10 vols (Weidmann, Berlin, 1906-75).

O. Seek, *Regesten der Kaiser und Päpste für die Jahre 311 bis 476* (Metzlersche, Stuttgart, 1919).

Imperial and royal documents

J.F. Boehmer, *Regesta Imperii* I: *Die Regesten des Kaiserreichs unter den Karolingern 751-918 (926)*; III: *Die Regesten des regnum Italiae und der burgundischen regna* I: *Die Karolinger im regnum Italiae 840-887 (888)* (Boehlau, Cologne, Vienna, 1991).

C.R. Brühl (ed.), *Codice diplomatico longobardo. Fonti dell'Istituto Storico Italiano* III, 1 (Istituto Storico Italiano, Rome, 1973).

F. Doelger, *Corpus der Greichischen Urkunden des Mittelalters und der Neueren Zeit. Reihe A. Regesten. Anteilung I. Regesten der Kaiserurkunden des östromischen reiches von 565-1453.* 5 vols (Oldenburg – Beck, Munich & Berlin, 1924-65).

E.L.C. Mullins, *Texts and Calendars: An Analytical Guide to Serial Publications.* 2 vols. *Royal Historical Society Guides and Handbooks* 7, 12 (Royal Historical Society, London, 1958-83).

Pipe Rolls. 1st series, 38 vols (Pipe Rolls Society, London, 1884-1925).

Pipe Rolls. 2nd series, 44 vols (Pipe Rolls Society, London, 1925-82).

Public Record Office, *Calendar of Charter Rolls (1226-1516).* 6 vols.

—— *Calendar of Patent Rolls (1216-1563).* 67 vols.

Regesta regum anglo-normannorum I: *1066-1100*, ed. H.W.C. Davis (Clarendon

Press, Oxford, 1913); II: *1100-1135*, ed. C. Johnson & H.A Cronne (Clarendon Press, Oxford, 1956): III: *1135-1154*, ed. C. Johnson, H.A Cronne & R. Davis (Clarendon Press, Oxford, 1968).

Regesta Imperii (Olms, Hildesheim, 1831-)

Rerum Britannicarum Medii Aevi Scriptores (= *Rolls Series*). 253 vols (1858-96).

R. Roehricht, *Regesta regni Hierosolymitani (MXCVII-MCCXCI).* 2 vols (Wagner, Innsbruck, 1893-1904).

P.H. Sawyer, *Anglo-Saxon Charters: An Annotated List and Bibliography. Royal Historical Society Guides and Handbooks* 8 (Royal Historical Society, London, 1968).

B. Thorpe (ed.), *Diplomaticarium Anglicum aevi saxonici: A Collection of English Charters, from the Reign of King Aethelbehrt of Kent AD 605 to that of William the Conqueror* (Macmillan, London, 1865).

Legislative and normative sources

F.L. Attenborough (trans. & ed.), *The Laws of the Earliest English Kings* (Russell & Russell, New York, 1963; reprinted 2000).

F. Calasso, *Medioevo del diritto. Le fonti* I (Giuffrè, Varese, 1954).

C. Chelazzi (ed.), *Catalogo della raccolta di statuti, consuetudini, leggi, decreti, ordini e privilegi dei comuni, delle associazioni e degli enti locali italiani dal medioevo alla fine del secolo XVIII.* 6 vols (Senato della Repubblica, Rome, 1943-63).

H. Conrad, *Deutsche Rechtsgeschichte* I: *Frühzeit und Mittelalter. Ein Lehrbuch* (Müller, Karlsruhe, 1962).

G. Gavet, *Sources de l'histoire des institutions et du droit français. Manuel de bibliographie historique* (Larose, Paris, 1899).

W.S. Holdsworth, *Sources and Literature of English Law* (Clarendon Press, Oxford, 1925; reprinted 1977).

H. Mitteis, *Deutsche Rechtsgeschichte: Ein Studienbuch* (7th edn. Beck, Munich & Berlin, 1961).

F. Olivier-Martin, *Histoire du droit français des origins à la Révolution* (Paris, 1948; 2nd edn. Centre National de la Recherche Scientifique, Paris 1988).

P.H. Winfield, *The Chief Sources of English Legal History* (Harvard University Press, Cambridge [Mass.], 1925).

Manuals and aids

T.A.M. Bishop, *Scriptores regis: Facsimiles to Identify and Illustrate the Hands of Royal Scribes in Original Charters of Henry I, Stephen and Henry II* (Clarendon Press, Oxford, 1961).

D.P. Blok, 'Les formulas de droit romain dans les actes privés au haut moyen âge, in *Miscellanea Mediaevalia in Memoriam J.F. Niermeyer* (Walters, Groningen, 1967).

L.E. Boyle, *A Survey of the Vatican Archives and of its Medieval Holdings* (Pontifical Institute of Medieval Studies, Toronto, 1972).

—— 'Diplomatics', in J.M. Powell (ed.), *Medieval Studies: An Introduction* (Syracuse University Press, New York, 1976), pp. 69-101.

J. Bristow, *The Local Historian's Glossary of Words and Terms* (3rd edn. Countryside Books, 2001; 1990).

F. Di Capua, *Fonti ed esempi per lo studio dello 'Stilus curiae romanae' medioevale* (Rome, Maglione, 1941).

P. Chaplais, *English Medieval Diplomatic Practice*. 2 vols (HMSO, London, 1975).

—— (ed.), *Diplomatic Documents Preserved in the Public Records Office* I: *1101-1272* (HMSO, London, 1964).

G.R.C. Davis, *Medieval Cartularies of Great Britian: A Short Catalogue* (Longman, London, 1958).

A. Dumas, 'La diplomatique et la forme des actes', *Le Moyen Âge* 42 (1932), pp. 5-31.

—— 'Études sur les classement des formes des actes', *Le Moyen Âge* 43 (1933), pp. 81-97, 145-82, 251-64; 44 (1934), pp. 17-41.

J. Earle, *A Hand-Book to the Land-Charters and Other Saxonic Documents* (Clarendon Press, London, 1888).

V. Federici, *Le scritture delle cancellerie italiane dal sec. XII al XVII* (Sansaini, Rome, 1934).

V.H. Galbraith, *An Introduction to the Use of Public Records* (Oxford University Press, Oxford, 1934).

L. Genicot, *Les actes publics (Typologie des sources du moyen âge* 3) (Brepols, Turnhout, 1972).

M. Gervers (ed.), *Dating Undated Medieval Charters* (Boydell Press, Woodbridge, 2000).

D.C. Greetham (ed.), *Textual Scholarship: An Introduction* (Garland, New York & London, 1995).

A Guide to Seals in the Public Record Office (Public Record Office, London, 1964).

H. Hall, *A Formula Book of English Official Historical Documents* II: *Ministerial and Juridical Records* (Cambridge University Press, Cambridge, 1909).

L.C. Hector, *Palaeography and Forgery* (St Anthony's Press, London, 1959).

—— *The Handwriting of English Documents* (2nd edn. Edward Arnold, London, 1966).

R. Kay & D. Heimann, *The Elements of Abbreviation in Medieval Latin Palaeography* (University of Kansas Libraries, Lawrence [KS], 1982).

M.D. Knowles, *Great Historical Enterprises* (Cambridge University Press, Cambridge, 1963).

K. Major, 'The teaching and study of diplomatic in England', *Archives* 8 (1968), pp. 114-18.

C.T. Martin, *The Record Interpreter: A Collection of Abbreviations, Latin Words and Names Used in English Historical Manuscripts and Records* (2nd edn. Stevens, London, 1912; reprinted 1949).

J. Mazzoleni, *Esempi di scritture cancelleresche, curiali e minuscule* (Libreria Scientifica, Naples, 1958).

M.F. Moore, *Two Select Bibliographies of Medieval Historical Study: Bibliography of Palaeography and Diplomatic* (Constable, London, 1912).

P. Ourliac & J. de Malafosse, *Histoire du droit privé* (Presses Universitaires de France, Paris, 1961).

C.M. Radding, *The Origins of Medieval Jurisprudence* (Yale University Press, New Haven & London, 1988).

Record Repositories in Great Britain (4th edn. HMSO, London, 1971).

F.M. Powicke & E.B. Fryde, *A Handbook of British Chronology* (2nd edn. Royal Historical Society, London, 1961).

P.H. Sawyer, *Anglo-Saxon Charters: An Annotated List and Bibliography* (Royal Historical Society, London, 1968).

F.M. Stenton, *Latin Charters of the Anglo-Saxon Period* (Clarendon Press, Oxford, 1955).

D.H. Thomas & L.M. Case, *The New Guide to the Diplomatic Archives of Western Europe* (2nd edn. University of Pennsylvania, Philadelphia, 1975; 1959).

D. Walker, 'The organization of material in medieval cartularies', in D.A. Bullough & R.L. Storey (eds), *The Study of Medieval Records: Essays in Honour of Kathleen Major* (Clarendon Press, Oxford, 1971), pp. 132-50.

A. Winchester, *Discovering Parish Boundaries* (2nd edn. Shire, Princes Risborough [Buckinghamshire], 2000; 1990).

A. Wright, *Court-Hand Restored, or, The Student's Assistant in Reading Old Deeds, Charters and Records* (9th edn. Reeves & Turner, London, 1879).

Select topics

G. Barraclough, *Public Notaries and the Papal Curia* (Macmillan, London, 1934).

P. Bonacini, 'Giustizia pubblica e società carolingia', *Quaderni Medievali* 31-2 (1991), pp. 6-36.

C.N.L. Brooke, 'Approaches to medieval forgery', in *ibid.*, *Medieval Church and Society: Collected Essays* (Sidgwick & Jackson, London, 1971), pp. 100-20.

L.F. Bruyning, 'Lawcourt proceedings in the Lombard kingdom before and after the Frankish conquest', *Journal of Medieval History* 11 (1985), pp. 193-214.

A. Cavanna, 'La civiltà giuridica longobarda', *I Longobardi e la Lombardia. Saggi* (Milan, 1978).

P. Chaplais (ed.), *Diplomatic Documents Preserved in the Public Record Office, 1101-1272* (HMSO, London, 1964).

———— 'The origin and authenticity of the royal Anglo-Saxon diploma', *Journal of the Society of Archivists* 3 (1965), pp. 48-60.

———— 'The Anglo-Saxon chancery: from the diploma to the writ', *Journal of the Society of Archivists* 4 (1966), pp. 160-76.

C.R. Cheney, *English Bishops' Chanceries, 1100-1250* (Manchester University Press, Manchester, 1950).

———— *The Study of the Medieval Papal Chancery* (Jackson, Glasgow, 1966).

———— *Notaries Public in England in the Thirteenth and Fourteenth Centuries* (Clarendon Press, Oxford, 1972).

W. Davies & P. Fouracre (eds), *The Settlement of Disputes in Early Medieval Europe* (Cambridge University Press, Cambridge, 1986).

P. Delogu, 'Il regno longobardo', *Storia d'Italia* I: *Longobardi e Bizantini* (Einaudi, Turin, 1980).

G. Diurni, *Le situazioni possessorie nel medioevo: età longobardo-franca* (Giuffrè, Milan, 1988).

J. Evans Grubbs, *Law and Family in Late Antiquity* (Oxford University Press, Oxford, 2000).

———— *Studies in Public Records* (Nelson, London, 1948).

S. Gasparri, 'Il potere pubblico nell'Italia longobarda', in C. Bertelli & G.P. Brogiolo (eds), *Il futuro dei longobardi: l'Italia e la costruzione dell'Europa di Carlo Magno* (Skira, Milan, 2000), pp. 94-7.

A. Gouron, *Juristes et droits savants: Bologne et la France médiévale. Variorum Collected Studies Series* CS679 (Ashgate, Aldershot, 2000).

J. Harries, *Law and Empire in Late Antiquity* (Cambridge University Press, Cambridge, 1999).

M. Kaser (trans. R. Dannenbring), *Roman Private Law* (Butterworth, London, 1968).

M.D. Knowles, *The Historian and Character and Other Essays* (Cambridge University Press, Cambridge, 1963).

A.J. Kosto, *Making Agreements in Medieval Catalonia: Power, Order and the Written Word. Cambridge Studies in Medieval Life and Thought* 51 (Cambridge University Press, Cambridge, 2001).

R.W. Leage, *Roman Private Law Founded on the 'Institutes' of Gaius and Justinian* (3rd edn. Macmillan & Co. – St Martin's Press, London & New York, 1961; 1930; 1906).

R.W. Mathiesen (ed.), *Law Society and Authority in Late Antiquity* (Oxford University Press, London & Oxford, 2001).

N.J. Menuge, *Medieval Women and the Law* (Boydell Press, Woodbridge & Rochester [NY], 2000).

B. Pohl-Resl, 'Legal practice and ethnic identity in Lombard Italy', in W. Pohl & H. Reintz (eds), *Strategies of Distinction: The Construction of Ethnic Communities, 300-800* (Brill, Leiden, Boston, Cologne), pp. 205-19.

R.L. Poole, *Lectures in the History of the Papal Chancery down to the Time of Innocent III* (Cambridge University Press, Cambridge, 1915).

F. Sinatti d'Amico, *Le prove giudiziarie nel diritto longobardo: legislazione e prassi da Rothari ad Astolfo* (Milan, 1968).

W. Ullmann, *Law and Jurisdiction in the Middle Ages. Variorum Collected Studies Series* CS283 (Ashgate, London, 1988).

P. Vinogradoff, *Roman Law in Medieval Europe* (Speculum Historiale, Cambridge, 1968).

C. Wickham, 'Land disputes and their social framework in Lombard-Carolingian Italy, 700-900', in *ibid.*, *Land and Power: Studies in Italian and European Social History, 400-1200* (British School at Rome, London, 1994), pp. 229-56.

R.G. Witt, *Italian Humanism and Medieval Rhetoric. Variorum Collected Studies Series* CS737 (Ashgate, Aldershot, 2001).

P. Wormald, *Legal Culture in the Early Medieval West: Law as Text, Image and Experience* (Hambledon Press, London, 1999).

Specialist journals

Scriptorium. Revue internationale des études relatives aux manuscrits / International review of manuscripts (1946-), Brussels.

Archiv für Diplomatik, Schriftgeschichte, Siegel- und Wappenkunde (1955-), Münster, Köln & Vienna.

Scrittura e civiltà (1977-), Rome.

7. Coins

Manuals and aids

C.E. Blunt, 'The coinage of Southern England 796-840', *British Numismatic Journal* 32 (1963), pp. 1-74.

I. Buck, *Medieval English Groats* (Greenlight, Witham, 2000).

A. Burnett, *Coins* (British Museum Press, London, 1991).

J. Casey & R. Reece (eds), *Coins and the Archaeologist* (2nd edn. Seaby, London, 1988).

R.H.M. Dolley (ed.), *Anglo-Saxon Coins* (Methuen, London, 1961).

—— *Anglo-Saxon Pennies* (London, 1964).

—— *Viking Coins of the Danelaw and Dublin* (Trustees of the British Museum, London, 1965).

E.T. Hall & D.M. Metcalf (eds), *Methods of Chemical and Metallurgical Investi-*

gation of Ancient Coinage. *Royal Numismatic Society Special Publication* 8 (Royal Numismatic Society, London, 1972).

S.C. Hawkes, J.M. Merrick & D.M. Metcalf, 'X-ray fluorescent analysis of some Dark-Age coins and jewellery', *Archeometry* 9 (1966), pp. 98-138.

H. Goodacre, *A Handbook of Coinage in the Byzantine Empire in three parts* (Spink, London, 1957; 1928-33).

P. Grierson, *Numismatics and History* (Historical Association Pamphlet G19, 1951).

—— *Numismatics* (Oxford University Press, London, Oxford & New York, 1975).

—— *Dark Age Numismatics: Selected Studies* (Variorum Reprints, London, 1979).

—— *Later Medieval Numismatics (11th-16th Centuries)* (Variorum Reprints, London, 1979).

—— & M. Blackburn, *Medieval European Coinage: With a Catalogue of Coins in the Fitzwilliam Museum, Cambridge* I: *The Early Middle Ages (5th-10th Centuries)* (Cambridge University Press, Cambridge, 1986).

E. Junge, *World Coin Encyclopaedia* (Barrie & Jenkins, London, Melbourne, Sydney, Auckland, Wellington & Johannesburg, 1984).

L.R. Laing, *Coins and Archaeology* (Weidenfeld & Nicolson, London, 1969).

I. Leimus & A. Molvogin, *Sylloge of Coins of the British Isles 51. Estonian Collections: Anglo-Saxon, Anglo-Norman and Later British Coins* (British Academy – Oxford University Press, London & Oxford, 2001).

D.M. Metcalf (ed.), *Coinage in Medieval Scotland (1100-1600)*. British Archaeological Reports British Series 45 (British Archaeological Reports, Oxford, 1977).

C.H.V. Sutherland, *English Coinage 600-1900* (Batsford, London, 1973).

J.D.A. Thompson, *Inventory of British Coin Hoards 600-1500* (Royal Numismatic Society, London, 1956).

The monetary history of medieval Europe

S. Armstrong, 'Carolingian coin hoards and the impact of the Viking raids in the ninth century', *Numismatic Chronicle* 158 (1998), pp. 131-64.

M.A.S. Blackburn, *Anglo-Saxon Monetary History* (Leicester University Press, Leicester, 1986).

—— & D.N. Dumville (eds), *Kings, Currency and Alliances: History and Coinage of Southern England in the Ninth Century* (Boydell, Woodbridge, 1998).

A.R. Burns, *Money and Monetary Policy in Early Times* (Kegan Paul, Trench, Trubner & Co., London, 1927).

J.F. Chown, *A History of Money from AD 800* (Routledge – Institute of Economic Affairs, London & New York, 1994).

S. Coupland, 'The early coinage of Charles the Bald', *Numismatic Chronicle* 151 (1991), pp. 21-158.

G. Dahl, *Trade, Trust and Networks: Commercial Cultures in Late Medieval Italy* (Nordic Academic Press, Lund, 1998).

J. Gies & F. Gies, *Merchants and Moneymen: The Commercial Revolution 1000-1500* (Barker, London, 1972).

D. Hill & D.M. Metcalf (eds), *Sceattas in England and on the Continent: The Seventh Oxford Symposium on Coinage and Monetary History*. British Archaeological Reports British Series, 128 (British Archaeological Reports, Oxford, 1984).

E.S. Hunt & J.M. Murray, *A History of Business in Medieval Europe* (Cambridge University Press, Cambridge, 1999).

K. Jacob, *Coins and Christianity* (Seaby, London, 1985).

D. Jacoby, *Trade, Commodities and Shipping in the Medieval Mediterranean. Variorum Collected Studies Series* CS572 (Ashgate, Aldershot, 1997).

S. Lebecq, *Marchand et navigateurs frisons du haut moyen âge.* 2 vols (Presses Universitaires de Lille, Lille, 1983).

R.S. Lopez & I.W. Raymond (eds), *Medieval Trade in the Mediterranean World: Illustrative Documents* (Columbia University Press, New York, 1955; reprinted 1990; new edition 2001).

C.S.S. Lyon, 'Historical problems of Anglo-Saxon coinage [1]', *British Numismatic Journal* 36 (1967), pp. 215-21.

―――― 'Historical problems of Anglo-Saxon coinage [2], the ninth century – Offa to Alfred', *British Numismatic Journal* 37 (1968), pp. 216-38.

―――― 'Historical problems of Anglo-Saxon coinage [3], denominations and weights', *British Numismatic Journal* 38 (1969), pp. 204-22.

―――― 'Historical problems of Anglo-Saxon coinage [4], the Viking age', *British Numismatic Journal* 39 (1970), pp. 193-204.

―――― 'Some problems in interpreting Anglo-Saxon coinage', *Anglo-Saxon England* 5 (1976), pp. 173-224.

D.M. Metcalf, J.M. Merrick & L.K. Hamblin, *Studies in the Composition of Early Medieval Coins* (Newcastle, 1986).

N.J.G. Pounds, *An Economic History of Medieval Europe* (2nd edn. Longman, London, 1994).

P. Spufford, *Money and its Uses in Medieval Europe* (Cambridge University Press, Cambridge, 1988; reprinted 1989).

J. Williams, J. Crib & E. Errington (eds), *Money: A History* (British Museum Press, London, 1997).

Specialist journals

The Numismatic Chronicle (1838-), London, Royal Numismatic Society.

Revue Numismatique (1838-), Paris.

Bollettino di numismatica (1983-), Rome.

Rivista italiana di numismatica e scienze affini (1898-), Milan.

8. The material record

Material culture and society

P.M. Allison (ed.), *The Archaeology of Household Activities* (Routledge, London & New York, 1999).

A. Appadurai (ed.), *The Social Life of Things* (Cambridge University Press, Cambridge, 1988).

A. Barnard & J. Spencer (eds), *Encyclopaedia of Social and Cultural Anthropology* (3rd edn. Routledge, London, 1998; 1997, 1996).

E.S. Chilton (ed.), *Material Meanings: Critical Approaches to the Interpretation of Material Culture* (University of Utah, Salt Lake City, 1999).

C. Geertz, *The Interpretation of Cultures* (Basic Books, New York, 1973).

C. Gosden, *Anthropology and Archaeology* (Routledge, London & New York, 1999).

M. Harris, *Culture, People, Nature: An Introduction to General Anthropology* (Longman, New York, 1996).

Journal of Material Culture (1996-), London.

A.B. Knapp, *Archaeology, Annales and Ethnohistory* (Cambridge University Press, Cambridge, 1992).

R. McGuire, *A Marxist Archaeology* (Academic Press, New York, 1992).

D. Miller, *Material Cultures* (University College London Press, London, 1997).

I. Morris, *Archaeology as Cultural History* (Blackwell, Oxford & Maldon [Mass.], 2000).

B. Orme, *Anthropology for Archaeologists: An Introduction* (Duckworth, London, 1981).

M.B. Schiffer & A.R. Miller, *The Material Life of Human Beings: Artifacts, Behavior and Communication* (Routledge, London & New York, 1999).

C. Tilley, *Reading Material Culture* (Blackwell, Oxford, 1990).

—— *The Art of Ambiguity: Material Culture and Text* (Routledge, London, 1991).

—— 'Interpreting material culture', in S.M. Pearce (ed.) *Interpreting Objects and Collections* (Routledge, London & New York, 1994), pp. 67-75.

Medieval archaeology

L. Barkan, *Unearthing the Past: Archaeology and Aesthetics in the Making of Renaissance Culture* (Yale University Press, New Haven & London, 1999; reprinted 2001).

M.W. Beresford, *The Lost Villages of England* (Lutterworth Press, London, 1954).

M. Carver, 'Digging for ideas', *Antiquity* 63 (1989), pp. 666-74.

—— 'Digging for data: principles and procedures for evaluation, excavation and post-excavation in towns', *Theory and Practice of Archaeological Research* 2 (1990), pp. 255-302 (Institute of Archaeology and Ethnology, Polish Academy of Sciences).

—— *Arguments in Stone: Archaeological Research and the European Town in the First Millennium. Oxbow Monograph* 29 (Oxbow, Oxford, 1993).

P.J. Crabtree, *Medieval Archaeology: An Encyclopaedia* (Garland, New York & London, 2001).

C. Daniell, *Death and Burial in Medieval England 1066-1550* (2nd edn. Routledge, London, 1998; 1997).

W.H.C. Frend, *The Archaeology of Early Christianity: A History* (Geoffrey Chapman, London, 1996).

S. Gelichi, *Introduzione all'archeologia medievale* (La Nuova Italia Scientifica, Rome, 1997).

R. Gilchrist, *Gender and Material Culture: The Archaeology of Religious Women* (Routledge, London, 1994).

J. Grenville, *Medieval Housing* (Leicester University Press, Leicester, 1997).

S. Gutierrez Lloret, *Arqueología. Introducción a la historia material de las societas del pasado* (Publicaciones de la Universidad de Alicante, Alicante, 1997).

D.A. Hinton, *Archaeology, Economy and Society: England from the Fifth to the Fifteenth Century* (2nd edn. Seaby, London, 1993).

R. Hodges, *Dark Age Economics: The Origins of Towns and Trade AD 600-1000* (Duckworth, London, 1982; reprinted 1989).

—— *Early Medieval Archaeology in Western Europe: Its History and Development. Headstart History Papers* (Headstart, 1991).

—— & P. Whitehouse, *Mohammed, Charlemagne and the Origins of Europe:*

An Introduction to Medieval History

Archaeology and the Pirenne Thesis (Duckworth, London, 1983; reprinted
1989).
D. Hooke, The Landscape of Anglo-Saxon England (2nd edn. Leicester University Press, London, 1998; 1985).
W.G. Hoskins, The Making of the English Landscape (Hodder & Stoughton,
London, 1955; reprinted Penguin, London, New York, Victoria, Ontario,
Auckland, 1985).
C. Karkov (ed.), The Archaeology of Anglo-Saxon England (Routledge, London
& New York, 1999).
G.D. Keevill, Medieval Palaces: An Archaeology (Tempus, Stroud, 2000).
J.K. Knight, The End of Antiquity: Archaeology, Society and Religion in Early
Medieval Europe (Tempus, Stroud & Charleston [SC], 1999).
R. Leech (ed.), Rapport sur la situation de l'archéologie urbaine en Europe (CID,
Rennes, 1999).
M. Mellor, Pots and People that have Shaped the Heritage of Medieval and Later
England (Ashmolean Museum, Oxford, 1997).
J. Moreland, 'Method and theory in medieval archaeology in the 1990s',
Archeologia Medievale 18 (1991), pp. 7-42.
P. Ottaway, Archaeology in British Towns: From the Emperor Claudius to the
Black Death (Routledge, London & New York, 1992).
P. Pulsiano, Medieval Scandinavia: An Encyclopaedia (Garland, New York &
London, 1993; reprinted 2001).
K. Randsborg, The First Millennium AD in Europe and the Mediterranean: An
Archaeological Essay (Cambridge University Press, Cambridge, 1991; reprinted 1993).
T. Rowley & T. Good, Deserted Villages (Shire, Princes Risborough [Buckinghamshire], 1982; reprinted 1995, 2000).
P.H. Sawyer (ed.), Medieval Settlement: Continuity and Change (Edward Arnold, London, 1976).
A. Schnapp, The Discovery of the Past (British Museum Press, London, 1999).
D. Whitehouse, 'Archaeology', in J.M. Powell (ed.), Medieval Studies: An Introduction (Syracuse University Press, New York), pp. 162-200.

G. Barker (ed.), Companion Encyclopaedia of Archaeology (Routledge, London
& New York, 1999).
P. Barker, Techniques of Archaeological Excavation (2nd edn. Batsford, London,
1982).
J. Collis, Digging up the Past: An Introduction to Archaeological Excavation
(Sutton, Stroud, 2001).
P. Drewett, Field Archaeology: An Introduction (University College London
Press, London, 1999).
E.C. Harris, Principles of Archaeological Stratigraphy (2nd edn. Academic
Press, London, 1989).
—— M.R. Brown & G.J. Brown, Practices of Archaeological Stratigraphy
(Academic Press, London, 1993).
I. Hodder, Theory and Practice in Archaeology (Routledge, London, 1992).
—— The Archaeological Process: An Introduction (Blackwell, Oxford & Maldon [Mass.], 1999).
M. Joukowsky, A Complete Manual of Field Archaeology (Prentice Hall, Engelwood Cliffs [NJ], 1980).
F. Petrie, Methods and Aims in Archaeology (Gollancz, London, 1904).

C. Renfrew & P. Bahn, *Archaeology: Theories, Methods and Practice* (3rd edn. Thames & Hudson, London, 2000).

M. Wheeler, *Archaeology from the Earth* (Oxford University Press, London & Oxford, 1956).

Dating methods

E.B. Banning, *The Archaeologist's Laboratory* (Plenum, Kluwer, 2000).

X. Delestre & P. Périn (eds), *La datation des structures et des objets du haut Moyen Age: méthodes et résultats* (Association française d'archéologie mérovingienne, Paris, 1998).

B.M. Fagan & C.E. Orser Jr., *Historical Archaeology* (Longman, New York & London, 1995).

G. Gibbon, *Explanation in Archaeology* (Blackwell, Oxford & New York, 1989).

J. Moreland, *Archaeology and Text. Duckworth Debates in Archaeology* (Duckworth, London, 2001).

Finds

K. Barclay, *Scientific Analyses of Archaeological Ceramics* (Oxbow, Oxford, 2000).

D. Brothwell, *Digging Up Bones* (3rd edn. Oxford University Press, London & Oxford, 1981).

E. Cooper, *Ten Thousand Years of Pottery* (4th edn. British Museum Press, London, 2000; 1988, 1981, 1972).

I.W. Cornwall, *Bones for the Archaeologist* (Dent, London, 1974).

C. Cumberpatch & P. Blinkhorn (eds), *Not So Much a Pot, More of a Way of Life. Oxbow Monograph* 83 (Oxbow, Oxford, 1997).

G. Dimbleby, *Plants and Archaeology: The Archaeology of the Soil* (John Baker, London, 1978).

J.G. Evans, *An Introduction to Environmental Archaeology* (Elek, London, 1977).

J. Henderson, *The Science and Archaeology of Materials* (Routledge, London, 2000).

E. Higgs & M. Jarman, 'Paleoeconomy', in E. Higgs (ed.), *Paleoeconomy* (Cambridge University Press, Cambridge, 1975), pp. 1-7.

I. Hodder, 'The contextual analysis of symbolic meanings', in S.M. Pearce (ed.), *Interpreting Objects and Collections* (Routledge, London & New York, 1994), p. 12.

N. Mills, *Medieval Artefacts* (Greenlight, Witham, 1999).

M. Parker Pearson, *The Archaeology of Death and Burial* (Sutton, Stroud, 1999).

J. Rackham, *Animal Bones* (California University Press – British Museum, London, 1994).

M. Shackley, *Environmental Archaeology* (George Allen & Unwin, London, 1981).

—— *Using Environmental Archaeology* (Batsford, London, 1985).

J.M. Skibo & G.M. Feinman (eds), *Pottery and People: A Dynamic Interaction* (Utah University Press, Utah, 1999).

A. Stirland, *Human Bones in Archaeology* (2nd edn. Shire, Princes Risborough [Buckinghamshire] 1999; 1986).

N. Stoodley, *The Spindle and the Spear: A Critical Enquiry into the Construction Meaning of Gender in the Early Anglo-Saxon Burial Rite. BAR 288* (British Archaeological Reports, Oxford, 1999).

Survey and other forms of archaeological investigation

W. Ashmore & A. Bernard Knapp, *Archaeologies of Landscape: Contemporary Perspectives* (Blackwell, Oxford & Maldon [Mass.], 1999).

G. Barker, *A Mediterranean Valley: Landscape Archaeology and Annales History in the Biferno Valley* (Leicester University Press, London & New York, 1995).

R. Francovich & H. Patterson (eds), *Extracting Meaning from Ploughsoil Assemblages* (Oxbow, Oxford, 2000).

M. Pasquinucci & F. Trément (eds), *Non-Destructive Techniques Applied to Landscape Archaeology* (Oxbow, Oxford, 2000).

S. Shennan, *Quantifying Archaeology* (Edinburgh University Press, Edinburgh, 1997).

—— *Experiments in the Collection and Analysis of Archaeological Survey Data* (University of Sheffield, Sheffield, 1989).

D.R. Wilson, *Air Photo Interpretation for Archaeologists* (Batsford, London, 1982; reprinted Tempus, 2000).

Journals

Medieval Archaeology (Journal of the Society of Medieval Archaeology; 1957-), London.

Journal of Material Culture (1996-), London.

Archéologie médiévale (Journal of the Centre des Récherches Archéologiques Médiévales, University of Caen; 1971-), Caen.

Cahiers Archéologiques. Fin de l'Antiquité et Moyen Âge (1945-), Paris.

Archeologia medievale (1974-), Florence.

Zeitschrift für die Archäologie des Mittelalters (1973-), Köln.

Boletin de arqueologia medieval (1987-), Madrid.

Index of Names